Black Hills Forestry

Black Hills
Forestry

A History

John F. Freeman

UNIVERSITY PRESS OF COLORADO
Boulder

© 2015 by University Press of Colorado

Published by University Press of Colorado
5589 Arapahoe Avenue, Suite 206C
Boulder, Colorado 80303

 The University Press of Colorado is a proud member of
the Association of American University Presses.

The University Press of Colorado is a cooperative publishing enterprise supported, in part, by Adams
State University, Colorado State University, Fort Lewis College, Metropolitan State University of
Denver, Regis University, University of Colorado, University of Northern Colorado, Utah State
University, and Western State Colorado University.

∞ This paper meets the requirements of the ANSI/NISO Z39.48–1992 (Permanence of Paper).

Library of Congress Cataloging-in-Publication Data

Freeman, John F. (John Francis), 1940–
  Black Hills forestry: a history / John F. Freeman.
    pages cm
  Includes bibliographical references.
  ISBN 978-1-60732-298-6 (cloth) — ISBN 978-1-60732-299-3 (ebook)
1. Forests and forestry—Black Hills National Forest (S.D. and Wyo.)—History. 2. Black Hills
National Forest (S.D. and Wyo.)—History. I. Title.
  SD144.S63F74 2014
  577.309783'9—dc23
                          2013037187

24   23   22   21   20   19   18   17   16   15   10   9   8   7   6   5   4   3   2   1

Cover photograph © Kari Greer Photography

Contents

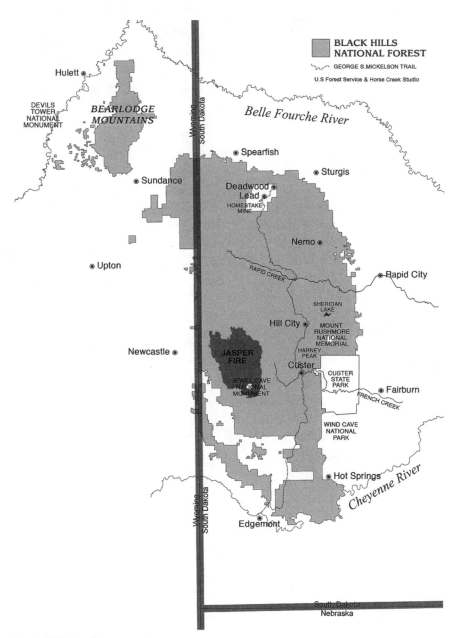

BLACK HILLS
NATIONAL FOREST

GEORGE S. MICKELSON TRAIL

U.S Forest Service & Horse Creek Studio

Hulett

DEVILS
TOWER
NATIONAL
MONUMENT

BEARLODGE
MOUNTAINS

Wyoming
South Dakota

Belle Fourche River

Spearfish

Sturgis

Sundance

Deadwood
Lead

HOMESTAKE
MINE

Nemo

Upton

RAPID CREEK

Rapid City

SHERIDAN
LAKE

Hill City

MOUNT
RUSHMORE
NATIONAL
MEMORIAL

HARNEY
PEAK

Newcastle

JASPER
FIRE

Custer

JEWEL CAVE
NATIONAL
MONUMENT

CUSTER
STATE
PARK

Fairburn

FRENCH CREEK

WIND CAVE
NATIONAL
PARK

Hot Springs

Cheyenne River

Wyoming
South Dakota

Edgemont

South Dakota
Nebraska

Map of Black Hills National Forest

Preface

In 1950 Howard R. Lamar, an eminent historian of the American West, wrote that "no adequate study of the Black Hills exists."[1] Since then, volumes of technical articles, monographs, and some readable books have been published on various aspects of the Black Hills, such as natural history, gambling and gold mining, timbering and sawmills, tourism, and Mount Rushmore. To date, however, no study has focused on the history of the Black Hills National Forest, its centrality to life in the region, and its preeminence within the national forest system.

My interest in the Black Hills came about through volunteer work in the Wyoming governor's office. I found myself in Hulett, population 400, called to advise residents on how a refurbished former school building might serve as the physical center for a community effort to stabilize and diversify the local economy. Hulett depended on the forest, with most working residents employed at the Neiman sawmill or by logging contractors. In 2007 I had no idea that the Black Hills National Forest was arguably the most commercialized national forest in the nation. On my first tour, I was struck immediately by the crass commercialism within and around the national forest.

To be perfectly candid, I arrived in the Black Hills with an ideologically tinged view of national forests. As a child, I had been taken into the Ozark National Forest for hiking and picnicking. At age fourteen, I spent a summer tramping with my dog in the Medicine Bow National Forest near Fox Park. I returned to Wyoming permanently during the height of the clear-cutting controversy, siding on aesthetic

grounds with anti-timbering advocates. It had yet to occur to me that a forest intensively cut for more than a century could be managed back into some form of natural
health or that the forest, like any living organism, could not be separated from its
dependent and interdependent parts—including loggers and miners, hunters and
hikers, private property in-holders, and the residents of communities within the
forest's boundaries.

Working in the office of a proactive governor certainly helps one shed one's righ-
teousness and naïveté because one is under pressure to solve, or at least lessen the
severity of, problems. In addition, it occurred to me that my prior work building
charitable endowments was similar in spirit to the work of a forester managing public forests. In both cases, we carry a picture in our mind of what we expect our community or our forest to look like in a hundred years, and we know the major results
of our work will not show until after we are gone.

My decision to write about the Black Hills National Forest was in part fortuitous
and in part historical. From my prior study of High Plains horticulture, I knew
that the Black Hills were the main seed source of ponderosa pine, the most popular conifer planted on the High Plains, and that Nebraska's Charles E. Bessey had
directed his early botany students to the Black Hills because of the unusual mixture
of floristic zones: Rocky Mountain Coniferous, Great Plains Grassland, Eastern
Deciduous, and Northern Coniferous—all within a relatively small, topographically isolated area.

With my own interest in French rural history—be forewarned that I am neither
an ecologist nor an environmental historian—I was intrigued that Gifford Pinchot
had pursued his formal forestry training in France. He knew about the French government's successes with restoring mountain forests and became captivated by the
notion of the duty of governments to protect public forests. In a troublesome parallel to his European findings, Pinchot had learned about deforestation around mining camps in the Black Hills. He knew firsthand about the favorable topography and
understood the timbering potential of the predominant ponderosa pine (chapters 1
and 2). By adapting science-based European forestry, he intended to transform the
Black Hills Forest Reserve into the nation's preeminent well-managed forest.

But first, Pinchot helped South Dakota senator Richard F. Pettigrew with the
landmark Forest Management Act, convinced Homestake Mining Company to
purchase the first stands of federal timber, and sent the entomologist Andrew
D. Hopkins to identify the insects damaging vast stands of marketable timber
and suggest measures for their control. Early forestry documented by Pinchot's
personal representatives in the Black Hills provided material for his famous *Use
of the National Forest Reserves*. By winning over the Black Hills stock grower and

influential Wyoming member of Congress Franklin W. Mondell, Pinchot brought about the consolidation of ownership and management of the forest reserves into the US Forest Service (chapters 3 and 4).

Over a period of fifty years (1910s–1950s), the Forest Service in the Black Hills did everything possible to ensure the largest possible sustainable harvests of commercial timber, with the criteria of sustainability worked out by well-trained and well-intentioned supervisors and their staffs. Managing for timber production encompassed far more than preparing sales, marking timber, and monitoring logging operations. It also included prevention and suppression of wildfires, thinning to encourage growth, and the construction of roads to enable operators to reach farther and farther into the forests. From the start, local businesses sought to capitalize on the beautiful scenery. The advent of automobile travel accelerated that effort, despite the Forest Service's reluctance to promote recreation. Nonetheless, the Forest Service was pressed to transfer land to the State of South Dakota for Custer State Park and was forced by congressional action to give up full control over land designated as the State Park Game Sanctuary. Though never so stated, the bitterest pill was the transfer of 1,200 acres within the most mountainous region of the national forest to the National Park Service for Mount Rushmore National Memorial (chapters 5–7).

As more and more people entered the national forest to enjoy its recreational and natural values, the Forest Service sought to accommodate those users and reconcile their various uses with the continuing emphasis on commercial timbering. With scientists joining the public in questioning the viability of managing forest stands as agricultural crops, the US Congress reacted with major pieces of legislation to rein in the public land agencies and give the public more say in their management. As a result, Forest Service professional staff expanded to include specialists in the natural and social sciences; and the forest planning processes mandated by legislation became more and more cumbersome, frustrated all interested parties, led to confrontations within the court system, and brought forestry virtually to a halt (chapters 8–11).

Meanwhile, the beetle epidemic that began in 1997 and the massive Jasper fire in 2000 led to a recognition within the agency as well as among the public that to preserve and protect public and private forestlands for all types of users, forestry could no longer concentrate on producing "outputs"; it needed instead to focus on restoring and maintaining the conditions that made those products possible. The 2012 "Black Hills Regional Mountain Pine Beetle Strategy" provided the framework for such a holistic approach and placed the Forest Service back in a position of leadership in conservation (chapter 12).

NOTE

1. Howard R. Lamar, *Dakota Territory, 1861–1889: A Study of Frontier Politics* (New Haven, CT: Yale University Press, 1956), 290.

Acknowledgments

My research depended upon unimpeded access to Forest Service staff and materials in the Black Hills. For that, I am most grateful to Blaine Cook, forest silviculturist, and to Frank Carroll, planning and public affairs staff officer (now retired) for the Black Hills National Forest. Both graciously responded to my many inquiries and provided useful insights. District rangers Robert Thompson and Steve Kozel helped dispel mistaken perceptions, and Black Hills National Forest supervisor Craig Bobzien confirmed my impression that the Black Hills National Forest is once again the flagship national forest Gifford Pinchot had envisioned.

Among the individuals with whom I talked, thanks in particular to Bob Averill, Tom Blair, Beth Burkhart, Gary Brundige, Bill Coburn, Shellie Deisch, Jim Margadant, Hollis Marriott, Bill McGrath, Roberta Moltzen, Jim Neiman, Colin Paterson, Bob Paulson, Hugh Thompson, Tom Troxel, and John Twiss. I am most grateful for the assistance of Cheryl Oakes, librarian-archivist at the Forest History Society; Roberta Sago, special collections librarian at Black Hills State University; Dee M. Salo, interlibrary loan librarian at the University of Wyoming; librarians at the Denver Public Library and the South Dakota School of Mines and Technology; and Ronald K. Hansen for preparing the map.

For critically reading the manuscript, I am deeply indebted to Steven W. Flanderka, Roger L. Williams, David A. Wolff, and the reviewers for the University Press of Colorado. I would like to thank Jessica d'Arbonne, acquisitions editor, and Darrin Pratt, director and acquiring editor, for their encouragement, friendly advice, and patience. Thanks to Cheryl Carnahan for her meticulous copyediting.

Black Hills
Forestry

Introduction

In an address to the annual meeting of the Agricultural History Society held in Washington, DC, April 15, 1937, Gifford Pinchot, long retired as first chief of the US Forest Service, took credit for creating American forestry. By forestry, he meant the science of managing stands of trees as agricultural crops. In his opinion, no American before him had worked forests in that way. Because the results of a forester's work do not appear during his lifetime, the forester is trained to take the long-term view, the application of which Pinchot called conservation.[1]

In taking credit for creating American forestry, Pinchot did not mean to detract from the preliminary work of those before him who had advocated for the protection of forests. Having knowledge of timber scarcities in Europe, some American colonies did try to regulate the sale and transport of timber; while the colonial government sought to reserve tall timbers for ship masts. Beginning in 1817, the US Congress passed a series of laws to create and protect certain tree plantations for naval timber.[2]

Beyond the military aspect, protecting and preserving forests had been of both economic and scientific interest to the founding fathers, enlightened agriculturists with intellectual roots in Europe. Andrea Wulf has argued that President James Madison (in retirement) was the first politician to speak publicly about the "excessive destruction of timber," to call for remedial action, and to express some understanding of the "balance of nature." In his "Address to the Agricultural Society of Albermarle" (1818), Madison noted that, through their successes, American farmers

DOI: 10.5876/9781607322993.c000

had increased the number of plants and animals "beyond their natural amount"; and he warned that by surpassing what we now call the historical range of variability, agricultural achievements could work against humanity's best interests.[3]

The eminent Vermonter George Perkins Marsh elaborated on those views in his address to the Agricultural Society of Rutland County in 1847. The views he expressed would become the theme of his major work, *Man and Nature or, Physical Geography as Modified by Human Action*: when human activity modifies nature to the extent that nature can no longer repair itself, such activity becomes detrimental to humanity in both the short and long term. Every Vermonter could see the results of timbering steep hillsides: erosion of topsoil, invasion of noxious weeds, and scattering of seeds to nearby arable lands. Marsh called for more careful selection of stands meant for timbering and suggested that the time had come to emulate those European nations in which timbering was regulated by law. Though not advocating government ownership of forests, Marsh appealed "to an enlightened self-interest to introduce the reforms, check the abuses, and preserve us from an increase of the [timbering] evils."[4]

As an early critic of the notion that America's natural resources are inexhaustible, Marsh added a moral dimension to the cause of forest conservation. "The destruction of the woods," he wrote, was "man's first physical conquest, his first violation of the harmonies of inanimate nature."[5] To restore disturbed harmonies, the agriculturist needed to "become a co-worker with nature in the reconstruction of the damaged fabric which the negligence or the wantonness of former lodgers has rendered untenable."[6]

But Marsh was no lover of pristine nature. In the case of forests, he favored growing trees for their timber, noting "the great general superiority of cultivated timber to that of strictly spontaneous growth." He believed the careful reader of late-eighteenth- and early-nineteenth-century French treatises on forestry would realize "that the sooner a natural wood is brought into the state of an artificially regulated one, the better it is for all the multiplied interests which depend on the wise administration of this branch of public economy."[7]

Despite *Man and Nature* and reports by scientists and federal officials who had observed the results of forest destruction, during the immediate post–Civil War period the US Congress continued to pass preemption laws; to transfer public lands to the states, which ended up in the hands of timber interests; and to grant public lands, many forested, to the railroads. In contrast, several states and territories on the Great Plains and in the Intermountain West had adopted legislation to protect forests and encourage tree planting. In 1851 the general assembly of Deseret enacted penalties for anyone wasting or otherwise destroying timber in the Wasatch Range, the source of water for farms in the Great Salt Lake Basin. In 1876 Colorado became the first state to write conservation of forests into its state constitution.[8]

Meanwhile, Nebraska had emerged as the preeminent tree-planting state; in 1869 the legislature provided property tax exemptions to settlers planting windbreaks, shade trees, and fruit trees and later made stock growers liable for damage to trees and shrubs caused by their herds. The Nebraska State Board of Agriculture established Arbor Day as a special day for the care and planting of trees.[9]

Nebraska US senator Phineas W. Hitchcock introduced the Timber Culture Act of 1873, which provided 160 acres of unappropriated public land to anyone who would agree to plant trees on 40 of those acres and keep them healthy for eight years. Deficiencies in the act, however, allowed speculators to amass claims, which led to its eventual repeal as part of the Forest Reserve Act (discussed later). That same year the American Association for the Advancement of Science recommended to Congress that a knowledgeable individual be hired to study the nation's existing timber resources, as well as their preservation and renewal, and proposed legislation for their protection. Although the legislative effort failed, Representative Mark H. Dunnell (R-MN) managed to attach a rider to the US Department of Agriculture appropriations bill for 1876, setting aside $2,000 for the study. Dunnell secured the appointment of Franklin Benjamin Hough—naturalist, physician, and longtime member of the association—to conduct the study.[10]

In fact, Hough had led the association's effort, outlined in his landmark paper "On the Duty of Governments in the Preservation of Forests." Because of the nation's absolute dependence on timber and on forests for water, Hough stated that the time had come for the United States to adopt a *system* to manage and regulate public forests. He praised the French government's actions to preserve forests, going back to the 1669 Forest Ordinance. But he recognized that France's autocratic approach would not work in the republican United States, where "we must begin at the centre of power, and that centre is the circumference. We must make the people themselves familiar with the facts and the necessities of the case."[11] Yet no matter how much the public knows, we still need laws to regulate and protect the woods, just as we have agreed to have laws for the management of roads and bridges and for other matters of public usefulness.[12]

Hough's appointment as forest agent in the Department of Agriculture marked the beginning of federally sponsored forestry, but public forests remained under the General Land Office in the Department of the Interior. Thus the situation, in the words of historian-archivist Harold Pinkett, was one "where one department, Agriculture, was placed in charge of forestry without forests, while another, Interior, remained in charge of forests without forestry."[13] In fairness, Carl Schurz, the distinguished secretary of the interior (1877–81), did establish a system of special agents to detect forest abuses, though Congress failed to appropriate sufficient funds for effective patrol over the hundreds of millions of acres; and he did recommend that forestlands in the public domain be withdrawn from sale to private parties.

Secretary Schurz's efforts combined with Hough's forestry reports—for which he was promoted from forest agent to chief of the Division of Forestry, still a one-person operation within the Department of Agriculture—undoubtedly contributed to increased interest in forest protection. At the first American Forestry Congress meeting at Cincinnati in 1882, its secretary, Bernhard Eduard Fernow, presented a paper recommending that owners of American woodlands adopt the principles of European forestry to improve their stands, reduce waste, and remain in business. A native of Prussia, Fernow was the first formally trained forester to practice in the United States and was a founding member of the American Forestry Association. In 1886 Fernow succeeded Hough as chief of the Division of Forestry. He used his position with the American Forestry Association to lobby for repeal of the Timber Culture Act, which became known as the Forest Reserve Act of 1891.[14]

During his last year at Yale (1889–89), Gifford Pinchot sought the advice of Fernow, as chief of the Division of Forestry, on how best to prepare for a career as a professionally trained forester. Pinchot had credited his father, a wealthy and philanthropic New York City merchant, with suggesting such a career. Pinchot père also owned a large estate at Milford, along the Delaware River in northeastern Pennsylvania, where he sought to restore the woods. Pinchot's parents gave him books on forestry, and the Yale Library contained more, but Gifford remembered that he had found only one book, Jules Clavé's *Etudes sur l'économie forestière* (1862), that dealt with "the application of Forestry to the forest."[15] At Fernow's recommendation and through family connections, Pinchot enrolled at the prestigious French national forestry school in Nancy, where Lucien Boppe, professor of silviculture, took him under his wing. It was Boppe, Pinchot recalled, who taught him that the "master quality" of the forester was the "forester's eye," an innate feel for what needed to be done. From field trips to nearby managed forests, Pinchot reported that he had gained his "first concrete understanding of the forest as a crop, and I became deeply interested not only in how the crop was grown, but also in how it was harvested and reproduced."[16] He was impressed, furthermore, that "the forest supported a permanent population of trained men . . . and not only a permanent population but also permanent forest industries, supported and guaranteed by a fixed annual supply of trees ready for the ax."[17] In a nutshell, this was what he and his successors would seek in the management of America's national forests.

After he left France, Pinchot spent one month with Superintendent Ulrich Meister at the Zurich municipal forest, which had been managed for timbering since the seventeenth century and was considered the most instructive forest in Europe. His experience in Switzerland convinced Pinchot of the urgent need for the US government to regulate timbering in public and, to some degree, privately owned forests. Shortly after his return to the United States, Fernow arranged for Pinchot's first public appearance as a forester. Before a joint meeting of the American Forestry Association and the American Economic Association, Pinchot read a paper on "Governmental Forestry Abroad" in which he favorably compared Swiss forestry, where foresters exercised professional discretion, to German forestry, where government rules covered the smallest details.[18]

Again through family connections, Pinchot landed his first job, as manager of the Biltmore Forest near Asheville, North Carolina. Proprietor George W. Vanderbilt II provided Pinchot with the opportunity to adapt into practice what he had learned in Europe. In December 1893 Pinchot moved to New York City to start his own business as "consulting forester," hiring his Yale classmate, Henry S. Graves, as his assistant. From that business, Pinchot and Graves launched their careers as public foresters, which would eventually lead them to the Black Hills.[19]

NOTES

1. Gifford Pinchot, "How Conservation Began in the United States," *Agricultural History* 11, no. 4 (October 1937): 255.

2. Harold T. Pinkett, *Gifford Pinchot, Private and Public Forester* (Urbana: University of Illinois Press, 1970), 6–8.

3. Andrea Wulf, *Founding Gardeners: The Revolutionary Generation, Nature, and the Shaping of the American Nation* (New York: Alfred A. Knopf, 2011), 205–7.

4. George Perkins Marsh, "Address Delivered before the Agricultural Society of Rutland County, Sept. 30, 1847," 17–19, at http://memory.loc.gov/ammem/today/sep30.html; accessed March 2010.

5. George Perkins Marsh, *Man and Nature or, Physical Geography as Modified by Human Action*, ed. David Lowenthal (Cambridge: Harvard University Press, 1965 [1864]), 119.

6. Ibid., 35.

7. Ibid., 260–61.

8. John Ise, *The United States Forest Policy* (New Haven: Yale University Press, 1920), 28.

9. John F. Freeman, *High Plains Horticulture, a History* (Boulder: University Press of Colorado, 2008), 19–20.

10. Harold K. Stern, *The U.S. Forest Service: A History* (Seattle: University of Washington Press, 2004), 11–13.

11. Franklin B. Hough, "On the Duty of Governments in the Preservation of Forests," *Proceedings of the American Association for the Advancement of Science*, August 1873, Portland, ME, 4, http://memory.loc.gov/ammem/amrvhtml/cnchron2.html; accessed February 2008.

12. Ibid., 6.

13. Pinkett, *Gifford Pinchot*, 9.

14. Ibid., 10–11.

15. Gifford Pinchot, *Breaking New Ground* (Washington, DC: Island, 1998 [1947]), 4.

16. Ibid., 11.

17. Ibid., 13.

18. Ibid., 35.

19. Ibid., 69–73.

1

Exploring the Forest

In the spring of 1897 Gifford Pinchot, acting as confidential forest agent to Interior Secretary Cornelius Bliss, endorsed the dispatch of his assistant, Henry Graves, to the Black Hills Forest Reserve to assess its timbering potential. Published in 1899, his report remains the primary written source for studies seeking to understand the nature of the pre-settlement forest. Although controversy remains as to the interpretation of the dynamics of natural disturbances, especially fires, the report does contain indisputable topographical facts that, combined with qualitative descriptions by earlier explorers, provide an overview of the forest setting.

Geographically, the Black Hills are situated between the Belle Fourche River on the north and the Cheyenne River on the south. They straddle the South Dakota–Wyoming state line, with the greater portion in South Dakota. "The Black Hills," Graves wrote, "constitute an isolated range of mountains with a general north-south trend, and are about 120 miles long and 40 miles wide."[1] While the entire range is geologically part of the same uplift, the Bearlodge Mountains in Wyoming are topographically separated from the main body of mountains in South Dakota. Altogether, the Black Hills actually span about 120 miles from north to south and 70 miles from west to east.

Most striking, the main body of the Black Hills is encircled almost entirely by a treeless, arid valley from several hundred feet to several miles in width, known as the Red Valley or Racetrack. Between this valley and the surrounding plains is the Hogback, a continuous rim of foothills intermittently covered by stands of conifers,

DOI: 10.5876/9781607322993.c001

rising abruptly from 200 feet to 800 feet on the inner or valley side and sloping gradually down to the plains on the outer side.

The surrounding plains range in elevation from 3,000 to 5,000 feet; the Black Hills generally are about 2,000 feet higher. The highest point is Harney Peak, elevation 7,241 feet, in the center of the most mountainous range, which includes the Needles and the Cathedral Spires, towering granite outcroppings from steep ridges above canyons and valleys. The lowest point is southeast on the Cheyenne River, elevation 1,900 feet, just before the river flows onto the Great Plains.

Graves called the limestone plateau, which runs north to south near the South Dakota–Wyoming state line, "the main backbone of the Black Hills." The plateau is fairly level and broad, up to 15 miles wide, broken by numerous swales that run into ravines at the heads of creeks that, in turn, flow through deep canyons and most often sink into the ground before reaching the Belle Fourche or Cheyenne Rivers. A narrower limestone plateau is located on the southeastern edge of the Black Hills.[2]

Although Graves did not specifically discuss climate, temperatures within the Black Hills have generally been less extreme, precipitation has tended to be higher, and wind velocity has usually been lower compared with the surrounding plains. In general, average temperatures decrease and average precipitation increases with higher elevations. Precipitation ranges from 16 inches to 29 inches annually, coming mostly during the months of April through July. The Black Hills have their share of snowstorms and occasional blizzards.

Graves estimated that the main forest reserve area was 2,600 square miles, of which 2,000 square miles were covered by trees. Overall, he described the Black Hills as "densely timbered, but the forest is broken in many places by parks and mountain prairies, and enormous tracts have been entirely denuded by forest fires." He attributed the broken condition of the forest—a large proportion of "defective and scrubby trees," windbreaks, treeless ridges, meadows, and mountain prairies—to "the destructive forest fires which have swept the Black Hills periodically for years and probably for centuries."[3] He believed the way to preserve the forest was to encourage natural reproduction and to prevent forest fires.

By preserving the forest, Graves really meant preserving the commercially valuable ponderosa pine that made up 95 percent of the trees in the entire forest. At the outset of our story, therefore, we should acknowledge the place of the ponderosa pine in the plant kingdom. The ponderosa pine belongs to the division Pinophyhta (woody plants), order Pinales (woody plants with cones as reproductive structures), class Pinopsida (simple leaves or needles), and family Pinaceae (pines). Within that family, the ponderosa pine belongs to the genus *Pinus* (true pines), species *ponderosa*, from the Latin for "great weight," first named by David Douglas—a Scottish

FIGURE 1.1. Ponderosa pine. Courtesy, USDA Forest Service, Black Hills National Forest, ForestPhoto.com.

botanist traveling in Oregon in the mid-1820s—and then described and published in 1836 by Peter and Charles Lawson, Edinburgh nurserymen. In 1880 the Lawsons further divided the ponderosa pine into three varieties or subspecies, of which our subspecies is called *scopulorum*, from the Latin for "pertaining to rocky sites." Thus the full scientific name of the Black Hills ponderosa pine is *Pinus ponderosa* Doug. ex P. Laws. & C. Laws., var. *scopulorum*.[4]

Since most plants have common names, which vary from time to time and from region to region, naturalists have found it wise to use their universally recognized scientific names as well. The case of the ponderosa pine is relatively clear because its scientific and common names are similar, though it also has been called western yellow pine, Rocky Mountain pine, and bull pine. In later years, when forest managers began to deal with entire plant communities and not just trees, scientific names would prove indispensable.

But to assess timber potential, Graves was charged with describing the character, extent, and condition of the tree stands in the Black Hills. Since the area had been surveyed and Graves had access to satisfactory topographic maps, he determined to approach his work by developing a simple classification system.[5] At first, he distinguished between marketable trees ready to be cut and non-marketable trees too small to cut; then he divided marketable trees into three classes: (1) trees averaging

20 inches in diameter and 80 feet in height, with straight trunks free of limbs up to 50 feet, growing in "crowded stands" on rich soils in protected sites, the largest such stand west of Spearfish Canyon; (2) "old trees" with the same diameter as the first class but averaging 65–70 feet in height, clear of limbs up to 40 feet, growing in less crowded stands, more exposed to natural disturbances, and covering the greater part of the Black Hills; and (3) trees smaller and shorter than those in the first two classes, averaging 14–17 inches in diameter, less than 60 feet in height, and located on ridges and steep slopes where the soils were "stony and thin."[6]

Among "old trees" in the un-timbered "original forest," Graves had seen clusters of non-marketable trees 40 to 100 years old. He was struck by the extreme density of these younger trees, from which he postulated ideal conditions for germination and growth of the ponderosa pine, foremost being location. "The old timber in canyon bottoms and side ravines is of superior development and quality," he wrote, "not only because the soil is rich and fresh, but because the trees are in protected situations."[7] Graves observed that stands on north slopes tended to be of better quality than those on south slopes because of more moisture and protection from fires. Also, he noted differences between the granitic or pre-Cambrian soils found in the central Black Hills and the limestone soils of the plateau country. He saw no differences in growth where stands were equally protected but, under similar climatic conditions, found that seeds germinated more readily in the "stronger" (more alkaline) limestone soils. He described ideal stand density as high enough to promote natural pruning of lower branches, thus providing more perfect lumber, and low enough to allow for maximum growth by diameter and height: "Trees prune themselves better on poor than on active soils."[8]

While acknowledging that he had stayed in the Black Hills for too short a time to ascertain the precise characteristics of the ponderosa pine, Graves did observe that natural reproduction appeared more than sufficient to ensure stand replacement. For example, he reported on a stand of saplings about 10 feet high with an estimated 7,000 to 8,000 trees per acre, far greater than today's recommended density for commercial timber stands. Again, he found the most prolific reproduction on broken forestland where older, seed-producing trees were evenly distributed or in small clusters not larger than 1 acre. Best growth seemed to occur along the forest edge and on hillsides where seedlings were exposed to light from above and on their sides.[9]

Graves was the first to report on forest fires in some detail, to distinguish between severe and less severe fires, and to assess their effect on forest growth. He concluded that most of the Black Hills had been burned by severe fire roughly every half century. By severe fires, he meant fires that burned so intensely that they destroyed the upper soil to the extent that seeds could not immediately germinate and that severely damaged or entirely denuded large swathes of forest. By less severe fires, he meant fires that burned close to the ground, destroying seedlings and saplings but inflicting only minor damage on older trees.

Indeed, Graves marveled at the fire tolerance of older trees and how their growth covered over and healed their fire scars. He described the case of a tree "about six inches in diameter . . . so severely burned that but three inches on one side had escaped injury. Not only had the tree succeeded in living, but the new growth had, within about 160 years, wrapped itself completely about the injured portion, even inclosing a disk of dead bark. A few years ago this tree was cut down for lumber and was apparently perfectly sound."[10] The effect of ground fires on smaller trees was a mixed blessing. Where fires burned only the upper, un-decayed layers of litter, ashes enriched the remaining humus and encouraged seed germination. But ground fires also destroyed seedlings, making room for a dense cover of grasses, shrubs, and, from his viewpoint, commercially useless trees such as aspen.[11]

The oldest severe fire for which Graves found empirical evidence had occurred sometime between 1730 and 1740. By counting annual tree rings, starting from just under the bark toward the rings scarred by fire, he dated trees at 160 to 170 years old, placing their germination shortly after a severe fire. Similarly, he found fire scars from the period 1790–1800, thus trees 100 to 110 years old. Since electrical storms were common, Graves had seen evidence of trees struck by lightning that, in turn, had caused wildfires. Most susceptible to ignition appeared to be patches of dead and dying trees in which he had found evidence of "bark borers, a species of Scolytidae, working under the bark," the first written mention of what Andrew D. Hopkins later identified as the Black Hills beetle.[12]

Regarding fires in the nineteenth century, Graves heard confirmation of his empirical observations. An early settler from Pactola, west of Rapid City, relayed conversations with Indians about their memories of severe fires around 1842, which they attributed to lightning strikes. Graves was unable to confirm stories told by the same Indians regarding fires their distant ancestors set as part of hunting for big game.[13] Controversy remains about those stories and, if true, whether game was driven by fire from the central forest into the foothills or simply from the foothills onto the plains.

Although the extent of human presence in the Black Hills before the 1870s remains obscure, we do know that by the late eighteenth century bands of nomadic Indians were moving over the adjoining plains; as the availability of buffalo declined, Indians entered the forest in search of other big game.[14] Pictographs found in the Black Hills suggest that the Lakota Sioux had become the predominant tribe by about 1800. As the westernmost group of the Sioux, the Lakota had migrated to the Black Hills from the upper Midwest. Originally a woodland tribe, it has been suggested that they camped within the forest during winter months.[15]

While the movement of nomadic tribes before the late eighteenth century remains unclear, we do know that sometime during the early 1740s Pierre Gauthier de Varennes, sieur de La Vérendrye, a soldier and fur trader stationed in Quebec, commissioned a party to search for the Western Ocean. Leading the party, his two sons, François and Louis-Joseph, traveled around the northern edge of the Black Hills, proceeded as far as the Big Horn Mountains, then abandoned their search and returned to Canada. The first written notice of the Black Hills is attributed to them. In their journal, they described the Black Hills as "for the most part well wooded with all kinds of timber."[16]

Although no European traveling in or around the Black Hills left written record during the second half of the eighteenth century, we can assume that fur trappers from several nations—France, Spain, Great Britain, and the United States—did travel in the area. Just prior to the Treaty of Paris in 1763, France had ceded Louisiana, including the Black Hills, to Spain as compensation for Spain's expected loss of Florida to Great Britain; by the Third Treaty of San Idelfonso in 1800, Spain secretly ceded Louisiana back to France. After the Louisiana Purchase in 1803, President Thomas Jefferson sent his aide, Meriwether Lewis, with William Clark to explore the newly acquired territory.

After the La Vérendrye brothers, Lewis provided the next fleeting description of the Black Hills. On October 1, 1804, along the Missouri River a few miles upstream from the mouth of the Cheyenne River (northwest of Pierre), Lewis and Clark met a French trader named Jean-Baptiste Valle. He informed them that he had spent the past winter far up the Cheyenne River "under the Black Mountains." He described the mountains as "very high" with "great quantities of pine," noted that snow remained on some parts of the mountains throughout the summer, and reported that "a great noise is heard frequently on those mountains." The last observation contributed to the mystery surrounding the Black Hills in the minds of early American explorers.[17] At an earlier stop, on September 16, Meriwether Lewis had found "Pine Burs" (cones) in driftwood a short distance up the White River from its confluence with the Missouri River. This led Charles Sprague Sargent, author of the monumental *Silva of North America*, to attribute the first collection of the ponderosa pine to Meriwether Lewis.[18]

Thomas Nuttall, the English botanist who had helped classify the botanical specimens collected by Lewis and Clark, was part of the 1811 American Fur Company expedition led by Wilson Price Hunt, which followed the Lewis and Clark route up the Missouri River. There is no evidence that Nuttall collected in the Black Hills or that any member of the Hunt party entered the forest.[19]

Not until 1823 do we get a firsthand written description of the forest itself. In the fall of that year, James Clyman—trapper, adventurer, and sometime diarist—accompanied the William H. Ashley expedition from St. Louis through the southern Black Hills, along the Cheyenne River, and west into the Powder River Basin. Though brief and inexact, Clyman did convey a general impression of the topography, from rolling hills covered by pine, "with here and there an open glade of rich soil and fine grass," to ascending ridges where, near the summits, the land became brushy with "scrubby" pine and juniper. Descending westward, the ridges turned into ravines so narrow that "horses had no room to turn," until the party reached a long plateau that eventually descended to the Cheyenne River.[20]

The little that is known about the Black Hills between 1823 and the military expeditions of the 1850s likely came from Indians who traded at Fort Laramie, at the spot on the plains where today the Laramie River flows into the North Platte River. It is said that the Indians traded gold nuggets from the Black Hills for merchandise at Fort Laramie.[21] Another source of information may have been a trading post known as Ogalallah, which apparently operated sporadically during the 1830s at the confluence of Rapid Creek and the Cheyenne River east of present-day Rapid City. Most likely, fur traders had built temporary and seasonal cabins along creeks in the foothills, but no records about the forest remain.[22]

In the course of westward development, the Black Hills was the last area to be explored. During the 1840s, the American military had established permanent posts at Fort Pierre to the east, Fort Kearny to the southeast, and Fort Laramie to the southwest. Between 1855 and 1875, the military sent a series of expeditions into the area for the purpose of protecting emigrants along established trails and reconnoitering new trails for prospectors en route to Montana.

Under a general principle of European law, the United States had gained sovereignty over the Black Hills region as a result of the Louisiana Purchase; thereby, it now possessed the exclusive right to buy land from the Indians, recognized by the federal government as the land's lawful occupants. Following the end of the Civil War, the US Department of War and the US Department of the Interior, through the Commission of Indian Affairs, competed against each other over the administration of lands reserved for the Indians; their differing approaches to seeking and keeping peace with and between the Indian tribes would be revealed in the Treaty of Fort Laramie (1868).[23]

For reasons both scientific and economic, each military expedition included a corps of naturalists to collect and assess information about the unexplored country. General William F. Harney led the first of these expeditions in 1855, accompanied by Lieutenant General Gouverneur Kemble Warren as topographic engineer, Ferdinand V. Hayden as geologist, W.P.C. Carrington as meteorologist, and Paul Max Engle as topographer. In a memoir included in Warren's *Explorations in the Dacota Country in the Year 1855*, Hayden recorded the first known notice about merchantable timber: the Black Hills "contain an inexhaustible quantity of the finest timber, mostly pine." He suggested that logs could be floated down the Belle Fourche and Cheyenne Rivers for inhabited places along the Missouri River, as he believed the Black Hills area would not be settled for a long time to come.[24]

Hayden and Warren returned to explore the mountainous region of the Black Hills with their own party in 1856–57. Together, they prepared the first maps of the area, later used by forester Henry Graves. Warren discovered and named Harney Peak after General Harney. Hayden found evidence suggesting the presence of gold in lower French Creek near the confluence with the Cheyenne River, confirming stories earlier relayed by Indians at Fort Laramie.[25] In 1859–60 Hayden again returned to the Black Hills, this time in a party led by Warren's successor, Captain William F. Raynolds. This party's charge was to investigate the geography, topography, climate, and possible routes for roads or rails "either to meet the wants or needs of military operations or those of emigration through, or settlement in, the country."[26] Hayden's reports had the effect of encouraging the Dakota Territorial Legislature to ask the US Congress in 1862, and again in 1866, for a scientific expedition to confirm the extent of mineral and timber resources in anticipation of the hoped-for opening of the Black Hills to settlement.[27]

By the 1868 Treaty of Fort Laramie, however, the United States agreed to recognize as reserved to the Lakota Sioux that part of Dakota Territory known as "West River," which included the Black Hills. The treaty specified that the Great Sioux Reservation be "set apart for the absolute and undisturbed use and occupation of the Indians." In return, the Sioux agreed to end their opposition to construction of the Union Pacific Railroad along the Platte River and to stop disturbing emigrant caravans. Settlers in Dakota Territory interpreted the treaty as favoring their counterparts on the central Great Plains.[28]

At best, the Treaty of Fort Laramie can be described as deficient. Not all authorized tribal chiefs signed the treaty; those who did sign agreed to allow "the construction of railroads, wagon roads, mail stations, or other works of utility or necessity, which may be ordered or permitted by the laws of the United States." The treaty's ambiguities would provide cause for questioning the federal government's sincerity in keeping the Black Hills closed to settlement. Whereas the military pledged to enforce the treaty and maintain the peace, civil authorities pledged to "insure the civilization of the Indians" by granting land out of reservation commons to families who wanted to settle and farm, offering elementary education to boys and girls ages six to sixteen, and supplying the needy with basic food, clothing, health services, and stipends.[29]

Continuing Sioux raids on westward travelers, combined with persistent stories about gold deposits, provided the rationale for General Philip H. Sheridan,

FIGURE 1.2. "Lime Stone Peak," William H. Illingworth, 1874 Custer expedition, and 2005 re-photograph. Courtesy, photo © Paul Horsted, http://www.dakotaphoto.com.

commander of the US Army's Department of the Missouri, to charge General Alfred H. Terry, Dakota District, to organize a reconnaissance expedition into the Black Hills. General Terry assigned the command to Lieutenant Colonel George A. Custer, stationed at Fort Abraham Lincoln near Bismarck, North Dakota. Much has been written about Custer's Black Hills expedition, July 2–August 30, 1874. Its official reports contained qualitative descriptions of the landscape and fine photographs by William H. Illingworth. The photographs were published in 1974, side by side with contemporary photographs that illustrated dramatic changes in forest cover.[30] Then in 2002, using excerpts from early eyewitness reports together with the Illingworth photographs and his companion photographs, Paul Horsted with Ernest Grafe compiled a first-rate chronicle, complete with maps and commentary, tracing the Custer expedition's route.[31]

As indication of its high profile, the Custer expedition brought along several news reporters, including Aris B. Donaldson, professor of rhetoric and English literature at the University of Minnesota, who reported for the *Saint Paul Daily Pioneer*.[32] An amateur botanist, Donaldson collected the first floristic specimens—forty-two different species—and forwarded them to the eminent botanist John Merle Coulter for identification; eventually, the specimens were moved to the herbarium at the New York Botanical Garden.

Reporters extolled the beauty of the Black Hills and speculated about its future use. The sentimentalist among them, Donaldson described the area as "the hunter's paradise," containing squirrels, hares, wolves, panthers, bears, deer, and elk. "Let the disciples of [the naturalist] Izaac Walton come here," he wrote, to "indulge in piscatorial sports and dreamy reveries." As if to foretell the coming of tourism, he wrote, "The lover of nature could here find his soul's delight; the invalid regain his health; the old be rejuvenated; the weary find sweet repose and invigoration; and all who could come and spend the heated season here, would find it the pleasantest summer home in America."[33]

Even the military men were dazzled by the area's floristic beauty. Custer named the valley of Cold Springs Creek, about 15 miles southeast of present-day Sundance, Wyoming, "Floral Valley." About that valley, Private Theodore Ewert noted in his diary: "A natural garden! One immense, vast flower bed! A paradise!" He described the "narrow and crooked valley, stretching away into the dim distance as far as the eye could see, and literally crammed with flowers. Every step of the horses would crush ten, fifteen beautiful wild flowers to the earth, and not as one might think of one variety."[34]

Other expedition members left observations on the general nature of the forest. Captain William Ludlow, who as chief engineer oversaw map making, wrote about both the density of tree stands and the meadows between them.[35] Chicago newspaper reporter William E. Curtis wrote, "None of us ever saw so dense and so extended a growth of pine."[36] Minnesota state geologist Newton H. Winchell made several references to the legacy of fires. About his ascent of Harney Peak, he wrote, "The trees had been thrown down by fire or tempest, often half consumed and left charred, and a thousand shrubs and small aspens . . . had made a perfect netted mesh, through which no horse could pass."[37] Similarly, Private Ewert described the difficulties of cutting swathes through downed trees, "sometimes six, seven and eight on top of each other, their branches interlocked," so wagons could get through.[38]

Then came the most exciting news from an economic standpoint: the two prospectors on the expedition found flakes of gold in the sand and gravel of French Creek, downstream from present-day Custer. One of them laid claim to the discovery and took out papers to organize the first mining district, arguably in violation of the Treaty of Fort Laramie. General Custer sent a courier with news of the discovery to Cheyenne, from which word was telegraphed to military headquarters in St. Paul and published in newspapers before the end of August.

Although the two prospectors did not have time to determine the geographic extent or value of the gold deposits, news of the discovery was enough to whet speculators' appetites. For his part, General Sheridan reiterated his standing order that trespassers into the reservation be stopped and those already within the reservation be driven out. At the same time, he urged the federal government to negotiate the purchase of the Black Hills. To calculate the value of such an offer, the commissioner of Indian affairs, in cooperation with the director of the US Geological Survey, commissioned Walter P. Jenney of Columbia University School of Mines and his assistant, Henry Newton, to survey the Black Hills for mineral deposits. With a military escort of 400 men commanded by Lieutenant Colonel Richard I. Dodge, the expedition left Cheyenne in March 1875 and returned in October.[39]

Jenney's expedition included an astronomer, photographer, topographer, head miner and ten laborers, and, as naturalist, Lieutenant William L. Carpenter. Although its primary objective was exploring for minerals, Jenney reported on the potential for timbering as well as farming in the Black Hills. He identified the ponderosa pine as by far the most commercially valuable tree. He had seen "old trees" such as the ones Graves later classified. For his part, Carpenter found a 100-foot-tall tree with a diameter of 35–40 inches in the lower French Creek area. He estimated that a merchantable tree would generally yield straight logs 30–50 feet long and 12–20 inches in diameter, eminently suitable for building houses and fences.[40]

Lieutenant Colonel Dodge reported not only on vast supplies of usable timber but also on rich valley soils that could produce fruits and vegetables, as well as luxuriant meadows that, he estimated, could support enough cattle to supply butter and cheese to the entire nation. As to "the absurdity of turning over such a country to miserable nomads," he expressed the opinion that the Sioux really did not want the country ("they never use it") but that "they are put up to this opposition [to sell] by interested agents, who hope to have the manipulation of millions of dollars which the Government may pay for the land, if the Indians only make row enough."[41]

Upon receiving news of the Jenney expedition and some expression of Sioux interest in negotiating the sale of the Black Hills, President Ulysses S. Grant instructed Secretary of the Interior Columbus Delano to appoint a negotiating commission. Chaired by Senator William B. Alllison (R-IA), the commission met in September 1875 with the grand council of the Sioux near the Red Cloud Agency in northwest Nebraska. Allison laid out proposals to lease or purchase the Black Hills; the Sioux declined the offers. As raids resumed, President Grant issued an executive order reaffirming that the Black Hills remained closed to prospectors and settlers while declaring that the military would no longer enforce the ban on entry to the reservation. By the end of the year, approximately 15,000 people had rushed to the Black Hills for gold. Their impact on the forest was immediate.[42]

NOTES

1. Henry S. Graves, "The Black Hills Forest Reserve," in US Geological Survey, *Nineteenth Annual Report, 1897–1898*, Part V: *Forest Reserves* (Washington, DC: Government Printing Office, 1899), 68.

2. Ibid., 69; Wayne D. Shepperd and Michael A. Battaglia, *Ecology, Silviculture, and Management of Black Hills Ponderosa Pine*, USDA Forest Service, Rocky Mountain Research Station General Technical Report 97 (September 2002): 1–3.

3. Graves, "Black Hills Forest Reserve," 72–73.

4. See William W. Oliver and Russell A. Ryker, "*Pinus ponderosa* Dougl. ex Laws," in *Silvics of North America,* ed. Russell M. Burns and Barbara H. Honkala (Washington, DC: USDA Forest Service, 1990), 1: 413–24.

5. Henry S. Graves, "Autobiographical Notes" (unpublished), transcribed by Jean M. Pablo, cabinet 8, drawer 1, folder 17, Black Hills National Forest Historical Collection, Leland D. Case Library for Western Historical Studies, Black Hills State University, Spearfish, SD.

6. Graves, "Black Hills Forest Reserve," 74–75.

7. Ibid., 75.

8. Ibid.

9. Ibid., 91–92.

10. Ibid., 84.

11. Ibid., 81–84.

12. Ibid., 87; Andrew Delmar Hopkins, "The Black Hills Beetle, with Further Notes on Its Distribution, Life History, and Methods of Control," *USDA Bureau of Entomology Bulletin* 56 (1905): 5–6.

13. Graves, "Black Hills Forest Reserve," 83.

14. Donald R. Progulske with Frank J. Shideler, "Following Custer," *South Dakota Agricultural Experiment Station Bulletin* 674 (1983): 4.

15. Jessie and Linea Sundstrom, "Exploration and Settlement," in *Black Hills National Forest Cultural Resources Overview,* ed. Lance Rom, Tim Church, and Michele Church (Custer: USDA Forest Service, Black Hills National Forest, 1996), I: 4a-1, 4a-2; Royal B. Hassrick, *The Sioux: Life and Customs of a Warrior Society* (Norman: University of Oklahoma Press, 1964), 65, 173, 176.

16. Quoted in Charles E. Deland, "The Vérendrye Explorations and Discoveries," *South Dakota Historical Collections* 7 (1914): 222. Francis Parkman, friend and correspondent of Pierre Margry who published the Vérendrye journal, noted that the brothers skirted the Black Hills from the north; see Parkman, *France and England in North America* (New York: Literary Classics of the United States, 1983 [1892]), 2: 593.

17. Gary E. Moulton, ed., *The Journals of the Lewis and Clark Expedition* (Lincoln: University of Nebraska Press, 1987) 3: 135; John M. Carroll and Lawrence A. Frost, eds., *Private Theodore Ewert's Diary of the Black Hills Expedition of 1874* (Piscataway, NJ: CRI Books, 1976), 1–2.

18. Charles Sprague Sargent, *The Silva of North America* (New York: Peter Smith, 1947 [1897]), 11: 82.

19. Roger L. Williams, *"A Region of Astonishing Beauty": The Botanical Exploration of the Rocky Mountains* (Lanham, MD: Roberts Rinehart, 2003), 37–38; Washington Irving, *Astoria, or Anecdotes of an Enterprise beyond the Rocky Mountains*, ed. Edgeley W. Todd (Norman: University of Oklahoma Press, 1964), 231.

20. Charles L. Camp, ed., *James Clyman, Frontiersman: The Adventures of a Trapper and Covered-Wagon Emigrant as Told in His Own Reminiscences and Diaries* (Portland, OR: Champoeg, 1960), 17–18.

21. Harold E. Briggs, *Frontiers of the Northwest: A History of the Upper Missouri Valley* (New York: D. Appleton-Century, 1940), 26.

22. Sundstrom, "Exploration and Settlement," 4a-4-5.

23. George W. Kingsbury, *History of Dakota Territory* (Chicago: S. J. Clarke, 1915), 1: 744, 753.

24. Quoted in James D. McLaird and Lesta V. Turchen, "Exploring the Black Hills, 1855–1875: Reports of the Government Expedition, the Scientist in Western Exploration, Ferdinand Vandiveer Hayden," *South Dakota History* 4, no. 2 (Spring 1974): 175.

25. Herbert S. Schell, *History of South Dakota*, 3rd ed. (Lincoln: University of Nebraska Press, 1961), 66–69; Sven G. Froiland, *Natural History of the Black Hills and Badlands* (Sioux Falls: Center for Western Studies, Augustana College, 1990), 49–50.

26. Quoted in James D. McLaird and Lesta V. Turchen, "Exploring the Black Hills, 1855–1875: Reports of the Government Expeditions, the Explorations of Captain William Franklin Raynolds, 1859–1860," *South Dakota History* 4, no. 1 (Winter 1973): 21.

27. McLaird and Turchen, "Scientist in Western Exploration," 192; John Milton, *South Dakota, a Bicentennial History* (New York: W. W. Norton, 1977), 24.

28. Schell, *History of South Dakota*, 88–89.

29. Treaty of Fort Laramie, *US Statutes at Large* 15 (1868): 635–40.

30. Donald R. Progulske and Richard H. Sowell, "Yellow Ore, Yellow Hair, Yellow Pine: A Photographic Study of a Century of Forest Ecology," *South Dakota Agricultural Experiment Station Bulletin* 616 (July 1974). Amanda G. McAdams sought to quantify the changes Progulske had illustrated through comparative photographs in "Changes in Ponderosa Pine Forest Structure in the Black Hills, South Dakota, 1874–1995" (MS thesis, Northern Arizona University, Flagstaff, 1995).

31. Ernest Grafe and Paul Horsted, *Exploring with Custer: The 1874 Black Hills Expedition,* 3rd ed. (Custer, SD: Golden Valley, 2005).

32. Ibid., 3.

33. Aris B. Donaldson, "The Black Hills Expedition [1874]," *South Dakota Historical Collections* 7 (1914): 573.

34. Carroll and Frost, *Private Theodore Ewert's Diary*, 41.

35. Grafe and Horsted, *Exploring with Custer*, 28.

36. Quoted in ibid., 34.

37. Ibid., 81.

38. Carroll and Frost, *Private Theodore Ewert's Diary*, 116.

39. Schell, *History of South Dakota*, 128–31.

40. Walter P. Jenney, "The Mineral Wealth, Climate and Rainfall, and Natural Resources of the Black Hills of Dakota," *US Geological and Geographical Survey of the Black Hills* (Washington, DC: General Printing Office, 1876), 69–70.

41. Wayne R. Kime, ed., *The Black Hills Journals of Colonel Richard Irving Dodge* (Norman: University of Oklahoma Press, 1996), 105.

42. John D. McDermott, "The Military Problem and the Black Hills, 1874–1875," *South Dakota History* 31, no. 3–4 (Fall-Winter 2001): 201–6; Howard R. Lamar, *Dakota Territory, 1861–1889: A Study of Frontier Politics* (New Haven: Yale University Press, 1956), 149–50.

2

Unbridled Use of the Forest

During the first quarter-century of settlement, from the advent of prospectors in 1874 up to the first sale of government timber in 1899, more than 1.5 billion board feet were cut in the Black Hills.[1] Annualized, that amount represents about two-thirds of what was cut in 2010; in the early days, however, timbering was concentrated around mining camps where loggers denuded entire hillsides, wasted more wood than they used, and degraded watersheds. It could be argued that long-standing federal land policies and an absence of federal regulatory enforcement contributed to such despoliation.

Following President Grant's deliberately ambiguous executive order, prospectors streamed into the French Creek area. The Custer town site was inhabited in early spring 1875, with a semblance of local government established in early 1876. By May, virtually the entire population had rushed to the northern Black Hills where, almost overnight, the town of Deadwood claimed a population of 5,000.[2] In Deadwood Gulch and environs, prospectors seeking gold struggled over masses of fallen timber. While such timber could be used as firewood, the prospectors needed solid lumber for their sluices—over which they panned to separate gold particles from sand and gravel—and for the sluice boxes by which they controlled stream flow.

Because of the great distances from civilization and the prohibitive costs of transportation, timbering in the Black Hills began at the most rudimentary level. At first, prospectors made do with basic tools—the ax, adze, and whipsaw; logging and

DOI: 10.5876/9781607322993.c002

milling were primitive. An early immigrant to Deadwood described the process: after chopping down a tree and trimming off its branches, two men dragged the cut log over a pit, where the log was held in place by a frame of timbers. The men hewed the log to create a piece of lumber approximately 1 inch thick and 12 inches wide. Then, one man stood on the frame and pulled the whipsaw up while the second man stood in the pit and pulled the saw down, cutting the board to a length of about 12 feet. By cutting the boards so they would interlock without the use of nails, the men could easily separate and move the boards from one placer site to another.[3]

Demand for lumber was such that the steam-powered sawmill soon replaced the hand-hewing process. This readily portable sawmill consisted of three elements: a wood-fired boiler, a large circular saw, and a carriage running on rails on which a log was moved past the saw. John Murphy from Nebraska is credited with assembling the first sawmill in Custer, which he had imported in pieces by ox or mule train from Cheyenne in February 1876. Murphy sold the sawmill in May, presumably to an owner who moved it to Deadwood where, by July, three sawmills were operating; each produced enough boards in one day to construct one house. Within a year, one of the mills added a planer, also powered by steam. Used to smooth surfaces and edges on sawn boards, the planer produced lumber suitable for doors, window frames, moldings, siding, ceilings, and flooring—all sold locally at premium prices.[4]

Just as prospectors caused the start of timbering, so too did they attract the first livestock. Mark Boughton from Wyoming is considered the first rancher to transfer his business to the Black Hills. In spring 1876 he sold his ranch near Cheyenne and trailed his cattle through unknown and unsettled country, anticipating high profits from the sale of beef and dairy products in the mining area.[5]

That summer, in the aftermath of the Battle of Little Big Horn, a new federal commission sought to negotiate the removal of the Sioux from the Black Hills. This time, the commission did not meet with the grand council but only with Sioux chiefs. Faced with imminent starvation and in return for federal assistance as long as needed, the chiefs agreed to give up claims to the Black Hills and to move their tribes to the Pine Ridge and Rosebud Reservations. On February 28, 1877, President Ulysses S. Grant signed the bill confirming that agreement with the Sioux chiefs, effectively repealing the 1868 Treaty of Fort Laramie.[6]

As is well-known, later generations of tribal leaders would challenge the validity of the agreement. In 1980 the US Supreme Court ruled the 1877 act unconstitutional and awarded the Sioux tribes $105 million as compensation for the taking of 7.3 million acres. The tribes declined the award because it did not include the land; the Supreme Court declined to hear their appeal.[7] In 2012 four Sioux tribes raised the monies necessary to purchase Reynolds Prairie Ranch, an inholding of 1,940 acres that the tribes continued to use as a key sacred site in their creation story.

The Oglala Sioux declined to participate in the fundraising, their president-elect stating "I'm still against buying something we own, but I'm thrilled the tribes are buying it."[8]

With the Black Hills no longer reserved for the Sioux after the 1877 act, the land reverted to the status of unappropriated US property. Prospectors who had earlier staked out claims found that recent arrivals used the new land status as an excuse to challenge those claims; those who had earlier staked out land for farming and timbering found prospectors "jumping" their land. Although the territorial legislature had drawn the boundaries for Custer, Lawrence, and Pennington Counties, no federal officials were yet present to survey the land or make allocations of any kind. In other words, those who made claims did so with no legal titles; they were squatters. Over time, most claimants retained their holdings, a matter that contributed greatly to the complexity of managing the future national forests.[9]

Historically, the federal government had encouraged private development as part of its policy to settle the West. Less publicized than homestead and preemption acts, the Timber and Stone Act of 1878, also known as the Free Timber Act, permitted miners and settlers to cut timber for personal use, free of charge, on "mineral lands" specifically identified as not suited for agriculture. Its intent seemed laudable, to assist families and small operators in making ends meet; had the act been enforced, limiting free timbering to "mineral lands" only, it would have provided insufficient timber for the intended uses. Moreover, like other preemption acts, this act contained ambiguities that would be exploited by small-scale logging operators and later by large mining companies and the railroads.

For the earliest prospectors and settlers, cutting trees and making logs had been secondary to their main occupations. In spring 1880, John Durst and Sons became the first operator for whom timbering was the primary occupation. The Dursts had purchased a portable sawmill in Cheyenne and transported it to a forest location west of Custer. There they produced the lumber used for home construction in Custer. After they exhausted local timber stands, they relocated to a site south of town.[10] Similarly, brothers Odo and Theodore Reder, immigrants from Pennsylvania, cut trees and operated portable sawmills around mining sites in the northern Black Hills. As those mining activities declined, Odo Reder moved his sawmill to the Custer area. After fire destroyed that facility, he built the first permanent sawmill and by 1893 had gained the reputation of operating the most efficient sawmill in the Black Hills. Meanwhile, his brother Theodore had set up a mill near Hill City and freighted lumber to Rapid City, where he expanded into the construction business.[11]

Henry Graves reported that by 1897, some timber stands had been entered for two successive cuttings. Initially, loggers had taken the largest trees that produced

FIGURE 2.1. Portable sawmill, ca. 1885. Courtesy, Black Hills National Forest Historical Collection, Leland D. Case Library for Western Historical Studies, Black Hills State University, Spearfish, SD.

the clearest logs; during second entry they cut smaller trees, though still 14 inches or more in diameter at stump level. Graves noted the "reckless waste of timber which has been going on for years." Where loggers found "a few spots of decay" or "logs [that] prove too knotty . . . either the whole tree is left lying in the woods or only one log is taken." Graves estimated that loggers wasted half of each tree cut, the equivalent of 1.5 cords of firewood for every 1,000 board feet transported out of the forest. Having seen "great masses of decaying saw logs" left behind, he noted that loggers cut more trees than they could mill to prevent their competitors from coming in.[12]

Graves found the worst evidence of deforestation within an 8-mile radius of Deadwood. By 1897 hard-rock mining, which required big timbers for mine shafts, had replaced placer mining. Two prospectors from Montana, Fred and Moses Manuel, had discovered and laid claim to a ledge of ore they named Homestake Lead, lead (pronounced "leed") being the name for a ledge of ore. On their claim about 3 miles south of Deadwood, the brothers dug a shaft and built a primitive mill to separate gold from ore. Within one year they sold the Homestake and nearby Golden Star claims to a group of investors including George Hearst,

FIGURE 2.2. Early deforestation around Deadwood. Courtesy, USDA Forest Service, Black Hills National Forest, http://www.ForestPhoto.com.

mining engineer and US senator from California; the investors incorporated the Homestake Mining Company in California.[13]

Homestake's requirements for mine timbers, lumber, and firewood grew rapidly. Since the Free Timber Act of 1878 pertained to domestic use only and since much surrounding forestland was federal, unappropriated, and without protection, Homestake simply proceeded to timber. Logging began around Lead; the company built and maintained its own narrow-gauge rail line, extending southeast as timber ran out. By 1883 the Black Hills and Fort Pierre Railroad had reached the eastern edge of the Black Hills. Henry Graves reported that Homestake operated three timber camps whose laborers supplied the mine with nearly 2 million board feet of timber annually.[14]

The advent of the railroads not only extended timbering into new areas but also contributed to the growth of ranching. By 1886 the Fremont, Elkhorn, and Missouri Valley Railroad skirted the eastern edge of the Black Hills from Chadron, Nebraska, through Buffalo Gap to Rapid City and then northwest to Belle Fourche. Buffalo Gap and Belle Fourche became major shipping points for cattle. The Burlington and Missouri River Railroad went through Edgemont at the southern edge of the Black Hills. From there, a line ran north to Custer and Hill

City, reaching Deadwood in 1891. In addition to delivering freight that included hardwood lumber not locally available, the railroads helped connect residents of the Black Hills communities to each other and to the rest of the nation, as well as to advance the development of tourism.[15]

The very earliest settlers had commented on the possibility of using the Black Hills as "a natural playground and sanitarium," even after loggers had shorn the forest of its "primitive luxuriance and beauty."[16] Around 1879, settlers discovered warm springs along Fall River in the southern Black Hills. A rheumatic named Joe Larive and his business partners opened the first commercial spa, which they sold in 1881 to a group of investors from Deadwood. The new owners formed the Hot Springs Town-Site Company and built the first boardinghouse. With the advent of the railroad in the early 1890s, Hot Springs claimed fifteen hotels, including the five-story Evans Hotel built of native stone. Developer Fred Evans added an indoor water park with a 150-foot-long pool, water slides, and other amenities. The Evans Plunge, still operating, was the first in what would become an ever-expanding number of "family entertainment" enterprises within and surrounding the forests of the Black Hills.[17]

In the most mountainous part of the Black Hills, logger Theodore Reder built the first destination resort. Working in the upper Sunday Gulch area near Hill City, Reder found a site he believed was perfect for an artificial lake and a hotel on its banks. In 1891 he obtained water rights, formed a company to raise capital, and hired a crew to build an earthen dam 30 feet high and 40 feet wide, creating Sylvan Lake with a surface of about 10 acres. After the dam was completed, Reder oversaw construction of a sixty-six-room hotel—a monumental feat considering the rocky terrain, the remoteness of the location, and the unavailability of skilled workers. Opened in summer 1895, the hotel proved too expensive for Reder to operate, so he sold it the following summer.[18]

Among the guests at Sylvan Lake Hotel that second summer was John Muir, the naturalist and founder of the Sierra Club. Muir described "this hollow in the rocky Black Hills" in a letter to his two daughters: "It is wonderful even to me after seeing so many wild mountains—curious rocks rising alone or in clusters, gray and jagged and rounded in the midst of a forest of pines and spruces and poplars and birches, with a little lake in the middle and a carpet of meadow gay with flowers."[19] Muir's advocacy for wild lands would find organized supporters in the Black Hills, but not until the 1970s.

Meanwhile, unbridled timbering throughout the nation renewed fear among members of the US Congress that the nation could run out of timber. On March 18, 1890, Representative William S. Hollman (D-IN) introduced a bill to repeal the 1873 Timber Culture Act. The House passed the repeal and sent it to the

Senate, which approved an amended version. When the House declined to concur, the repeal bill went to a six-member conference committee that included Senator Richard F. Pettigrew (R-SD) and Representative John A. Picker (R-SD), clear recognition of the importance of timbering to South Dakota. The conference committee reported the bill, with a last-minute rider by Senator Preston B. Plumb (R-KS). To a query about the rider's specific contents, Representative Lewis E. Payson (R-IL) responded that it simply enabled the president to temporarily set aside forested public lands, primarily for the protection of watersheds, until Congress passed legislation to open those lands for use. As with much significant legislation, the rider came about not as the product of deliberate and farsighted statecraft but as the result of parliamentary maneuvering that, according to Gifford Pinchot, allowed it to be "slipped through Congress without question and without debate." Most members of Congress, including the South Dakota delegation, did not realize what they had voted for.[20]

President Benjamin Harrison signed the repeal of the Timber Culture Act on March 3, 1891. The Plumb rider, which became known as the Forest Reserve Act, read as follows: "That the President of the United States may, from time to time, set apart and reserve, in any State or Territory having public lands bearing forests, in any part of the public lands wholly or in part covered with timber or undergrowth, whether of commercial value or not, as public reservations, and the President shall, by public proclamation, declare the establishment of such reservations and the limits thereof."[21]

With passage of the Forest Reserve Act, Congress and the president set into motion a fundamental change in federal land policy: from selling public lands to encourage settlement and earn income for the federal government to keeping public lands in public hands for the public good and still earn income for the government. Within a month of passage, President Harrison set aside the first forest reserve, the Yellowstone Park Timber Land Reserve (renamed Shoshone National Forest in 1908), encompassing 1.2 million acres bordering on Yellowstone National Park. When the issue of actively managing public forests arose, Senator Pettigrew would claim authorship of the Forest Reserve Act; his biographer, however, acknowledged the absence of evidence for that assertion. In any event, shortly after passage of the Forest Reserve Act, Senator Pettigrew did seek forest reserve status for a 10-square-mile area around Harney Peak for the purpose of creating a national park, but he gave up that effort in light of local opposition.[22]

During the seven years between the creation of the first reserves and the beginning of their management, timbering in the Black Hills continued unfettered. In preparing the first botanical catalog of the Black Hills, Per Axel Rydberg described the damage mining and timbering caused to the flora. His professor, Charles E.

Bessey, economic botanist at the University of Nebraska, had obtained a commission from the US Department of Agriculture, Division of Botany, for his star student to collect vascular plants in the Black Hills. In crisscrossing the region by train and on foot, Rydberg collected around 700 different species. He noted that vast stands of ponderosa pine had been made barren "by the ravages of lumbermen, mining companies, fire, and cyclones, nothing being left but stumps, fallen logs, and the underbrush." With sawmills scattered all across the Black Hills, "it will be no wonder if in a short time the dark pine forest is gone and the name 'Black Hills' has become meaningless."[23]

Recall that in the late 1870s, Secretary of the Interior Schurz had made valiant attempts to police the public forests. He had sought to limit timbering to trees 8 inches in diameter or larger and did establish a system of special agents to detect forest abuses. Whether any of the early forest agents visited the Black Hills is unclear.[24] In 1894 Secretary of the Interior Michael Hoke Smith requested assistance from the military to protect the forest reserves from illegal encroachments but was turned down on constitutional grounds. Between 1894 and 1897, the Department of the Interior through the General Land Office did station at least one special agent in the Black Hills. As a result, timber trespass charges were filed against, among others, Fish Hunter Company for illegally cutting 4 million board feet on mining claims and for wanton waste of trees, against Homestake Mining Company for cutting undersized trees, and against Odo Reder for numerous charges of timber thievery.[25]

Before the end of his term, President Harrison set apart another 13 million acres of public lands by creating fifteen more reserves. His successor, Grover Cleveland, added 5 million acres and then declined to create more reserves until Congress passed legislation that would enable the federal government effectively to manage the forest reserves.[26]

Enter Gifford Pinchot. Through personal connections, he knew that Charles Sprague Sargent, director of Harvard's Arnold Arboretum, had been pressing for a presidential commission to recommend to Congress a plan for the management of public forests. Knowing about Pinchot's interest in forests, Sargent invited him to a meeting in New York in December 1894 with William A. Styles, editor of *Garden and Forest*, and Robert U. Johnson, associate editor of *Century Magazine*. Both magazines had editorialized for a presidential commission, which had also been endorsed by the American Forestry Association. At Sargent's meeting, the participants drafted a bill to create a presidential commission under auspices of the American Forestry Association; nothing came of it until a second meeting at Sargent's home near Boston in June 1895, with Pinchot, Styles, and Wolcott Gibbs, emeritus Harvard professor of chemistry and physics. Apparently, Pinchot had invited Gibbs in his capacity as president of the National Academy of Science, believing the academy's mission, to conduct research on behalf of government agencies, would make it a more acceptable choice for sponsorship than the American Forestry Association.

Pinchot served as intermediary for the conversations that eventually led Secretary of the Interior Hoke Smith to formally request that Gibbs appoint the National Forest Commission. In February 1896 Gibbs named Henry L. Abbot (hydrographer, Engineering Department of the US Army), Alexander Agassiz (curator, Harvard Museum of Comparative Zoology), William H. Brewer (professor of agriculture and Pinchot's former teacher at Yale), Arnold Hague (geologist, US Geological Survey), Sargent as chair, and as secretary Gifford Pinchot, the only non-member of the National Academy of Science. Gibbs instructed the National Forest Commission to answer three principal questions: (1) what portions of the forests on unapportioned public lands should be reserved, not transferred to private owners? (2) How should the reserved forests be used so nearby inhabitants could draw upon needed forest products without negatively affecting the permanency of the forests? (3) How should the federal government administer those forestlands to ensure "continuous, intelligent and honest management?"[27]

Hague and Pinchot did the bulk of the commission's work, starting with preliminary investigations, interviews, and recommendations. With a $25,000 appropriation from Congress, the commission collected information, primarily from the US Geological Survey and the General Land Office. During summer 1896 members traveled throughout the West, inspecting forested lands and conversing with local residents. Pinchot and his assistant, Henry Graves, had started in late spring, traveling to Montana and then on to the Pacific Northwest where they knew that an existing forest reserve was under attack from both politicians and wool growers. Commission members Abbott, Brewer, Hague, and Sargent, accompanied by John Muir, arrived by train at Hot Springs on July 5, 1896; traveled by wagon to Sylvan Lake Hotel; spent the night; returned to the mainline at Edgemont, and from there took a train through the northern Rockies.[28]

President Grover Cleveland requested that the commission report be ready by November 1 so he could include its recommendations in his last annual message to Congress. Commission members agreed to recommend thirteen new forest reserves for a total of 21 million acres, including the Black Hills. Sargent wrote that the forest of the Black Hills "has suffered seriously from fire and the illegal cutting of timber" and that it "should be protected and made permanently productive" because the mines depended on the timber and the settlers depended on the watershed.[29]

On the matter of reserve administration, Hague and Pinchot favored keeping the forest reserves open for public use and gradually introducing scientific forest management under the direction of professional foresters. Others favored closing the forest reserves immediately, with support of the military if needed, to prevent further forest despoliation but without a specific management plan. As a result of disagreements, the commission postponed completion of its work and failed to meet the president's deadline.[30]

Less than a month before he left office, President Cleveland invoked the Forest Reserve Act to proclaim creation of the thirteen new reserves on 21 million acres. His message included the Black Hills Forest Reserve of 967,680 acres, the number the commission was prepared to recommend.[31] Reaction from Black Hills residents against the president's "midnight surprise" was swift and strongly opposed, based on fear that the proclamation would close the forest to all present and future development, even force the evacuation of communities within reserve boundaries. In fact, quite the opposite would happen, thanks to Senator Pettigrew changing his mind in favor of accepting federal management of the reserves.

NOTES

1. One board foot equals 12 inches by 12 inches by 1 inch. Recently, the US Forest Service began measuring logs by volume as well; 1 cubic foot of ponderosa pine contains about twelve board feet.

2. Jessie Sundstrom and Linea Sundstrom, "Exploration and Settlement," in *Black Hills National Forest Cultural Resources Overview,* ed. Lance Rom, Tim Church, and Michele Church (Custer: USDA Forest Service, Black Hills National Forest, 1996), 1: 4a–10, 4a–11.

3. John S. McClintock, *Pioneer Days in the Black Hills,* ed. Edward L. Senn (Norman: University of Oklahoma Press, 2000 [1939]), 52; Watson Parker, *Gold in the Black Hills* (Norman: University of Oklahoma Press, 1966), 57–58, 76.

4. Martha Linde, *Sawmills of the Black Hills* (Rapid City: Fenske, 1984), 2–3; Carl A. Newport, *Forest Service Policies in Timber Management and Silviculture as They Affect the Lumber Industries: A Case Study of the Black Hills* (Pierre: South Dakota Department of Game, Fish, and Parks, 1956), 9.

5. McClintock, *Pioneer Days,* 77; John Rolfe Burroughs, *Guardians of the Grasslands: The First Hundred Years of the Wyoming Stock Growers Association* (Cheyenne: Pioneer Printing, 1971), 39.

6. Herbert S. Schell, *History of South Dakota,* 3rd ed. (Lincoln: University of Nebraska Press, 1961), 143.

7. Linda Green Hobbs, "Sioux Lose Fight for Land in Dakota," *New York Times,* January 19, 1982.

8. Quoted in http://www.cbsnews.com/news/tribes-raise-9m-to-buy-sacred-south -dakota-land/; accessed December 2012. See also Linea Sundstrom, "The Sacred Black Hills: An Ethnohistorical Review," *Great Plains Quarterly* 17, no. 3–4 (Summer-Fall 1997): 206–8.

9. "Annals of the Black Hills," typescript, p. 4, 1948 draft with 1967 addition, Black Hills National Forest supervisor's office, Custer, SD (hereafter BHNF).

10. Linde, *Sawmills of the Black Hills*, 5.

11. Ibid., 8–11.

12. Henry S. Graves, "The Black Hills Forest Reserve," US Geological Survey, *Nineteenth Annual Report, 1897–1898*, Part V: Forest Reserves (Washington, DC: Government Printing Office, 1899), 88–89. One cord measures 4 feet by 4 feet by 8 feet.

13. *Homestake Centennial, 1876–1976* (Lead, SD: Homestake Mining Company, 1976), 5–6.

14. Newport, *Forest Service Policies*, 10–11; Graves, *Black Hills Forest Reserve*, 90.

15. Sundstrom and Sundstrom, "Exploration and Settlement, 1: 4a–14.

16. McClintock, *Pioneer Days*, 7; Annie D. Tallent, *The Black Hills, or, the Last Hunting Ground of the Dakotahs: A Complete History of the Black Hills of Dakota, from Their First Invasion in 1874 to the Present* (St. Louis: Nixon-Jones, 1899), 107.

17. Suzanne Barta Julin, *A Marvelous Hundred Square Miles: Black Hills Tourism, 1880–1941* (Pierre: South Dakota State Historical Society Press, 2009), 8–11.

18. Ibid., 33; Linde, *Sawmills of the Black Hills*, 9–10.

19. John Muir to daughters Helen and Wanda, Sylvan Lake, July 6, 1896, in William Frederic Badè, ed., *The Life and Letters of John Muir* (Boston: Houghton Mifflin, 1924), 2: 301.

20. John Ise, *The United States Forest Policy* (New York: Arno, 1972 [1920]), 117; Harold K. Steen, "The Beginning of the National Forest System," USDA Forest Service, History Unit FS-488 (May 1991): 18–20, 85; Gifford Pinchot, *Breaking New Ground* (Washington, DC: Island, 1998 [1947]), 85.

21. An Act to Repeal Timber Culture Laws, section 24, *US Statutes at Large*, 51 (1891): 1103.

22. Wayne L. Fanebust, *Echoes of November: The Life and Times of Senator R. F. Pettigrew of South Dakota* (Freeman, SD: Pine Hill Press, 1997), 209–10.

23. Per Axel Rydberg, "Flora of the Black Hills of South Dakota," *Contributions from the U.S. National Herbarium* 3, no, 8 (June 1896): 476–77. See also Roger L. Williams, *"A Region of Astonishing Beauty": The Botanical Exploration of the Rocky Mountains* (Lanham, MD: Roberts Rinehart, 2003), 164–65.

24. Newport, *Forest Service Policies*, 12–13.

25. Ise, *United States Forest Policy*, 121; Linde, *Sawmills of the Black Hills*, 11.

26. Harold K. Steen, *The U.S. Forest Service: A History* (Seattle: University of Washington Press, 2004 [1976]), 27–28.

27. Pinchot, *Breaking New Ground*, 87–93; Steen, *U.S. Forest Service*, 30–32.

28. Gerald W. Williams and Char Miller, "At the Creation, the National Forest Commission of 1896–97," *Forest History Today* (Spring-Fall 2005): 33–37; John Muir to Wanda Muir, Hot Springs, SD, July 5, 1896, in Badè, *John Muir*, 2: 299–300.

29. Charles Sprague Sargent to Wolcott Gibbs, February 1, 1897, copy, BHNF.

30. Pinchot, *Breaking New Ground*, 105–7.

31. Steen, "Beginning of the National Forest System," 30–31.

3

Federal Administration of the Forest Reserve

Under the headline "Civilization Stabbed," the *Custer Weekly Chronicle* reported that President Cleveland's February 22, 1897, executive order "may be safely regarded as one of the most vital blows at civilization, so far as the Black Hills is concerned, that has ever been perpetrated by the ruler of any nation in the history of modern or ancient times."[1] Anticipating immediate closure of the forest to everyone—miners, ranchers, farmers, tourists, and inhabitants of communities within the forest—local newspapers reflected unanimous opposition to creation of the Black Hills Forest Reserve. Within ten years, however, the newspapers would reflect general acceptance, even appreciation of the stewardship role performed by the US Forest Service.

The reversal in local opinion was a result of the political skills and sensibilities of Senator Richard F. Pettigrew and Homestake counselor Gideon C. Moody, assisted by Gifford Pinchot, still consulting forester and secretary to the National Forest Commission. Pettigrew had moved to Dakota Territory in 1869 as a government surveyor, settled in Sioux Falls where he practiced law, developed real estate (including gold mining interests in the Black Hills), and served in the territorial legislature and as territorial delegate to the US House of Representatives. Elected to the US Senate when South Dakota became a state in 1889, he joined the Free Silver Republicans and later became a Populist at heart. Moody had reached Dakota Territory in 1864 after serving as a colonel in the Union Army. Trained as an attorney, he, too, had served in the territorial legislature—as speaker for two terms—and

DOI: 10.5876/9781607322993.c003

sat on the territorial supreme court before his election as US senator from South Dakota, also in 1889. Defeated in his bid for reelection two years later, he returned to his home in Deadwood, where he would distinguish himself as legal counsel and lobbyist for the Homestake Mining Company. Moody and Pettigrew had worked together in politics; their business interests in the Black Hills meshed.[2]

In the immediate aftermath of President Cleveland's executive order, Senator Pettigrew had endeared himself to the electorate by vociferously opposing the Black Hills Forest Reserve; but he also knew that for Homestake to survive and support the local economy, it needed timber from the reserve. The "perfect furor of excitement" about reports telegraphed from Washington caused business and civic leaders to call a series of community meetings to galvanize opposition and prepare petitions seeking relief. At the invitation of the mayor, probably William R. Steele, Moody addressed a mass meeting in Deadwood. He warned the crowd about the "incalculable disastrous injury to our mining and dependent industries" caused by President Cleveland's "outrageous act." If upheld, not a single mine would be "worth a hen coop with a dozen hens and a rooster." Moody did not accuse the president of bad intentions, only that he had been deceived by his interior secretary, David R. Francis, "and some unheard of commissioner [actually, four members of the National Forest Commission], who, it is alleged, visited this section."[3]

Following Moody's speech, an ad hoc committee of three residents, including Moody, drafted an entreaty to the president. "We are directed by a large public meeting now being held here," their telegram began, "voicing the feeling of thirty thousand vitally interested residents of western South Dakota to respectfully ask for you to suspend the executive order . . . until people can be heard protesting against it . . . This reserve if maintained will effect [sic] disastrously all the mining and dependent industries in this region and largely compel its depopulation."[4] A similar message was sent by Mayor L. P. Jenkins on behalf of the citizens of Lead and adjacent mining camps, asking the president to defer execution of his proclamation as it related to the Black Hills "until a thorough investigation of the [reserved] land and conditions prevailing here can be made and the matter can be more fully placed before you in its true light."[5] Still other messages were sent from Custer, Edgemont, Hill City, Spearfish, and Sturgis, all emphasizing the disastrous economic consequences of closing the forest and, in the process, grossly inflating the population of the affected communities.[6]

In Washington, Senator Pettigrew signed on to a bill sponsored by Senator Clarence D. Clark (R-WY) to invalidate the president's proclamation. Meanwhile, Secretary of the Interior Francis had summoned Pinchot, in his capacity as secretary of the National Forest Commission, to assist Representative John F. Lacey (R-IA) in preparing an amendment to the budget bill that would allow for timber sales as well as forest protection within the reserves. By declining to sign the budget bill, President Cleveland left President William McKinley no choice, after taking office, than to call a special session of Congress.[7]

With the forest reserves still scheduled for closure, a delegation of legislators including Senator Pettigrew plus Homestake's Moody met with the new president, asking that he cancel his predecessor's proclamation. When that proved impossible legally, Pettigrew looked for assistance in drafting a bill to keep the reserves open. He met with the new interior secretary, Cornelius N. Bliss, and followed up by sending the secretary a map of the Black Hills. Pettigrew meant to illustrate the unreasonableness of the proposed reserve area, in which every township was occupied by permanent settlers and several towns as well as mining claims would have to be abandoned if the reserve was closed. Moody, too, called on Secretary Bliss and obtained assurance that Homestake could continue timbering on reserve lands, paying nothing to the federal government. It should be noted that Moody represented Homestake, a major contributor to the National Republican Party, at the time Bliss had served as party treasurer.[8]

Homestake's apparent acceptance of the principle of the forest reserves encouraged Charles D. Walcott, director of the US Geological Survey, to seek out Senator Pettigrew. Walcott argued that the senator could perform a great service to the nation, as well as to his South Dakota constituents, by proposing legislation for the managed use and protection of the reserves. Pettigrew consented and asked Walcott to draft legislation, which Walcott did after discussions with President McKinley, Secretary Bliss, General Land Office commissioner Binger Hermann, and members of the National Forest Commission. Pinchot later described Walcott as "a man of first-class ability, who knew Congress like the back of his hand" and was thoroughly familiar with South Dakota's economics and politics.[9]

Pettigrew, too, met with the forest commission but got nowhere because of the unyielding stance of the two members who favored using the military to protect the reserves. Pettigrew did, however, successfully convince fellow senators, from both the East and the West, to accept what would turn out to be a genuine legislative compromise.[10] By all accounts, crafting that compromise and ushering it through the necessary legislative steps created an unattractive sight. Credit for passage belonged to Pettigrew and his congressional friends and to Moody, Pinchot, and Walcott for their behind-the-scenes work. The final draft, adopted as an amendment to the budget bill, was signed by President McKinley on June 4, 1897. Variously called the Organic Act of 1897 and the Forest Management Act of 1897, the amendment is generally considered the most significant piece of congressional forest legislation until it was replaced by the National Forest Management Act of 1976.

"Forestry Reserve Quashed!" The headline back home in the Black Hills reflected neither the compromise nor the concessions. In reporting that President Cleveland's proclamation had been "knocked into smithereens by Congress," the *Custer Weekly Chronicle* reprinted a telegram from Homestake's Moody. "The bill as it now stands," Moody explained, "revokes absolutely the proclamation of the president of February 22nd [1897] until March 1st next, and gives the president power to continue the revocation after that date if he so thinks proper." Again for local consumption, Moody allowed that "the champion of this measure is Senator Pettigrew, and whatever may be said about him politically, the fact stands that he has in this forestry reserve question, which is so vital to the interest of the Hills, proved himself [a tireless] friend of the Black Hills."[11]

More accurately, the Forest Management Act of 1897 suspended but did not revoke President Cleveland's proclamation. Suspension gave the US Geological Survey time to establish reserve boundaries and to deposit copies of surveys, field notes, and maps for public inspection at survey offices in the six affected western states. Residents in and around the reserves had felt left out of the process that had led to the president's proclamation. Suspension provided time for them to calm down and rationally review the situation.

The Forest Management Act delineated the purposes of the reserves: "to improve and protect the forest within the reservation, or for the purpose of securing favorable conditions for water flows, and to furnish a continuous supply of timber for the use and necessities of citizens of the United States."[12] Lands deemed more valuable for agricultural and mineral purposes were specifically excluded from the reserves, including several sections (about 5,000 acres) in the Deadwood-Lead area that to this day are administered by the Bureau of Land Management, successor to the General Land Office.

Much to Gifford Pinchot's liking, the act affirmed the principle of federal ownership and management of all forest reserves and enabled the secretary of the interior to "make such rules and regulations and establish such service as will insure the objects of such reservations, namely to regulate their occupancy and use and to preserve the forests thereon from destruction."[13] The secretary was specifically authorized to provide protection against fires and "depredations" such as trespass, waste, and despoiling. In brief, the all-important, costly responsibility for preventing and fighting forest fires rested with the federal government, a tremendous gift to forest users and nearby communities.

Prior to the Forest Management Act of 1897, the federal government could either give away timber on federal land or sell timber with the land, but it could not sell the timber separately from the land. Pinchot attributed much of the unbridled timbering on federal lands to the failure of earlier law to separate timber from land.[14]

The act specified that timber sales were limited to dead, mature, or large-growth trees (an item used much later by opponents of clear-cutting in the all-important Monongahela case). Sales could be made for no less than appraised value, individual trees had to be marked by an appointee of the Department of the Interior, and timber cut in one state or territory could not be exported to another state or territory as requested by the Homestake Mining Company to ensure its timber supply. The act still allowed settlers and miners to obtain the free use of timber and stone "for firewood, fencing, buildings, mining, prospecting, and other domestic purposes."[15]

Private parties who owned property surrounded by federal lands (inholders) retained access, though the secretary of the interior was authorized to establish rules. Furthermore, the "in lieu" section of the act allowed an inholder to exchange a claim or a patent that had not been fully developed or "perfected" for a tract of vacant federal land not to exceed the size of the tract covered by the relinquished claim or patent. In effect, a timber or mining company could divest itself of cut-over land or an exhausted claim in exchange for an equal area of federal land outside the reserves. Pinchot, Walcott, and others had strongly opposed the "in lieu" provision. Last but not least, the act gave the president, and through him the secretary of the interior, broad powers to modify any existing or future executive order regarding any reserve, "and by such modification may reduce the area or change the boundary lines of such reserve, or may vacate altogether any order creating such reserve."[16] Broad executive powers, yes; guaranteed permanence of the forest reserves, no.

Within a month after President McKinley signed the Forest Management Act, Director Walcott hired A. F. Dunnington of Rapid City, a topographer well-known for his work on other government surveys, as chief of the first crew to begin survey work in the Black Hills. Using the conventional rectangular system of township, range, and section, the party of sixteen established boundaries and marked corners using steel stakes with brass caps on which location and elevation were inscribed. A second party of sixteen set out to prepare a topographical map, and a third party, yet to be assembled, would identify parcels most valuable for agriculture to be excluded from the reserve.[17]

That same summer Walcott toured the Black Hills to reassure local inhabitants that the reserve was open for their use. In Deadwood, he explained that the Forest Management Act authorized the federal government at once "to prevent the wanton destruction of timber by irresponsible parties" and to ensure sufficient timber for local sawmills.[18] In Custer, he acknowledged that President Cleveland's proclamation could have been interpreted to mean "that nothing but trees were privileged to live and grow in this part of Uncle Sam's domain." In truth, the public retained the same privilege to use the forest as before, with the added assurance that the federal government would aim to prevent wasteful logging and destructive fires. Anticipating more extensive forestry, Walcott advised local audiences of the network of patrol stations and teams of firefighters established by the Canadian government to protect its public forests.[19]

Secretary of the Interior Bliss, meanwhile, delegated to General Land Office commissioner Binger Hermann the task of drafting the rules and developing the organizational structure for administering timbering in the reserves. Those rules included appraisals in advance of sales, published notice of sales at least sixty days in advance, and a requirement that stands valued in excess of $500 must be divided among several parties. For the first time, operators needed permits to place saw-mills on reserve land. For administrative purposes, Hermann assigned the Black Hills Forest Reserve to the same regional district as the Big Horn and Yellowstone Reserves, with headquarters at Sheridan, Wyoming. Until funding for forest offi-cers became available on July 1, 1898, the Department of the Interior continued to rely on its special agents; their primary task remained that of pursuing the most egregious trespassers.[20]

In view of Interior's deficient record of protecting federal lands, Director Walcott had taken it upon himself to ask Pinchot to intervene with Secretary Bliss. The day after President McKinley signed the Forest Management Act, Pinchot traveled to Washington to meet Bliss, whereupon Bliss contracted with Pinchot to become the secretary's confidential forest agent "to examine and report upon the suspended Reserves, their condition and needs, their forests, and their relations to lumbering, agriculture, mining, grazing, commerce and settlement." Bliss also asked Pinchot to prepare guidelines for evaluating requests for reserve boundary adjustments, as well as "a practical plan for the establishment of a Forest Service, with specific recom-mendations for individual Reserves."[21]

Pinchot began his work once again with a trip to forest reserves in Montana, Idaho, and Washington before reaching the Black Hills in October 1897. At Custer, he met up with Henry Graves who, as noted, had been sent to assess timber poten-tial more accurately than could be expected of a conventional survey crew. Graves described his few days with Pinchot, including a hike up Harney Peak, as "a joy to me and we had a fine time together," reminding us that despite their focus on economic forestry, both men greatly appreciated the beauty of the forests.[22] After Harney Peak, Pinchot left Graves to tour the Black Hills—mostly on horseback—taking note of the effects of fire, wind, and insects on the forest and listening to stock growers and farmers worried about declining supplies of water, which they attributed to deforestation. After ten days on tour, Pinchot rode into Deadwood where he met a Dr. Carpenter, superintendent of the Deadwood and Delaware Smelter, second in size to the Homestake Mining Company. Then he went on to Rapid City where he conferred with C. W. Greene, Interior's special agent for the

Black Hills, and officials of the General Land Office. From them he learned that several Homestake mine claims had been staked for the sole purpose of cutting timber. With that information, Pinchot saw an opportunity, returned to Deadwood, and solicited and received an audience with Homestake superintendent Thomas J. Grier and counselor Gideon Moody.[23] Here, then, we have a self-confident, thirty-two-year-old easterner negotiating successfully with the two highest-level representatives of the largest gold mining company in the nation, also representative of the most powerful political force in South Dakota. Homestake's consent to federal protection paved the way for federal management of the forest reserves.

Pinchot recorded the main points of his audience as follows: Homestake agreed to purchase timber from the federal government and to stop timbering surreptitiously and expressed a willingness to advance $10,000, or more if needed, to enable the Department of the Interior to set up a system for managing timber sales. Grier and Moody recognized that laws and regulations would help ensure a supply of timber for the long term; in return, they received assurances from Pinchot that the price for standing timber would be kept to a minimum. Grier and Moody concluded, according to Pinchot, that it would be "a good thing for them to make a bid for timber, or otherwise notify the government that they favored the reservation policy as now existing." In addition, they favored extending the boundaries of the Black Hills Forest Reserve to include all the forested areas of the Black Hills, provided that those lands identified as agricultural be set aside for that purpose; further, they committed their workforce to assist the government in fighting forest fires, something Homestake had already begun the prior summer.[24]

Before leaving the Black Hills, Pinchot sent a summary of his findings to Secretary Bliss. The boundary lines of the Black Hills Forest Reserve remained inaccurate and would require considerable adjustment. He had seen how the combination of forest fires and illegal timbering had devastated large areas, especially in the northern Black Hills. In addition, he had sensed "a general change of opinion in regard to the Reserve, both among the ranchers and among those interested in mining." He continued, "I have talked with no one who was not strongly in favor of preserving the timber, and I am convinced that the application of simple measures, to be described in a subsequent report, will, if carried out, bring substantially the whole population into cooperation with the government to this end." That subsequent report (see page 45) was completed three years later but never published.[25]

Despite pledges by Grier and Moody, as well as Pinchot's assessment of favorable public opinion, it appeared that Black Hills residents still hoped the reserves would be suspended permanently. In January 1898 Moody was back in Washington, reportedly lobbying for that very purpose. Faced with opposition from both executive and legislative branches, he still managed to extract some concessions to

FIGURE 3.1. Gifford Pinchot. Courtesy, Black Hills National Forest Historical Collection, Leland D. Case Library of Western Historical Studies, Black Hills State University, Spearfish, SD.

Homestake. Commissioner Hermann revised rules so mining companies could purchase a year's supply of timber at one time rather than be limited to timber from the previously allowed 160 acres. For Homestake, that meant cutting 2 million rather than 600,000 board feet annually. Moody also settled an earlier case brought by the federal government against Homestake; the company agreed to pay $75,000—the price that would have been paid for standing timber cut illegally—plus fines.[26]

In his report on the Black Hills Forest Reserve, Henry Graves expressed the opinion that General Land Office rules failed to consider the economics of timbering. Rules properly required operators to use the entire saw-timber portion of every cut tree, to use branches and treetops for cordwood, and to dispose of remaining slash; but the rules failed to take into account the fluctuating prices of lumber, high costs of freight, and competition among sawmills. Only Homestake, with its large size, could afford to operate according to the rules. In view of virtually unanimous local support for federal protection against forest fires, wasteful logging, and timber fraud, Graves recommended the implementation of a practical "system" to ensure such protection as "the first and most necessary step in forest management." Forestry, he added, encompassed much more than enforcement: managing stands for perpetual use required "the intelligent direction and control of lumbering."[27]

That direction began in a less than satisfactory way when, in spring 1898, Commissioner Hermann appointed Henry G. Hamaker as the first supervisor of the Black Hills Forest Reserve. Little is known about Hamaker's background except that he came from Indiana and had worked for the Bureau of Indian Affairs as a logging supervisor on the Chippewa Reservation in northern Minnesota.[28] Pinchot grew to dislike Hamaker; he remembered him as a strictly political appointee "utterly without experience" who had never seen a western forest before arriving in the Black Hills.[29]

Hamaker reached the Black Hills in August 1898. Within three months of his arrival, President McKinley enlarged the Black Hills Forest Reserve by 211,630 acres through the addition of unappropriated federal land in Wyoming. The president also agreed to boundary adjustments proposed by Senators Pettigrew and James H. Kyle (R-SD).[30] Hamaker divided the entire reserve into twenty districts, each containing roughly 60,000 acres and each to be overseen by a district ranger. He hired 20 men from a list of 219 local applicants; after the expected appropriations failed to materialize, he reduced that number to 10. None of these early rangers were trained formally in forestry; they were entrusted with management for the conservative use of timber according to rules and regulations devised by the General Land Office.

The rangers' most important duty, as publicized locally, was to exercise "utmost vigilance to guard against forest fires" and, when fires occurred, to suppress them as quickly as possible.[31] On at least three separate occasions, however, settlers complained that neither Hamaker nor his rangers troubled themselves to fight such fires. Regarding one of those cases, a member of a US Geological Survey team testified that the nearest district ranger had checked on a small fire, determined that it would burn itself out, and thus taken no action. Some days later the ranger revisited the site and found the fire uncontrollable; it burned for thirty-seven days and destroyed valuable timber. All the while, it was said that Supervisor Hamaker had "kept himself carefully concealed."[32]

In addition to forest officers' alleged indifference, that same surveyor testified that some ranchers and settlers had failed to report fires out of fear that they would be evicted from the reserve. Distinguishing between legitimate homesteaders and unauthorized intruders necessarily put rangers in awkward positions. On the one hand, rangers were instructed to stay away from homesteads; on the other hand, they needed to document trespassers, serve them with due notice to leave, and inform the US attorney about those who failed to move out in the allotted time.[33]

Rule makers at the General Land Office added to the frustrations of settlers living in and around the reserves. In a matter as petty as gathering dead or damaged trees for firewood, Hamaker was required to notify residents through local newspapers that they needed to make written application to him. He would forward the requests to Washington, which needed up to sixty days to reach a decision. If approved, the cost would be fifteen cents per cord, except that residue gathered from completed logging sites remained free of charge. After receiving not even a single application, Hamaker expressed his frustration; he could not authorize such permits in a timely fashion. Under pressure from the South Dakota congressional delegation, the Washington bureaucrats changed their minds; Hamaker then announced that residents could collect as much firewood as needed for domestic use without permits or fees, so long as they disposed of their slash. How such a directive could be enforced remains obscure.[34]

Seeking to introduce order where little or none existed and where distances were great and the number of rangers limited was no easy task. As of July 1900, settlers needed to obtain grazing permits for their cattle and horses, but regulations imposed no limits on the numbers of head and no fees. Some ranchers continued to graze their livestock on the reserve without permits; others left their animals in the forest during the winter of 1900–1901, though Hamaker had ordered the forest temporarily closed.[35] The following spring, Congressman Charles H. Burke (R-SD) failed to convince Commissioner Hermann to rescind his order to remove stock fences installed by ranchers within the reserve. Burke contended that ranchers needed those fences to secure pasturage for their respective herds; Hermann argued that fences impinged on homesteaders. From the very beginning, forest administrators had to cope with users competing for forest resources.[36]

On the overriding issue of timber sales, subsequent to Pinchot's conversations with Superintendent Grier and counselor Moody, Homestake Mining Company began compiling the information necessary to make application to purchase timber in the reserve. As indication of its willingness to operate according to General Land Office rules, Homestake gave up mining claims made deceitfully in order to cut timber.[37] On April 8, 1898, Grier submitted an application, proposing to cut trees in eight sections (5,120 acres) near Nemo, about 15 miles southeast of Deadwood. The General Land Office assigned Special Agent Greene to inspect the proposed sale sites but, given his principal preoccupation with trespass cases, he never visited the sites. Instead, Hamaker received instructions to inspect the proposed sale sites; he was to assess stands from the perspective of official policy, "to supply present and future needs for timber within the state by providing for the use of timber which can be cut without detriment to the reservation," but not to overvalue the timber, as the government was more interested in meeting local demand than in earning revenue.[38] The minimum price, set at $1 per 1,000 board feet of green saw-timber, became the agreed-upon price.

Hamaker surveyed the proposed sites in late fall and submitted his findings to the General Land Office in April 1899. He recommended that logging be confined to burned-over areas; Homestake countered, and the General Land Office agreed that cutting only dead trees would be too costly and would not yield the quality of timber required. Homestake pledged to remove slash and cut cordwood, paying 15 cents per cord, defined as a stack of firewood 4 feet by 4 feet by 8 feet. While Hamaker advertised for additional bids, Homestake sought permission to begin logging, claiming impending shortages. Washington declined that request, though it was understood that there would be no more bids. Cutting could begin only upon formal award of a bid, sixty days after the end of the advertising period.

In November 1899, two years after Pinchot had obtained Grier's agreement to purchase timber and eighteen months after Homestake submitted its formal application, the General Land Office awarded the sale; the agency then sent someone from its Denver office to begin marking trees and to explain pertinent rules and regulations to Homestake loggers and, presumably, to Hamaker and his rangers. Actual timbering began during the last week of December 1899.[39] Sale contracts stipulated that only trees measuring 8 inches or more in diameter measured at breast height (dbh)—considered 4.5 feet aboveground—could be cut. During the eight-year duration of the contracts, Homestake would cut 15.5 million board feet of saw-timber and 5,100 cords of wood, using the prevailing method of clear-cutting by which virtually all trees in a given stand would be cut.[40]

Although more selective methods of timbering were yet to be adopted, Timber Case #1 set the precedent for federal management of the national forests. Credit for reaching that milestone goes primarily to the officers of Homestake Mining

Company for their willingness to purchase timber from the federal government and to Gifford Pinchot for convincing them that such an arrangement was in their best business interest.

In view of his success with Homestake and given the untenable situation of the General Land Office managing the reserves without professional foresters, Pinchot embarked on a quiet campaign to bring the reserves under the auspices of the US Department of Agriculture. In late April 1898, during deliberations over appropriations for executing the Forest Management Act, Director Walcott confided to Pinchot that, if the US Geological Survey were not assigned management of the reserves, he would advocate for Pinchot to take over management as head of the Division of Forestry. When the Geological Survey failed to win the assignment, Walcott approached Secretary of Agriculture James "Tama Jim" Wilson about naming Pinchot to the position of chief of the Division of Forestry, recently vacated by Bernhard Fernow who left to become dean of the new forestry school at Cornell University. Fernow had worked for passage of the Forest Management Act but viewed the division's role as provider of scientific information. In contrast, Pinchot envisioned the division as promoter of actual forestry.[41]

Philosophically, Wilson agreed with Pinchot about managing forests as agricultural crops. A former agricultural experiment station director, Wilson was committed to the application of the sciences to all forms of economic development. He hired Pinchot away from his position as confidential forest agent in the Department of the Interior, effective July 1, 1898, and gave him programmatic carte blanche, though within the confines of a modest budget. Pinchot hired Henry Graves as assistant; but since administration of the reserves remained under Interior, Pinchot and Graves turned their efforts to advising landowners on the management of private woodlands. That is, they did so until the General Land Office, recognizing its own operational deficiencies and lack of expertise, requested that the Division of Forestry prepare a separate "working plan" for timbering within each forest reserve.

Pinchot's explanation of how one federal agency requested assistance from another, seemingly competitive federal agency revealed his method of operating and appeared entirely credible. In 1896 he had befriended Hiram H. Jones, a young employee of the General Land Office who helped prepare the National Forest Commission report. Then in 1899, with Pinchot's help, Jones drafted the letter requesting assistance from Acting Commissioner William A. Richards to Secretary of the Interior Ethan Allen Hitchcock. Secretary Hitchcock forwarded Richards's request to Secretary Wilson, and Pinchot drafted Wilson's response. Pinchot later reminisced, "The play had been Pinchot to Jones to Richards to Hitchcock to Wilson to Pinchot."[42]

Pinchot chose the Black Hills Forest Reserve as the reserve most urgently in need of federal management because of continuing destructive timbering practices, the vast potential for timbering, and nearby communities' dependence on the forest. He noted that Black Hills timber was in greater demand than that from all other forest reserves combined, that local residents generally favored federal management, and that General Land Office ineptitude in handling Timber Case #1 illustrated the immediate need for professional forestry.[43] By the time he made his selection, Pinchot likely knew about Graves's observation that scientific forestry in the Black Hills would be relatively uncomplicated because of the prolific reproduction of the ponderosa pine, the varying ages of trees, favorable topography, and an existing system of roads.[44]

Immediately upon notification of his appointment and with his own money, since government appropriations would not begin until July 1, Pinchot hired Edward M. Griffith as forest assistant. He sent Griffith to the Black Hills to prepare for the next summer's fieldwork, meant to "give complete and explicit directions for the harvesting of the forest crop in the Black Hills in such a way [as] to perpetuate the supply of native timber." A native of New York City, Griffith, too, had attended Yale, spent a year abroad studying forestry, and worked at Biltmore Forest.[45] Secretary Wilson memorialized Griffith's trip to the Black Hills as the first step toward the application of scientific forestry to all federal forestlands. The local press viewed Griffith's trip in less lofty terms, as preparing the blueprint for generating more jobs and more revenues for the region over the long term.[46]

On May 1, 1900, Griffith left Spearfish with a crew of a dozen students for Potato Gulch, an area of 10,234 acres 12 miles to the southwest. Their task was to take various measurements from which to extrapolate timber volume and estimate potential timber yields for the entire reserve. Pinchot liked the idea of using students, not simply because they worked for less money, helping to stretch limited budgets, but because of his interest in attracting and training young people for forestry. He expressed delight about Griffith's crew, a "fine collection of spirited young colts . . . nearly all enthusiastic, rejoicing in a hard life in the open and in strenuous physical work. Most of them were destined to make successful foresters and leaders."[47] Among them were Hugh M. Curran, who would develop a system for classifying ponderosa pine forests as to their quality for timbering, and Richard P. Imes, who would return to the Black Hills as the first supervisor of Harney National Forest. After Griffith's crew left at the end of summer, he remained, inspecting every township and nearly every section within the reserve.[48]

Griffith heard considerable local criticism of the Hamaker administration: applicants waited twelve to sixteen months for decisions on applications to purchase timber while being assured by forest officers that they might hear at any time. Similarly, settlers who had helped fight forest fires and signed payment vouchers had to wait months for their pay, which "led to a very bitter feeling against the Department. Many settlers say that, after the way they have been treated[,] they will never fight another forest fire, unless it is threatening their homes."[49]

On the administration of timber sales, Griffith reported that standing timber had often not been marked as required, encouraging indiscriminate logging and violations of sale contracts. On one sale, the ranger in charge claimed he had marked 6 million board feet; however, Griffith had found fewer than one in ten logs stamped "US." On another sale, the ranger had handed over his marking hatchet (the end opposite the blade made the "US" stamp) to the loggers. Given that situation, Griffith recommended that Hamaker inspect each major timber cut at least monthly and be allowed to hire a secretary to assist with office work so he could spend more time in the field.

Griffith criticized the General Land Office for its failure to take market conditions into account when setting standards for appraisals. He found assessments on merchantable trees too low and those on damaged trees too high. He recommended a sliding appraisal scale to encourage quick removal of burned trees (half-price) and beetle-infested trees (one-fourth price). Far ahead of his time, Griffith recommended that every tree marked for cutting should be removed in its entirety from the forest stand and that loggers be held liable financially for collateral damage. Rangers, not loggers, needed to determine skidding routes, and roads should be kept to a minimum, all for the protection of young growth. He accused local forest officers of failing to ensure that treetops were cut into cordwood and slash piled for burning. To make adherence to the rules more likely, he recommended that the forest supervisor be authorized to issue permits for up to 100 cords of firewood without waiting for higher approval and urged Washington to send a special agent to the rail yards at Edgemont to stop out-of-state shipments of timber in violation of the Forest Management Act.[50]

Deficiencies in federal forest laws enabled unscrupulous parties to undermine the established process of timber administration. Griffith acknowledged that, under the "in lieu" provision, a settler could sell timber on his land and, once all the trees were cut, relinquish that land to the federal government for an equal number of acres elsewhere in the public domain. Or an honest logger could purchase a stand of timber from the federal government, only to have a squatter claim that same land as a homestead and then extort the logger into paying twice for a given timber stand.[51]

In his report, Griffith expressed the view that forestry was more than administering timber sales. Much more needed to be managed to ensure a timber supply over the long term. Although critical of squatters, he recommended finding ways to channel their interests into agriculture. He had seen forest stands separated by narrow strips of fertile land. By cultivating these strips, farmers created excellent fire breaks; when forest fires did occur, farmers had a selfish interest in helping extinguish them.[52] Similarly, Griffith recommended that, in return for fighting fires, settlers within the reserve be allowed to range their cattle free of charge and in unlimited numbers. He believed the scarcity of water in certain sections and the mountainous terrain in others would naturally limit those numbers. He estimated that the Black Hills Forest Reserve could support three to four times as many head as the roughly 5,000 that grazed in 1900; by grazing unused grasslands, cattle would effectively reduce the danger of ground fires. Regulations allowing each settler a maximum of 120 head of cattle had proven ineffective and unpopular. A settler with fewer than the allowable number could apply for a permit to cover the full 120, helping a friend or neighbor who held more than 120 head. He added, "The rangers do not know who has permits, the section in which the cattle are supposed to range, or the cattle brands, and so cannot pretend to enforce the law. Consequently, the settlers range as many cattle as they please, laugh at the law, and are led to break other forest reserve laws."[53]

With protection of watersheds understood as part of ensuring the conservative use of timber, Griffith recommended no timbering on steep slopes, limits on cutting around headwaters and along year-round streams, and a ban on clearing aspens and willows along stream banks. At the same time, he recommended removing trees that encroached on natural clearings because he deemed those areas more valuable for farming and grazing than for timbering. As a variation on Director Walcott's reference to fire patrols in Canada, Griffith suggested that rangers adopt fire watch routines: "The rangers should be obliged to ride to some high point twice every day during the dry season, once in the morning and again in the afternoon, and go at once to any fire which they see, no matter whether it is on their range or not."[54] Yet Griffith acknowledged that the forest rangers received less pay than Homestake's least skilled laborers and even had to furnish and maintain their own horses. Moreover, in a précis prepared for *The Forester*, he noted that "unfortunately these men are not trained foresters and often do not understand their work or sympathize with the forest reserve movement." As a result, he argued for professional training as well as higher salaries.[55]

By the time Griffith completed his working plan for the Black Hills, the General Land Office had replaced Hamaker with Seth Bullock, a local celebrity; on Griffith's recommendation and with Pinchot's support, the General Land Office had separated administratively the Black Hills Forest Reserve from the Wyoming reserves. Those two steps did much to assuage the complaints Griffith had recorded during his trip to the Black Hills, though more needed to be done to establish scientific forestry.

NOTES

1. *Custer Weekly Chronicle*, February 27, 1897.

2. Wayne L. Fanebust, *Echoes of November: The Life and Times of Senator R. F. Petti-grew of South Dakota* (Freeman, SD: Pine Hill Press, 1997), 104, 189.

3. *Custer Weekly Chronicle*, February 27, 1897; quotations in *Black Hills Daily Times*, February 26, 1897, 1.

4. Night wire from G. C. Moody, Fred Seipp, and C. W. Carpenter to President of the United States, Deadwood, February 27, 1897, copy, Black Hills National Forest supervisor's office, Custer, SD (hereafter BHNF).

5. Night wire, L. P. Jenkins, Mayor and Chairman Presiding, and R. H. Discoll, Secretary, Lead, to President of the United States, February 25, 1897, copy, BHNF.

6. *Custer Weekly Chronicle*, February 27, 1897.

7. Gifford Pinchot, *Breaking New Ground* (Washington, DC: Island, 1998 [1947]), 110–13.

8. Richard F. Pettigrew to Cornelius Bliss, Washington, DC, March 17, 1897, copy, BHNF; Carl A. Newport, *Forest Service Policies in Timber Management and Silviculture as They Affect the Lumber Industries: A Case Study of the Black Hills* (Pierre: South Dakota Department of Game, Fish, and Parks, 1956), 16.

9. John Ise, *The United States Forest Policy* (New York: Arno, 1972 [1920]), 132; *Custer Weekly Chronicle*, April 10, 1897; Pinchot, *Breaking New Ground*, 114–16.

10. Fanebust, *Echoes of November*, 293–94; G. Michael McCarthy, "The Forest Reserve Controversy: Colorado under Cleveland and McKinley," *Journal of Forest History* 20, no. 2 (April 1976): 85.

11. *Custer Weekly Chronicle*, June 5, 1897.

12. An Act Making Appropriations for Sundry Civil Expenses for Fiscal Year Ending June Thirtieth 1898 [includes Forest Management Act of 1897], *US Statutes at Large* 30 (1897), 34–36.

13. Ibid., 36.

14. Pinchot, *Breaking New Ground*, 24.

15. Pinchot, *Breaking New Ground*, 116; Ise, *United States Forest Policy*, 140; Forest Management Act 30.

16. Pinchot, *Breaking New Ground*, 118; Forest Management Act, 30.

17. *Custer Weekly Chronicle*, July 10, 1897, August 14, 1897, 1.

18. *Deadwood Daily Pioneer-Times*, August 6, 1897, copy, BHNF.

19. *Custer Weekly Chronicle*, August 14, 1897.

20. Newport, *Forest Service Policies*, 18–19.

21. Harold K. Steen, ed., *The Conservation Diaries of Gifford Pinchot* (Durham, NC: Forest History Society, 2001), 78; quotations from Pinchot, *Breaking New Ground,* 123.

22. Henry S. Graves, "Autobiographical Notes" (unpublished), 54, transcribed by Jean M. Pablo, cabinet 8, drawer 1, folder 17, Black Hills National Forest Historical Collection, Leland D. Case Library for Western Historical Studies, Black Hills State University, Spearfish, SD (hereafter cited as BHSU Case Library).

23. Pinchot, *Conservation Diaries*, 84–85.

24. Memo by Gifford Pinchot, November 3, 1897, copy, BHNF; Henry S. Graves, "The Black Hills Forest Reserve," US Geological Survey, *Nineteenth Annual Report, 1897–1898*, Part V: *Forest Reserves* (Washington, DC: Government Printing Office, 1899), 85.

25. Gifford Pinchot to Cornelius N. Bliss, Custer, November 5, 1897, copy, BHNF.

26. *Custer Weekly Chronicle,* January 15 and 22, February 5, 1898; Newport, *Forest Service Policies*, 19.

27. Graves, "Black Hills Forest Reserve," 89, 96.

28. *Rapid City Daily Journal*, September 10, 1898, 1, cited in Brian G. Krick, "Mountain Farmers: Supervisors of the Black Hills National Forest, 1898–1995" (MA thesis, University of South Dakota, Vermillion, 2001), 1.

29. Pinchot, *Breaking New Ground*, 163.

30. *Custer Weekly Chronicle*, September 24, 1898.

31. Ibid., May 20, 1899, 1.

32. Transcript of testimony by a Mr. Heron, US Geological Survey, Washington, DC [1901], 2, copy, Pinchot Papers, Library of Congress, cabinet 8, drawer 1, folder 4, BHSU Case Library.

33. Ibid.; *Custer Weekly Chronicle*, March 11, May 13, 1899.

34. Ibid., July 8, 1, September 23, 1899, 1.

35. Ibid., August 18, 1900, 1, March 9, 1901, 1.

36. Ibid., June 15, 1901, 1.

37. Richmond L. Clow, "Timber Users, Timber Savers: The Homestead Mining Company and the First Regulated Timber Harvest," *South Dakota History* 22, no. 3 (Fall 1992): 227.

38. Ibid., 229.

39. Ibid., 229–31; F. J. Poch, forest assistant, "History of Government Timber Sale No. 1," typescript, part of "Cumulative Silvical Report, Black Hills National Forest," 1929, BHNF.

40. Arthur F.C. Hoffman and Theodore Krueger, "Forestry in the Black Hills," in *USDA Yearbook* (Washington, DC: US Department of Agriculture, 1949), 320.

41. Pinchot, *Conservation Diaries*, 88, 92; Pinchot, *Breaking New Ground*, 134; "Report of the Secretary of Agriculture," in *USDA Yearbook* (Washington, DC: US Department of Agriculture, 1898), 44–45.

42. "Report of the Forester," in *USDA Annual Reports* (Washington, DC: US Department of Agriculture, 1901), 329; Pinchot, *Breaking New Ground,* 173.

43. Pinchot, *Breaking New Ground*, 173–74.

44. Graves, "Black Hills Forest Reserve," 97; Newport, *History of Black Hills Forestry*, 27.

45. Herman H. Chapman, "Edward Merriam Griffith, 1872–1939," *Journal of Forestry* 38, no. 1 (January 1940): 62–63.

46. "Report of the Secretary of Agriculture," in *USDA Yearbook* (Washington, DC: US Department of Agriculture, 1900), 51; *Custer Weekly Chronicle*, February 10, 1900.

47. Pinchot, *Breaking New Ground*, 175.

48. "Report of the Secretary of Agriculture" in *USDA Yearbook* (Washington, DC: US Department of Agriculture, 1901), 329.

49. Griffith to Commissioner of General Land Office, Spearfish, October 12, 1901, 1–2, copy, Pinchot Papers, Library of Congress, in loose-leaf binder, vol. 2, BHSU Case Library.

50. Ibid., 2–5; Edward M. Griffith, "A Working Plan for the Black Hills Forest Reserve, South Dakota" [1901], 63–67, copy, National Archives, BHSU Case Library.

51. Griffith to Commissioner, October 12, 1901, 6–7.

52. Edward M. Griffith, "The Black Hills Forest Reserve," typescript, 6–8, copy, Pinchot Papers, BHSU Case Library; *Custer Weekly Chronicle*, December 1, 1900.

53. Griffith to Commissioner, October 12, 1901, 7–8.

54. Griffith, "Black Hills Forest Reserve," 8–11, 44.

55. Edward M. Griffith, "The Black Hills Forest Reserve," *The Forester* (November 1901): 289.

4

Rooseveltians and Black Hills Forestry

In his celebrated first message to the US Congress on December 3, 1901, President Theodore Roosevelt outlined his conservation agenda, dividing it into forests and waters as reflected in the interests of two trusted advisers: Gifford Pinchot, forester in the US Department of Agriculture, and Frederick H. Newell, hydrographer for the US Geological Survey. Roosevelt declared that "the fundamental idea of forestry is the perpetuation of forests by use. Forest protection is not an end of itself; it is a means to increase and sustain the resources of our country and the industries which depend upon them. The preservation of our forests is an imperative business necessity."[1] He did not neglect to mention that the nation's water supply, particularly in the arid West, depended on the forests or that the forest reserves should be preserved for wildlife—all requiring protection from fire and from overgrazing by livestock.

Roosevelt expressed the upbeat view that public opinion throughout the country had come to appreciate the value of forests in creating and maintaining national wealth and that westerners in particular, recognizing the "practical usefulness" of the forest reserves, demanded their protection and extension. The president raised the issue that responsibility for the forest reserves fell to three separate federal agencies: the General Land Office for protection, the US Geological Survey for mapping and description, and the Bureau of Forestry for working plans and advancement of practical forestry. Noting that the separation of responsibilities had prevented "that effective co-operation between the Government and the men who utilize the

DOI: 10.5876/9781607322993.c004

resources of the reserves, without which the interest of both must suffer," President Roosevelt recommended that Congress consolidate the various forest functions within the Department of Agriculture.[2]

Even before that formal statement of forestry principles and before Roosevelt succeeded McKinley as president, Pinchot had been at work on then–vice president Roosevelt's forestry agenda. It is a good bet that Pinchot had something to do with Henry G. Hamaker's resignation as supervisor and, even more likely, with the selection of Seth Bullock as Hamaker's successor (1901–6). Hamaker happened to be in Washington in early April 1901, when he submitted his resignation; he did not return to the Black Hills but went directly to Colorado to manage his personal mining interests.

At the same time, South Dakota senators James Kyle and Richard Pettigrew pressed Department of the Interior officials to appoint Bullock as supervisor.[3] A Canadian by birth, Bullock had prospected in Montana and served as a deputy sheriff before moving to Deadwood during the gold rush of 1876. With a partner, he opened a hardware store, engaged in other businesses including mining and ranching, and became immensely popular—best known to future generations as the sheriff of Lawrence County. Howard R. Lamar described Bullock as the quintessential frontier politician. He even looked the part of a western lawman.[4]

Bullock's nomination for forest supervisor received the hearty endorsement of his friend, the vice president. In a recent biography of Bullock, David Wolff dated the beginning of that friendship to 1892, when the two men first met at a crossing over the Belle Fourche River near Spearfish. Roosevelt, in his capacity as federal civil service commissioner, was riding with two other men from his ranch at Medora, in southwestern North Dakota, to the Pine Ridge Reservation. Bullock was riding the range checking his own cattle, but, always the lawman, he found Roosevelt's party unkempt (after 200 miles on the trail) and inquired into its purpose. "Seth received us with rather distant courtesy at first," Roosevelt reminisced, "but unbent when he found out who we were, remarking, 'You see, by your looks I thought you were some kind of tin-horn gambling outfit, and that I might have to keep an eye on you!'"[5]

Bullock next saw Roosevelt in 1898 when invited, as captain of Grigsby's Cowboys—an army corps called into service but never deployed—to celebrate victory in the Spanish-American War. From that time on, Bullock revered Roosevelt as a hero and did whatever he could to assist him politically. Roosevelt reciprocated with genuine friendship. In fall 1900 Bullock traveled with Roosevelt as he campaigned for vice president and organized a huge rally for the candidate in Deadwood.[6]

Roosevelt's endorsement of Bullock as forest supervisor would be understandable from a partisan political viewpoint alone. But such indebtedness likely converged with a specific interest in the Black Hills expressed by Roosevelt's friend Gifford Pinchot. Their friendship had begun in 1897 when Roosevelt, upon recommendation of a mutual family acquaintance, invited Pinchot to become a founding member of the Boone and Crockett Club, a select group of hunters seeking to conserve big-game hunting. At the time, Pinchot was consulting on the Adirondack forests; in 1898, after Roosevelt became governor of New York, Pinchot convinced him to establish a state forest commission.[7] Given Pinchot's genius for connecting forestry and politics, it is inconceivable that he did not pull his oar for Bullock.

During Bullock's first summer (1901) as supervisor, Pinchot once again visited the Black Hills—this time accompanied by his field assistant, Edward M. Griffith, and Andrew D. Hopkins, state entomologist of West Virginia. Pinchot had requested, and Secretary Wilson had agreed, to put Hopkins on contract through the US Department of Agriculture's Division of Entomology to identify definitively and recommend methods to control the insects destroying the ponderosa pine. In 1899 Hopkins had identified and named the destructive southern pine beetle, *Dendroctonus frontalis* Hopk. Like many distinguished scientists of his era—the botanist Aven Nelson of Wyoming comes to mind—Hopkins was mostly self-educated. He ended his formal education at age seventeen, when he took over his grandfather's farm. Through attendance at Farmers' Institutes (precursors to the Cooperative Extension Service), he met the director of the West Virginia Agricultural Experiment Station, wangled a job, and eventually rose to the position of associate director. At some point, he was granted a doctorate before moving to the Division of Entomology. Like Aven Nelson, he had an innate sense for nature and an acute ability to observe.[8]

Hopkins spent four days in the Black Hills (September 1–4, 1901), traveling with Pinchot and Griffith from Spearfish through the forest reserve to Lead. Along their route, Hopkins observed vast numbers of ponderosa pine dying or dead; affected trees ranged in diameter from 4 inches to the largest trees and occurred in clusters of a few trees to hundreds and even thousands. Settlers and others told Hopkins that they had begun to notice dying timber about 1895; the evidence suggested to him that the destruction had been going on for a much longer period and that much of the devastation attributed to forest fires had actually been caused by insects.[9]

Because of the brevity of his visit, Hopkins depended on local descriptions of the offending insect's habit and behavior. In his field report, he quoted from a letter—postmarked from Lead, August 12, 1899, and accompanied by an insect specimen—addressed to the Division of Entomology, worth re-quoting for its clarity and simplicity on a subject of continuing and immense concern:

> [Last Wednesday] there was a southwest wind, and a swarm of them [pine beetles] came. My dwelling is in what was a grove of young native Black Hills pine. The bugs

FIGURE 4.1. Mountain pine beetle on match tip. Courtesy, USDA Forest Service, Black Hills National Forest, Custer, SD.

settled on the house like a plague of locusts. At night they left the house and scattered about. I have examined the trees, and with one exception do not find that they attacked them. This one excepted tree is a sight. Hundreds of bugs settled on it during the night, and by morning they had buried themselves out of sight in the trunk. As they bored their way in, the dust from the boring, which was very fine, filtered out from the top to the bottom of the tree like fine sawdust, and fell about the tree on the ground. They could be plainly heard at their work as they bored into the wood. The tree was a vigorous young pine about fifteen feet high and six inches in diameter at the ground, and there is no apparent reason why they should select it more than others.[10]

Supervisor Hamaker and others had described the insect variously as a "worm" or a "bug." Hopkins described it as "a small, black, bark-boring beetle, belonging to a species heretofore unknown to science." Since it did not have a specific name, he named it *Dendroctonus ponderosae*, from the Greek for "killer of trees," and gave the type-species (the example he thought best exemplified the characteristics of the genus) location as Piedmont, about 12 miles northwest of Rapid City. The species became known scientifically as *Dendroctonus ponderosae* Hopk. Hopkins suggested the popular name, "the pine-destroying beetle of the Black Hills," because he thought, incorrectly, that it was unique to the Black Hills, Today, the popular name is mountain pine beetle.[11]

After examining hundreds of individual trees, Hopkins prepared the classic description of the adult beetles: strong in body, dark-brown to black in color, one-sixth to one-quarter inch in length. As to their behavior:

> The beetles attack living and healthy large and small pine trees, enter the bark on the main trunk, and each pair excavates a long, nearly straight, longitudinal gallery through the inner bark, usually grooving the surface of the wood. Eggs are deposited along the sides of this gallery and hatch into minute white grubs (larvae), which excavate mines through the bark at right angles to the primary gallery. These mines are extended and enlarged as the larvae increase in size, and when full grown each individual excavates a broad, oval cavity in the bark, in which it transforms to a soft, white pupa, and then to the adult, which bores out through the bark and flies, with other adults of the same and other broods, in search of other living trees in which to excavate galleries and deposit eggs for another brood.[12]

Hopkins identified the beetles as "the primary cause of the trouble." Only later did scientists discover that a significant contributor to killing the trees are fungal spores or microorganisms from the genera *Ophiostoma* and *Ceratocystis*, commonly known as blue-stain because they discolor the outer wood or sapwood. Carried into the trees by the beetles, these microorganisms produce a thread-like mass (mycelium) that enters the food-conducting tissue (phloem) and then expands, eventually blocking the food supply to the tree.[13]

For the forester and the logger, Hopkins provided a short field guide to identify trees infested by the beetles. The first sign of beetle attack is reddish dust found on the loose outer bark or at the base of the trees. Such a sign can be confirmed by cutting away some outer bark to check for galleries and beetles in their various stages of development. Next and easier to see, small masses of resinous substance or pitch on the outer bark exude from the beetles' entrance galleries. From some distance, needles of dying trees first turn a pale yellow at the tops and tips of branches, gradually becoming yellow throughout and eventually turning red; most needles fall off during the second or third year following attack.[14]

Acknowledging that he did not know enough about the life habits and history of the beetles to suggest ways to eliminate them—their endemic or habitual presence in the forest was yet to be understood—Hopkins reaffirmed General Land Office policy to encourage cutting and removal of dying timber. Removing the number of infested trees in a timely manner reduced the size of the "attacking force" to a point where, combined with natural predators, healthy trees could protect themselves. By cutting the infested trees and removing their bark, loggers would be exposing and destroying the larvae while providing themselves with commercial timber.

In addition to identifying the insect and suggesting remedies, Pinchot had asked Hopkins to investigate the extent to which timber operators who had purchased beetle-infested stands at reduced prices were actually cutting healthy timber. Toward that end, Hopkins inspected a tie-timber sale near Cheyenne Crossing, about 20 miles south of Spearfish. There he found that of 207 ties, only 55 showed evidence of beetle kill; the remaining ties came from healthy, living trees.[15]

Given the destruction of merchantable timber the mountain pine beetle caused in the Black Hills, Pinchot convinced Secretary of Agriculture Wilson to create a Division of Forest Insect Investigation within the Bureau of Entomology and to appoint Hopkins as its head. Shortly after taking that job in 1902, Hopkins sent his first hire, Jesse L. "Jack" Webb, to Elmore near Cheyenne Crossing to further study the beetle's life history and habits. Webb had earned a master's degree in forest entomology under Hopkins at West Virginia University, the first such degree awarded in the nation.

Webb spent five months (May 28–October 30) at Elmore, where he conducted experiments on trap trees. He cut over 200 healthy trees in an effort to attract beetles to those trees and away from an otherwise healthy stand; once the beetles were attracted and before their young began to emerge, the trap trees would be destroyed, ostensibly reducing the overall beetle population. Hopkins visited the site in August 1902 and again in June 1903, after which he still recommended the timely cutting of infested trees, de-barking them on-site, and transporting them out of the forest.[16] He, too, criticized General Land Office regulations for what he considered excessive time allotted to advertising and other timber sale preparations, as well as the Homestake Mine clause in the Forest Management Act, prohibiting shipment of timber out of state. Under such rules, he felt "it was practically impossible to accomplish anything of importance" in controlling bark beetle epidemics.[17]

Meanwhile, Seth Bullock used his personal popularity to enlist settlers in an ongoing campaign to exterminate the beetles. Through local newspapers, he publicized Hopkins's expert advice: cutting infested trees during the winter months and peeling the bark to expose and destroy larvae, which "with the assistance of birds and other natural causes will in a very short time do away with the beetle pest."[18] He offered the free assistance of his rangers to identify infested trees on private lands, if settlers asked; this constituted early recognition of the fact that, with the intermingling of public and private public land in the Black Hills, public and private landowners needed to work together. Bullock did proceed with what seemed like a quixotic effort—offering bounties on squirrels, which he believed ate the eggs of the woodpeckers that preyed on the beetles.[19]

Again thanks to his popularity, Bullock managed to organize a volunteer fire department that, according to a boast in the local press, covered the largest area of any fire department in the world. According to General Land Office regulations, every holder of a grazing lease was required to participate in fire fighting. Bullock divided the department into twenty-five brigades covering all ranger districts. He instructed that as soon as a lessee spotted a fire, the lessee needed to notify the closest ranger and remain on the scene until the ranger arrived. If needed, the ranger in charge could call on neighboring rangers, volunteers, and temporary help from other districts. From Washington, Bullock received permission to suspend grazing fees for lessees who had not volunteered as firefighters. On the other hand, barring proof of legitimate absence, Bullock meant to revoke the permit of any lessee who refused to volunteer. How well this worked in practice is unclear. The same rules applied to loggers, but their cooperation in preventing fires seems to have rarely materialized.[20]

Timber operators strongly resisted the cutting of beetle-infested trees because such trees produced inferior lumber when not harvested soon enough after attacks. With support from Washington, Bullock took steps to make the process of timber sales less cumbersome. Prospective purchasers of dead timber valued at less than $20 could make an application and receive immediate approval from the supervisor; purchasers of dead or living timber valued at $21–$100 needed only the supervisor's approval but had to wait for the sale to be recorded in Washington. For larger proposed sales, the supervisor first decided whether such sales were advisable for ensuring future sales and protecting watersheds, then set conditions under which the trees needed to be cut. Once the prospective purchaser had agreed to sale conditions and completed the application form, the application with the supervisor's recommendation was sent to Washington for approval. Following approval, the sale was advertised locally to attract additional bids. If no further bids came in, the supervisor could award the bid to the sole applicant.[21]

In the matter of enforcing rules and regulations, during Bullock's first summer, rangers did collect enough evidence of illegal timbering to temporarily close down Lepke and McLaughlin Company; that action likely contributed to an overall reduction in illegal timbering during the Bullock administration. Without a doubt, personal acquaintanceships made it easier for Bullock and his rangers to nudge operators to abide by the rules. Presumably, President Roosevelt's pardon of Odo Reder, imprisoned for timber thievery, contributed to better relations between forest officials and timber operators.[22]

By the end of his first full year in office, Bullock could refer with pride to the General Land Office annual report, which listed revenues from sale of timber on the Black Hills Forest Reserve in the amount of $25,432, greater than revenues of $20,270 from all other forest reserves combined.[23] Yet in one of those rare cases in which official reporting could be checked against an insider's independent assessment, around the time Bullock took office, the General Land Office had sent Edward Tyson Allen to conduct an audit of timber management. Son of a Yale professor who moved to forested country near Mt. Rainier, the younger Allen, in the capacity of porter, first met Pinchot on one of his trips to the Pacific Northwest in 1896 or 1897 and kept in touch with Pinchot after Allen became a ranger and took on research assignments for the General Land Office.[24] Highly regarded by Pinchot though he had no formal forestry training, Allen turned to Pinchot for specific instructions on the Black Hills audit, having received no direction from his agency. Allen served as Pinchot's confidential forest agent, forwarding insights unrestricted by bureaucratic protocol. Both men recognized the limits of their informal relationship. At one point, Allen hesitated to bother Pinchot with detailed observations, even asking whether Pinchot preferred that he correspond with Filibert Roth, head of the newly created Division of Forestry within the General Land Office. Pinchot returned the courtesy, fearing that he was burdening Allen with too much letter writing: "If, however, things come up which you think I ought specially to know, I shall be glad to hear from time to time, especially if I can be of use."[25]

While in the Black Hills, Allen began work on a policies and procedures manual for the reserves that would be issued by the General Land Office in early 1902. Forest historian Harold Steen has suggested that the manual's content and style were Pinchot's, even though Pinchot credited authorship to Allen; quite likely, the two men collaborated.[26] In any case, we can safely assume that, through Allen, Pinchot obtained from the Black Hills the sort of useful information that would serve him well as author of his own forest manual, published shortly after he became chief of the US Forest Service.

To Pinchot, Allen portrayed Bullock as more local booster and consummate politician than rules enforcer and accomplished administrator. He noted that even after Bullock had been in office for several months, his rangers remained mostly inadequately trained and too few in number—still ten—to effectively oversee timbering. Bullock, on the contrary, had complained directly to Roosevelt that Washington kept sending out dandies while he wanted men "who could sleep out in the open with or without a blanket and put out a fire and catch a horse thief."[27] Allen confided to Pinchot that Bullock "is violently opposed to the policy of appointing eastern students and I think will make it impossible for them to do anything if they come. He lost his temper when he heard of the appointment of [two Yale men] as head rangers and it took a good deal of smoothing down to make him see that they could be a great help to him if he will let them."[28] Along with Representative Eben W. Martin (R-SD), Bullock later pursued the matter with the president in Washington. Bullock reminded Roosevelt that the Black

Hills Forest Reserve was the most important reserve in the nation because of its high timber value; Bullock did not want full responsibility for its management unless he could name his own staff. Roosevelt agreed and instructed Secretary of the Interior Hitchcock to confirm the appointments of those rangers Bullock had selected.[29]

Allen expressed the opinion that Supervisor Bullock would never make an ideal forest officer but, with some coaching, would be better than most. "His great fault is lack of energy," meaning that Bullock sought to delay making decisions. Further, he disdained instructions from Washington. "But as soon as he finds that you [Pinchot] hold the whip," he would readily acquiesce.[30] Undoubtedly recognizing that Pinchot sought to professionalize the US Forest Service, Bullock pursued establishment of a department of forestry at the School of Mines in Rapid City (founded in 1885, now South Dakota School of Mines and Technology) or at Spearfish Normal (founded in 1883, now Black Hills State University), which came to naught but further suggested Bullock's strong preference for hiring local people.[31]

Concerning his own relationship with Bullock, Allen noted that after waiting an entire fall for Bullock to assign six men to mark timber near Elmore as part of continuing research Hopkins had begun on the mountain pine beetle, Allen had been assigned three men in mid-December. By the time they arrived at the work site, heavy snows had fallen, making marking all but impossible.[32]

Forest research may not have been of pressing interest to Bullock, but forest restoration projects did begin under his administration. Starting in his first year, he hired local youths to collect cones and extract seeds in preparation for sowing on logged and fire-damaged areas within the reserve. In addition, Charles A. Scott—soon to be the first supervisor of the Nebraska National Forest—and three young assistants collected seeds and seedlings around Nemo. The Black Hills became the principal source of ponderosa pine seeds for the federal government's Bessey Nursery near Halsey in the Sandhills; the Nebraska National Forest became the principal recipient of seedlings for experimental sowing.

As a consummate politician anxious to please constituents, Supervisor Bullock weighed in on the side of settlers still without legal title to their inholdings. He persuaded Representative Martin to introduce legislation, passed by the US Congress and signed by President Roosevelt, giving claimants two additional years to produce evidence that they had been on the land prior to President Cleveland's 1897 executive order. The new legislation allowed any claimant who "has failed, by reason of ignorance of the proclamation of the President, or of the filing of the township plat or survey, or from unavoidable accident or condition, or from misunderstanding of the law, to place his claim of record within the statutory period."[33]

Recall that Pinchot's early interest in the Black Hills stemmed in part from the presence of communities dependent on the forest and the extraordinary intermingling of federal and non-federal land. Indeed, the very first regulation in his forest manual read in part: "The Forest Service will do all in its power to protect [persons having valid claims within forest reserves], and will grant preference for the use of privileges to actual residents in or near forest reserves." At the same time, forest officers would "make special efforts to discover and report fraudulent claims and to prevent the perfection of title to them."[34] Difficulties for forest officers arose not only because of the "free and easy" attitude toward the use of public land but also because the Forest Service, as manager of forestlands, was put in the position of investigating claims and enforcing the law while the General Land Office still served as the agency for approving or disapproving the validity of claims, which led to criticism of the Forest Service for preventing development.[35]

During summer 1905 inholders seeking permanent title to their lands had banded together as the Black Hills Forest Reserve Home Builders Association. Organizers sponsored a "mass meeting" at Hill City, attended by over 100 people, and invited US representative Martin in the hope of obtaining his sponsorship of a bill giving them title to agricultural land. Seth Bullock spoke briefly, assuring everyone that Congress would be friendly toward them.[36]

Indeed, Congress was friendly. Representative Martin informed his constituents that President Roosevelt had signed the Forest Homestead Act on June 11, 1906. The act permitted qualified homesteaders who had settled on agricultural lands within the reserves before January 1, 1906, to take ownership and allowed those who did not qualify as homesteaders the chance to purchase up to 100 acres of agricultural land upon payment of $2.50 per acre.[37] Bullock's successor cautioned his rangers that just because someone had settled on a piece of land, that land was not necessarily agricultural. Rangers needed to assess whether land was in fact agricultural and, if so, to advise prospective homesteaders to make application directly to Washington, the surest way to obtain fair hearings.[38] Congress would pass additional homestead legislation, increasing allowable acreages and reducing residency periods. In addition, special legislation would allow ranchers in Lawrence and Pennington Counties to apply for use of forestlands deemed more valuable for grazing and for growing crops.[39] During the decade 1906–16, approximately 100,000 acres of federal land in the Black Hills were released to homesteaders.

In representing the Roosevelt administration, Supervisor Bullock emphasized the economic necessity of conservative forestry. In a speech to the Black Hills Mining Association, he explained that "the permanent industries of the Black Hills are wholly dependent upon timber and water: destroy one, and those industries will disappear; while, if both are destroyed, the 'richest 100 miles square' will become a desert."[40] In an address to the American Forestry Congress in Washington, DC, he argued that a stable supply of timber and water required "intelligent and practical forestry which can best be obtained under forest reservations, laws administered with business-like methods."[41]

Regarding a stable supply of water, beginning in 1904, one of the nation's earliest reclamation projects took place on the northern edge of the Black Hills, along the Belle Fourche River; decades later, the Bureau of Reclamation constructed an irrigation project on the southern edge, along the Cheyenne River. Both projects included reservoirs—Belle Fourche, completed in 1908; Angostura, in 1949; and Keyhole, in 1952—that in time would attract even more recreationists to the Black Hills.

Indeed, during Supervisor Bullock's tenure, business interests in Hot Springs successfully lobbied the South Dakota congressional delegation to introduce legislation establishing Wind Cave, thirteen miles north of town, as a national park. The cave was discovered in 1881 when a party happened upon a flow of cool air emerging from a small opening in the ground; early promoters dug out an entrance so spelunkers could get into the cave. Surface land had been claimed for farming but never proven. In 1902 President Roosevelt attached the site (now 28,295 acres) to the Black Hills Forest Reserve, appointed Bullock as supervisor, and instructed that the closest ranger be put in charge. On January 9, 1903, the president signed legislation making Wind Cave the first cave in the nation designated a national park; it was transferred to the National Park Service in 1916.[42]

As yet, the only tourist destination within the mountainous portion of the Black Hills Forest Reserve was Sylvan Lake Resort. In August 1904 Bullock took Secretary Wilson, Senator Alfred B. Kittredge (R-SD), and Representative Martin on a forest inspection trip that included a day of rest at the resort. The local newspaper speculated that "their visit will result in much good to the Hills, and especially to legislation affecting the reserve."[43] The fact that Bullock, an employee of the Department of the Interior, served as guide to the secretary of agriculture presaged the imminent transfer of the reserves from Interior to Agriculture.

Gifford Pinchot had been laying the groundwork for transfer at least since passage of the Forest Management Act in 1897. Setting up Secretary of the Interior Hitchcock's request to Secretary of Agriculture Wilson to allow Pinchot to assist in preparing timbering plans for the reserves constituted a critical step. Pinchot's success with the Homestake Mining Company served to enlist the all-important support of Superintendent Thomas Grier who, together with Frederick E. Weyerhaeuser of the prominent West Coast lumber family, would help with final lobbying on behalf of the transfer act.[44]

Placing all forest functions under a single agency raised the specter of stronger and tighter control of the forest reserves, meaning less flexibility for forest users.

Smaller timber operators feared that, as a result of the transfer, the Department of Agriculture would hire professional foresters who had graduated from eastern colleges rather than local men who knew the local area. "A technical knowledge of forestry," the *Custer Weekly Chronicle* editorialized, "is not as essential in a forest ranger as a knowledge of the country and of the correct treatment of forest fires, which can only be acquired by long residence in the region." More to the point, rangers must also know the people with whom they deal: "This knowledge is not possessed by the average college graduate who is unused to western customs and western life." Abandoning Supervisor Bullock's practice of local hiring, the editorial continued, "would undo much of the good work that has been done in allying the apprehension of the population" toward President Cleveland's executive order.[45] To assuage local fears, Bullock may have been among those who lobbied successfully for inclusion of this provision in the transfer act: "That forest supervisors and rangers shall be selected, when practicable, from qualified citizens of the States and Territories in which the said reserves, respectively, are situated." [46]

The transfer act, less than one page in length, was signed by President Roosevelt on February 1, 1905. It was one of several acts promulgated that year that gave Pinchot full control over all forest reserves. In Pinchot's opinion, the transfer act provided the means necessary to put "technical practical forestry" in place and to give the forest reserves "their fullest permanent usefulness."[47] As testimony to Pinchot's political skills, the final version garnered the support not only of the timber and mining industries but also of the railroads. Western members of Congress, who had consistently opposed creation of the forest reserves, voted for the bill, among them Senator Francis E. Warren (R-WY) and Representative Franklin W. Mondell (R-WY). Both stockmen, they initially feared, and then were persuaded otherwise by Pinchot, that the Department of Agriculture would promulgate and enforce stronger grazing regulations than the Department of the Interior. Mondell, who grazed cattle and sheep in the Newcastle area, did prevent specific mention of fees in the act; but US attorney general William H. Moody expressed the opinion that the act allowed the secretary of agriculture "to make a reasonable charge" in connection with the use and occupation of the forest reserves.[48]

Moreover, the act stipulated that "all money received from the sale of any products or the use of any land or resources" of the forest reserves be placed in a special fund for a period of five years, until expended "for the protection, administration, improvement, and extension" of the reserves.[49] The appropriations bill for the Department of Agriculture, passed in March 1905, further strengthened Pinchot's hand by giving forest officers the authority to make arrests for violations of laws and regulations relating to the reserves and did away with the "in lieu" option that had allowed the unscrupulous to exchange denuded forestlands for federal lands elsewhere but still prohibited out-of-state shipment of timber.[50]

With the transfer act came name changes, from Bureau of Forestry to Forest Service and from "forest reserves" to "national forests." Both changes reflected Pinchot's political sensibility and foresight. The impression he least wanted to convey was that the new consolidated agency was a bureaucracy or that public forests were closed to productive use. Just prior to official transfer on July 1, 1905, Pinchot put out his famous forest manual. As if to emphasize its eminent practicality, *The Use of the National Forest Reserves, Regulations and Instructions*, published with a strong binding and solid bevel-edged weather-resistant cover, fit into a forest ranger's shirt pocket.[51] Though greatly expanded over the years from the original 142 mini-pages (to more than sixteen linear feet of notebooks until recently put in electronic form), its basic premise remains intact: "where conflicting interests must be reconciled the question will always be decided from the standpoint of the greatest good of the greatest number in the long run."[52]

In introducing the *Use of the National Forest Reserves*, Pinchot took an excerpt from Secretary Wilson's letter of instructions to the forester, following the president's signature of the transfer act. That letter, which Pinchot apparently drafted, set forth the general policy for the Forest Service: "In the administration of the forest reserves it must be clearly borne in mind that all land is to be devoted to its most productive use for the permanent good of the whole people, and not for the temporary benefit of individuals or companies. All the resources of the forest reserves are for *use*, and this use must be brought about in a thoroughly prompt and businesslike manner, under such restrictions only as will insure the permanence of these resources."[53]

In the *Use of the National Forest Reserves*, Pinchot provided assurance to legitimate settlers that their rights would be protected and that, in the administration of the forest reserves, "local questions will be decided upon local grounds." In addressing the matter of use permits, Pinchot instructed forest officers to be guided by the spirit of the regulations and to take the side of permittees if at all possible, always keeping in mind that the conservative use of forest resources "in no way conflicts with their permanent value." To maintain that balance, the Forest Service as steward reasonably required permits for any and all uses of the reserves.[54]

In the matter of grazing permits, their purpose was threefold: ensuring the conservative use of grazing land, the permanent well-being of the stock-growing industry "through proper care and improvement of the grazing lands," and settlers' continued use of the range. Pinchot instructed that every effort be made "to assist the stock owners to a satisfactory distribution of stock on the range in order to secure greater harmony among citizens, to reduce the waste of forage by tramping in unnecessary movement of stock, and to obtain a more permanent, judicious, and profitable use of the range."[55] Thereby, he introduced the concept of carrying capacity that, in the late 1970s, would be expressed in animal unit months. Pinchot acknowledged that, beginning in January 1906, a grazing fee would be charged: it would start at twenty to thirty-five cents per head for the grazing season and gradually increase as lumber market conditions, transportation facilities, and demand for forest range warranted.[56]

Taking the side of ranchers, Bullock had argued that Pinchot's fees were unreasonably high because they did not fully recognize stock grower assistance in fire prevention and fire fighting. Since most stock growers in the Black Hills grazed fewer than 100 head, Bullock recommended no fees on the first 100 head and a levy of ten cents per head above that number. In fact, the levies would start at twenty cents per head for cattle belonging to settlers who resided within reserve boundaries and thirty cents per head for cattle grazing within the reserves but belonging to stock growers who lived outside the boundaries; local stock growers' associations were invited to appoint voluntary boards to advise the Forest Service on future fees. Permittees were limited in building corrals and erecting fences, required to allow free access to water for any stock grazing under permit, and required to pay for damages to roads and trails. Grazing season in the Black Hills was set for May 15 through October 15.[57]

The *Use of the National Forest Reserves* restated procedures for timber sales as outlined in Allen's earlier manual, though Pinchot conveyed an enabling rather than a prescriptive spirit: "All timber on forest reserves which can be cut safely and for which there is actual need is for sale." Anyone except those who had violated the law could purchase timber, limited in quantity only by the capacity of the forest (preventing overcutting and injury to young growth) and by protection against monopolists and speculators. As a first step in the process, applicants for purchase of timber were invited to confer with the nearest forest officer. On deciding local questions locally: "Inquiries or applications should never be sent to Washington direct[ly]. Remittances of money or complaints against the conduct of local officers are the only communications which applicants or purchasers should make to the Washington office during any stage of a sale."[58]

The greatest benefit provided by federal management of the national forests would be protection of timber and watersheds. Within that context, Pinchot reminded forest officers of their responsibility to instruct the public on the agency's conservation agenda. He set the tone for his officers to communicate with settlers, loggers, miners, other forest users, and the general public. Prevention being the most effective and least expensive form of protection, Pinchot advised his officers to "cheerfully and politely tell hunters, campers and others about the rules and regulations governing camp fires. An officer who loses his temper or uses improper language in talking with persons who are careless . . . fails in one of his principal duties." While the approach should always be one of "cooperation and good will, it is equally important to have it well understood that reserve interests will be protected by every legal means." Congress had fixed a variety of penalties for violation of forest regulations.[59]

To make the Forest Service more professional, Pinchot inaugurated a policy of hiring staff on the basis of merit, demonstrated by passing competitive civil service examinations "along practical lines" and including "tests in the actual performance of field work." Hiring preferences for supervisors and rangers still went to qualified residents of the states in which the respective national forests were located.[60] Part of Pinchot's genius in organizing the Forest Service was the unprecedented way he sought to balance centralized authority in Washington with decentralization at the local forest level. Secretary Wilson's letter of instruction to Pinchot noted that the general policy of the Forest Service "can be successfully applied only when the administration of each reserve is left largely in the hands of the local officers, under the eye of thoroughly trained and competent inspectors."[61]

Initially, forest supervisors reported directly to the forester in Washington; Pinchot established a section of inspectors directly responsible to him. Within two years, however, he had created six regional districts, with each supervisor reporting to the respective district forester in Washington; only the district foresters reported directly to the forester. As a way of bridging headquarters to the individual forests, Pinchot rotated supervisors into Washington to serve temporarily as district foresters. In December 1908 Pinchot moved the district foresters into their respective regions. His rationale was twofold: closer connection between the direction of work and its execution and closer technical oversight of forest supervisors. The Black Hills National Forest came under the jurisdiction of the Denver district, now known as Region 2.[62]

NOTES

1. Gifford Pinchot, *Breaking New Ground* (Washington, DC: Island, 1998 [1947]), 90.

2. Ibid., 188–91.

3. *Custer Weekly Chronicle*, May 11, 1901.

4. Howard R. Lamar, *Dakota Territory, 1861–1889: A Study of Frontier Politics* (New Haven: Yale University Press, 1956), 166.

5. David A. Wolff, *Seth Bullock, Black Hills Lawman* (Pierre: South Dakota Historical Society Press, 2009), 126–27; Theodore Roosevelt, *An Autobiography* (New York: Library of America, 2004 [1913]), 373.

6. *Custer Weekly Chronicle*, October 6, 1900; Wolff, *Seth Bullock*, 143–45.

7. Pinchot, *Breaking New Ground*, 144–45.

8. C. Wayne Berisford, "Andrew Delmar Hopkins—a West Virginia Pioneer in Ento-mology," *West Virginia University Agricultural and Forestry Experiment Station Circular* 155 (January 1992): 20–24; Malcolm M. Furniss, "A History of Forest Entomology in the Inter-mountain and Rocky Mountain Areas, 1901–1982," USDA Forest Service General Technical Report, RMRS-GTR-195 (2007): 1–3; see also Roger L. Williams, *Aven Nelson of Wyoming* (Boulder: Colorado Associated University Press, 1984).

9. Andrew Delmar Hopkins, "Insect Enemies of the Pine in the Black Hills Forest Reserve: An Account of Results of Special Investigations, with Recommendations for Pre-venting Losses," *USDA Division of Entomology Bulletin* 32 (1902): 7–8.

10. Ibid., 8.

11. Ibid., 9.

12. Ibid., 10.

13. Furniss, "History of Forest Entomology," 40n1.

14. Hopkins, "Insect Enemies," 19.

15. Ibid., 21–23.

16. Furniss, "History of Forest Entomology," 2–3, 43–44; *Custer Weekly Chronicle*, November 22, 1902; Andrew Delmar Hopkins, "The Black Hills Beetle, with Further Notes on Its Distribution, Life History, and Methods of Control," *USDA Bureau of Entomology Bulletin* 56 (1905): 6–7.

17. Hopkins, "Black Hills Beetle," 19.

18. Bullock quoted in *Custer Weekly Chronicle*, September 27, 1902.

19. Ibid., August 26, 1905; Wolff, *Seth Bullock*, 153.

20. *Custer Weekly Chronicle*, August 24, November 23, 1901; E. A. Sterling, "Attitude of Lumbermen toward Forest Fires," in *USDA Yearbook* (Washington, DC: US Department of Agriculture, 1904), 136.

21. Allyson Brooks, Brad Noisat, and Linda Sundstrom, "Logging," in *Black Hills National Forest Cultural Resources Overview,* ed. Lance Rom, Tim Church, and Michele Church (Custer: USDA Forest Service, Black Hills National Forest, 1996), 1: 5b–4; *Custer Weekly Chronicle*, December 2, 1905.

22. Gifford Pinchot to Secretary James Wilson, Custer, August 1, 1901, copy, Pinchot Papers, loose-leaf binder, vol. 2, Leland D. Case Library for Western Historical Studies, Black Hills State University, Spearfish, SD (hereafter BHSU Case Library); *Custer Weekly Chronicle*, October 12, 1901.

23. Martha Linde, *Sawmills of the Black Hills* (Rapid City: Fenske, 1984), 102.

24. Shirley W. Allen, "E. T. Allen," *Journal of Forestry* 43, no. 3 (March 1945): 222–23.

25. Edward T. Allen to Gifford Pinchot, Lead, December 6, 1901, and Pinchot to Allen, Washington, DC, November 4, 1901, copies, Pinchot Papers, vol. 2, BHSU Case Library.

26. Harold K. Steen, *The U.S. Forest Service: A History* (Seattle: University of Washing-ton Press, 2004 [1976]), 58.

27. Quoted in Kenneth C. Kellar, *Seth Bullock: Frontier Marshal* (Aberdeen, SD: North Plains, 1972), 120.

28. Edward T. Allen to Gifford Pinchot, Lead, December 17, 1901, copy, Pinchot Papers, vol. 2, BHSU Case Library.

29. *Custer Weekly Chronicle*, February 1, 1902.

30. Edward T. Allen to Gifford Pinchot, December 17, 1901.

31. *Custer Weekly Chronicle*, May 24, 1902.

32. Edward T. Allen to Gifford Pinchot, Lead, December 17, 1901.

33. Quoted in *Custer Weekly Chronicle*, April 19, 1902.

34. Gifford Pinchot, *The Use of the National Forest Reserves: Regulations and Instructions* (Washington, DC: US Department of Agriculture, 1905), 13.

35. Henry Clepper, *Professional Forestry in the United States* (Baltimore: Johns Hopkins Press, 1971), 62–63.

36. *Custer Weekly Chronicle*, July 8 and 22, 1905.

37. Ibid., May 5, June 16, 1906.

38. Ibid., June 23, 1906.

39. Ibid., August 12, 1916.

40. Quoted in "Annals of the Black Hills," typescript, p. 49, 1948 draft with 1967 addition, Black Hills National Forest supervisor's office, Custer, SD.

41. Quoted in *Custer Weekly Chronicle*, January 14, 1905.

42. Ibid., August 30, 1902; Suzanne Barta Julin, *A Marvelous Hundred Square Miles: Black Hills Tourism, 1880–1941* (Pierre: South Dakota State Historical Society Press, 2009), 15–18.

43. *Custer Weekly Chronicle*, August 13, 1904.

44. Pinchot, *Breaking New Ground*, 255.

45. *Custer Weekly Chronicle*, February 1, 1902.

46. An Act Providing for the Transfer of Forest Reserves from the Department of Interior to the Department of Agriculture, Public Law 58–34, *US Statutes at Large* 33 (1905): 628; Carl A. Newport, *Forest Service Policies in Timber Management and Silviculture as They Affect the Lumber Industry: A Case Study of the Black Hills* (Pierre: South Dakota Department of Game, Fish and Parks, 1956), 28.

47. "Report of the Forester," in *USDA Annual Reports* (Washington, DC: US Department of Agriculture, 1905), 199.

48. Pinchot, *Breaking New Ground*, 271–72.

49. Act for Transfer of Forest Reserves, 628.

50. An Act Making Appropriations for the Department of Agriculture for the Fiscal Year Ending June 30, 1906, Public Law 58–138, *US Statutes at Large* 33 (1905): 873; Pinchot, *Breaking New Ground*, 257–58.

51. Described in Steen, *U.S. Forest Service*, 78.

52. Pinchot, *Use of the National Forest Reserves*, 11.

53. Ibid., 10.

54. Ibid., 11–19.

55. Ibid., 20–21.

56. Ibid., 30.

57. *Custer Weekly Chronicle*, February 10 and 17, November 4, 1905; "Report of the Forester," in *USDA Annual Reports* (Washington, DC: US Department of Agriculture, 1906), 267.

58. Pinchot, *Use of the National Forest Reserves,* 31–32, 41.

59. Ibid., 65–67.

60. Ibid., 82–83.

61. Pinchot, *Breaking New Ground,* 262.

62. "Report of the Forester," in *USDA Annual Reports* (Washington, DC: US Department of Agriculture, 1907), 343; "Report of the Forester," in *USDA Annual Reports* (Washington, DC: US Department of Agriculture, 1908), 440; Newport, *Forest Service Policies,* 30–31.

5

Pinchot's Legacy

Managing the Timber

"The Black Hills Will Have Perpetual Timber Supply. Forest Service Has Placed Forests under Intensive Management." So read a 1922 headline for a story about the first long-range plan in the nation for the management of national forest timber stands. Prepared by Black Hills National Forest supervisor George A. Duthie and publicized jointly with Harney National Forest supervisor John F. Conner to emphasize its broad application, the plan meant to "insure the proper handling of a forest to produce a continuous crop of greatest possible volume, and permit an annual harvest just as the farmer harvests his alfalfa field each year."[1]

The concept of harvesting timber while maintaining growing stock, like distributing earnings from an endowment fund without touching the principal, was not new in 1922. The Rooseveltians had found the concept entirely consistent with their notion of public usefulness, which they had inherited from the founding fathers. By the time the Bureau of Forestry was renamed the Forest Service and the reserves were renamed national forests, most Black Hills residents had come to recognize the benefits of federal administration to ensure continuous supplies of timber. Representative Freeman T. Knowles (R-SD), an early opponent of the reserves, acknowledged that he had been wrong in 1897. After eight years of experience, he concluded "that the establishment of the reserve has been and will be of inestimable benefit to the Black Hills."[2]

Even after President William H. Taft fired Gifford Pinchot in 1910, the fact that he had appointed Henry Graves as forester meant forestry would continue to

DOI: 10.5876/9781607322993.c005

advance according to Pinchot's principles. Just as his predecessors had, President Taft made changes in forest boundaries as well as in forest administration. By way of review, President Cleveland had created the Black Hills Forest Reserve, 967,680 acres in South Dakota; President McKinley had added 244,000 acres in Wyoming; and upon Pinchot's recommendation, President Roosevelt had established the Bearlodge Forest Preserve, 136,784 acres north of Sundance, administratively attached to the Black Hills National Forest. Pinchot's rationale: "If this forest is not protected from careless and [in]discriminate logging methods and the ravages of the pine bark beetle, the settlers hitherto depending upon it for their timber supply will be forced to go to the Black Hills reserve at considerable increased cost."[3] In 1908 President Roosevelt consolidated the Forest Service lands in northeast Wyoming into the Sundance National Forest.

Ostensibly to ensure more effective management, in 1910 President Taft divided the Black Hills National Forest into a northern section, which kept the name and remained headquartered in Deadwood, and a southern section designated Harney National Forest, headquartered in Custer. Following the division, boundaries of the latter contained 642,550 acres, reduced to 508,037 acres in 1914 as a result of lobbying for more agricultural designation of land and a land exchange with the State of South Dakota that made possible the creation of Custer State Park. In 1915 President Woodrow Wilson consolidated the Sundance National Forest into the Black Hills National Forest; together with the Harney National Forest, the acreage within national forest boundaries would amount to 1,316,742 acres in 1930, of which 1,025,911 acres were in federal ownership and most of the remaining 290,831 acres in private hands. The two national forests would be merged into one by President Dwight D. Eisenhower in 1954.[4]

Gifford Pinchot may have wished otherwise, but Seth Bullock's immediate successors were not formally trained foresters; professional foresters were not yet available. Supervisor John Fremont Smith (1906–7) had been hired by Supervisor Henry Hamaker and, while serving as ranger, had earned the distinction of securing the first conviction of a rancher caught violating grazing rules. The fact that Smith resigned after a brief tenure to manage an orchard, which he had purchased on Colorado's Western Slope, suggests a farming background.[5] His successor, Edwin M. Hamilton (1907–9), was working as a logger when Bullock hired him. He held the position "chief inspector of logs" when promoted to supervisor and later returned to timber as a sawmill manager in Sheridan.[6]

From extant correspondence between Supervisor Smith and one of his rangers, we obtain a glimpse into the trials and tribulations of early rangers in the Black Hills. Without a doubt, George C. Smith (no relation) was a decent, hardworking officer, ever aware of his limitations. Born in 1872 and raised on a farm in

Kansas, he moved to the Sundance area in 1894 and spent the next five years as a laborer in the timber industry. After obtaining his own homestead, he began farming, though working out of season at sawmills or wherever else he could earn wages. In early 1906, Supervisor Smith hired George Smith on a six-month probation as assistant ranger to patrol for timber and grazing trespassers and forest fires; fifteen months later, he promoted Smith to deputy ranger for the newly created Bearlodge Forest Reserve. By then George Smith had become a forest inholder with the purchase of 800 acres, which he leased to a rancher for grazing since he himself possessed no cattle.[7]

To allow him to carry out his official duties, the Forest Service had issued George Smith a service badge (no uniforms yet) plus tools and supplies for surveying boundaries and appraising timber stands: a 66-foot surveyor chain, surveyor pins and tripod, a 100-foot steel tape, rulers for measuring timber, and the official marking hatchet. In addition, Smith had sought to borrow, but had yet to receive, from the US Department of War a 7-foot by 9-foot tent until he could build a permanent summer cabin in the forest.[8]

Supervisor Smith reminded George Smith that his charge extended beyond the Bearlodge Reserve to include the Wyoming portions of the Black Hills National Forest. The vast size of his territory overwhelmed George Smith. "I really need some help here," he wrote, "as there is so much patented timber land, with so few Section corners, that it is hard to tell just what I am doing." He continued, "I believe there will be some attempts to run in stock that has no right on the Forest, and with so much opposition to the making of these Reserves, it will be a very hard matter for one man to be effective." Consequently, he requested that a second forest officer be hired and stationed near Alladin, northeast of Sundance. He recommended a Mr. Madison as someone who "knows the country, will take the Civil Service exam, and will make a good ranger." But he added, "If I can't get any help, I shall surely do the best I can."[9]

John Smith supported the request and forwarded it to Washington. He also asked George Smith to interview George C. Butterfield, assess his ability compared to Madison's, and, if in his opinion neither is "a good man," suggest someone else. After much back and forth, Washington did authorize a temporary forest guard position and the hiring of Butterfield on the condition that he pass the civil service examination if the position became permanent.[10]

Perhaps because of his expanded responsibilities, George Smith inquired how he might advance himself within the Forest Service. At his supervisor's suggestion, Smith wrote directly to Pinchot, asking whether there was any way he could "study up" on the Forest Service and obtain promotion without interfering with his current work. "I am satisfied with my present position," he wrote, "and I wouldn't want you to think that I wanted a raise without earning it." From the forester's office, Clyde Leavitt responded that civil service examinations for higher positions required technical knowledge that "can hardly be secured outside a Forest School." But Leavitt informed Smith that the Forest Service had just inaugurated a plan to circulate basic books about forestry. Leavitt copied Supervisor Smith, who supplied George Smith with a list of twelve books from which he could choose those he would like to have mailed to Sundance.[11]

As to the principal task of regulating timbering, Deputy Ranger Smith clearly did the best he could, though his successes paled against the enormity of the task. In the case of loggers timbering on the north end of the forest, he tried valiantly to stop them from delivering timber to mills until after they had piled their slash. Knowing that the loggers operated their own stock farms, he allowed additional time for hay season; but when they ignored his request, he sent the requisite form letter informing them of the imminent seizure of their logs and lumber and that any removal of forest products before slash had been piled "to the satisfaction of the Forest Officer in Charge" would be considered trespassing under penalty of federal law. The outcome of that effort is unknown.[12]

Sawmill operators posed a different challenge. In the case of Fred Brooks, who operated a sawmill on private land within the national forest, George Smith asked Brooks on at least three occasions to install devices on his equipment to prevent sparks from igniting nearby flammable materials. Expressing a view that still prevails among some operators, Brooks insisted that since his mill was on private property, he could not be compelled to do anything ordered by an agent of the federal government. Smith responded that with extreme fire danger as a result of unusually dry conditions, sparks from the sawmill threatened the surrounding forest. Brooks remained intransigent, so Smith requested an injunction to force closure of the mill; but Supervisor Smith, uncertain about the legalities, instructed his ranger to advise Brooks instead that he would be held responsible for any damage to the public forest caused by his mill operation.[13]

George Smith encountered difficulties with inholding settlers as well: "They tear and destroy the Boundry notices and Fire Warnings as fast as I put them up; if it continues I am going to bring somebody to account for it."[14] Again, we don't know the outcome. Given the urgent need to remove diseased timber, however, Smith hoped a quick way could be found to confirm yet-unproven homestead claims, giving settlers some incentive to cut beetle-infested timber. Moreover, a satisfied and secure people would benefit the forest.[15] When Crook County commissioners requested free timber for their road and bridge department, Supervisor Smith urged his ranger to convince the commissioners to use beetle-infested timber, noting that the Burlington Railroad had cut such timber for its bridges. In addition,

Supervisor Smith instructed George Smith to publicize the availability of infested timber at little or no cost and to encourage special arrangements between loggers and sawmill operators so that all concerned could benefit from using such timber.[16]

As part of conservative forestry and undoubtedly initiated by the forester in Washington, reforestation efforts in the Black Hills commenced in earnest under Supervisor Smith. His successor, Supervisor Hamilton, is credited as the first to publicize such efforts and to employ college students for re-seeding and planting seedlings. During summer of 1906 or 1907, about 30,000 ponderosa pine and 10,000 Douglas fir (*pseudotsuga menziesii*) seedlings from the Bessey Nursery were set out on the Roubaix burn, southeast of Deadwood. Also part of conservative forestry, scientific research began early in the Black Hills. James W. Tuomey of the Yale School of Forestry visited the Roubaix site in the summer of 1907 in preparation for a study of growth rates of the ponderosa pine.[17] Meanwhile, an early forest assistant wrote general descriptions of trees and shrubs he had found in the forest; and in 1915 a forest examiner, using accepted Latin nomenclature, identified more than seventy species of trees and shrubs, some commercially valuable and others not.[18]

Yale produced the first professionally trained foresters to serve as supervisors in the Black Hills: Paul D. Kelleter over the Black Hills National Forest (1909–18) and Richard P. Imes as first supervisor of the Harney National Forest (1910–16). Kelleter, class of 1904, had begun his career at forest headquarters in Deadwood and then worked briefly in the Lolo National Forest of Montana before returning to the Black Hills.[19] Pinchot thought well enough of Kelleter to accept his invitation (see page 74). Kelleter clearly subscribed to Pinchot's vision of the Forest Service as a field agency. "All effort is made in the plan of organization to make it possible for the Forest Rangers to spend practically all of their time in the field," confining record keeping and reporting, to the greatest extent possible, to the supervisor's office.[20]

In the *Use of the National Forest Reserves*, Pinchot stated that he required from supervisors two monthly reports—one on the progress of timber sales and the other on grazing permits issued—and four end-of-year reports: on free use (timber), grazing and range conditions, fires, and miscellaneous work such as cabin building and trail construction. Pinchot required every supervisor "to keep a diary, in which he will record for each day of service his work and movement and the progress and notable happenings of his reserve."[21] The only diary held in the Forest Service historical collection at Black Hills State University belonged to Kelleter. Although sporadic and abbreviated, entries over a six-year period (1909–15) testify to his time in the field and his engagement in the routine business of the forest. Just one example: for October 27, 1909, Kelleter recorded that he left Hill City at 7:00 a.m., taking three hours to ride a distance of 15 miles to inspect a fire-fighting crew near Pactola. He returned to Hill City by 7:00 p.m., in time for a meeting on forest policy with a Mr. Gregg who arrived by train from Deadwood. Two days later, with the Pactola fire getting worse, Kelleter telephoned Rapid City (lines were just being strung in the area) for an additional 65 fire fighters and supplies. On October 30 he telegraphed US Army headquarters in Omaha, requesting 100 soldiers from Fort George G. Meade near Sturgis; with the fire under control, they were able to return to camp on November 1. Back in his office at Deadwood, Kelleter took two days to catch up on routine office work and prepare a special fire report for Washington.[22]

In addition to seeking to protect the forest from fires and insects, the supervisor's routine included oversight of grazing that, if not carefully regulated, Pinchot and others considered damaging to the forest. By Kelleter's time, stock and wool growers had organized into effective lobbies, especially in Wyoming. Among their most outspoken advocates was Congressman Franklin W. Mondell (R-WY) from Newcastle. Because sheep were generally more destructive than cattle, Pinchot's *Use of the National Forest Reserves* allowed for sheep in the forests only "where special conditions warrant such privileges."[23]

During his first year as supervisor, Kelleter requested Pinchot's presence to help address the concerns of livestock producers. Pinchot arranged for a stopover in the Black Hills en route to the West Coast. With Kelleter, he embarked on a four-day inspection trip by wagon team to the south and west of Deadwood. Newcastle-area wool growers owned about 40,000 sheep and controlled the area's grazing land, except for national forest land they sought for summer grazing. In advance of Pinchot's visit, Kelleter scheduled two public meetings to hear comments for and against opening the forest to sheep. His rangers publicized both locations to attract participation from homesteaders and stock growers as well as wool growers.

The first meeting took place on a Saturday evening at a lumber camp west of Nahant (about 15 miles south of Deadwood). Standing on a wagon bed, Kelleter introduced Pinchot, who said a few words before listening to the approximately 120 men in attendance. According to a ranger who was present, wool growers argued that since sheep were permitted to graze in other national forests, it was unfair to ban them from the Black Hills. Pinchot responded that, indeed, sheep grazed elsewhere on national forest lands but outside wooded areas; because sheep, unlike cattle, graze in tight bands and forage very close to the ground, they harm or destroy tree seedlings. Stand mortality caused by the mountain pine beetle meant that new growth needed the fullest protection to ensure forest renewal. Pinchot added that compared to any other national forest, the Black Hills housed the greatest concentration of small farmsteads within its boundaries; seasonal movement of sheep through those properties would be intrusive as well. At the end of testimonials, Kelleter took a head count vote that went three to one against opening the forest to

FIGURE 5.1. Mountain pine beetle infestation, 1925. Courtesy, N. C. Robert, USDA Forest Service, Harney National Forest, http://www.ForestPhoto.com.

sheep. As the meeting disbanded, Kelleter and Pinchot remained with a few men and, again according to the ranger present, conversed until dawn. The second meeting, at a ranch on the Limestone Plateau, produced the same results. Before boarding a train at Newcastle, Pinchot advised Kelleter to maintain the ban on sheep. In later years, Pinchot reminisced that he hated sheep and concurred with John Muir's assessment of them as "hoofed locusts."[24]

Upon learning that the sheep ban would remain, Representative Mondell and Senator Clarence D. Clark (R-WY)—resident of Evanston, also a major sheep grazing area—renewed their efforts to overturn the Forest Service ban. Their appeal to President Taft coincided with the dismissal of Pinchot, at which time they lobbied the president to appoint Albert F. Potter as special representative to review the grazing situation in the West. A former wool grower in Arizona, hired by Pinchot as grazing specialist and promoted to assistant forester (to whom Pinchot handed over his keys when dismissed), Potter became the Forest Service's first chief of grazing under Henry Graves.

As part of his review of grazing, Potter spent a week in the Black Hills—together with Harney National Forest supervisor Richard Imes—meeting with business

R. P. Imes
Forest Supervisor
uly, 1910 - June, 1916

FIGURE 5.2. Supervisor Imes, ca. 1910–15. Courtesy, Black Hills National Forest Historical Collection, Leland D. Case Library for Western Historical Studies, Black Hills State University, Spearfish, SD.

interests in Custer, stopping to converse with settlers along the route from Custer to Newcastle, and ending with a meeting of wool growers from Wyoming. Before his departure, Potter told Imes he would recommend continuation of the ban on sheep; he had found water from various springs and watering places insufficient to allow for sheep without serious damage to farmlands and to livestock belonging to inholders. Potter's recommendation held with President Taft and did more than any other action to incur, in Imes's opinion, "the everlasting enmity [of Senator Clark and Representative Mondell] for the Forest Service."[25]

The alienation of the legislators disappointed Supervisor Imes; he had taken satisfaction in cultivating public opinion for the Forest Service. He would reminisce about how, after three years of effort, he had won over an opposition newspaper editor who then agreed to publish articles about the Forest Service; in fact, Imes wrote the articles on behalf of a reporter. Recall that Imes had been connected to the Black Hills since summer 1900 when, after completing his freshman year at Yale, he worked as a student aide to Edward Griffith. He did not finish his degree at Yale but took employment with the Forestry Division and later with the Forest Service, appearing as forest inspector in the Black Hills during summer 1907.[26]

Both Clark and Mondell had left office by the time Imes's successor, John F. Conner (1916–35), allowed 4,800 sheep into the national forest on a five-year experimental basis. Because of a four-year depression in cattle prices, Conner had seen valuable forage unused, which he believed added to the fire danger. Having grown up on a stock farm near Spearfish, Conner noted that stock growers had come to realize that cattle and sheep could graze complementarily. After graduating from Spearfish Normal School, Conner had started as a forest guard, remained in the Black Hills, and moved up through the ranks to become supervisor of Harney National Forest. Well-respected locally, he participated actively as a member of numerous civic organizations, including president of the Custer Commercial Club.[27]

Both locally and from a system-wide perspective, Conner was overshadowed by his contemporary, George Duthie. A native of Michigan, he had earned a master's degree in forestry from the University of Michigan in 1909. That summer, under Supervisor Kelleter, he began work as a forest agent assigned to the reforestation project on the Roubaix fire site. He was transferred to an administrative position under Supervisor Imes and in 1911 earned the appointment of deputy supervisor of the Pike National Forest, where he oversaw reforestation on the slopes of Pikes Peak. After two years he moved to the position of supervisor of the Medicine Bow National Forest before returning to the Black Hills as supervisor of the Black Hills National Forest (1918–30). Duthie never abandoned his interest in reforestation, drafting the bill that authorized the State of South Dakota to receive matching grants for reforestation and fire protection under the Clarke-McNary Act of 1924.[28]

In the Pinchot tradition, Supervisor Duthie helped popularize forest conservation in general as well as, through his plan, conservative forestry. That plan was founded on the most accurate, most detailed inventory of standing timber to date, accompanied by site-specific prescriptions for timbering and a timber budget, all with the goal of making timbering in the Black Hills National Forest sustainable.

In general terms, the plan contained five major strategies: thinning to improve the commercial value of stands; building roads to make timber stands more accessible to local loggers; promoting permanently fixed, rather than mobile, sawmills; replanting deforested areas of the forest; and accelerating efforts to protect against fires and insects.[29]

In seeking to explain how and why a managed approach to forestry benefited people and their communities, Duthie contrasted the "timber mining" of the past with the "timber harvesting" outlined in his plan: "Harvesting the tree crop means regulated cutting always with a view to keeping the woodland actively employed in the production of crops. Mining the timber means taking the accumulated wealth without making provision for the future productiveness of the land."[30]

Duthie envisioned stable local communities as integral to sustainable timber harvesting, which meant there needed to be a continuous, reliable supply of logs. He explained that if a timber stand supplying a community was cut over too rapidly and milled too quickly, a community would be left without a supply and would lose its business base until a new crop matured. Duthie clearly favored permanent sawmills located in towns over portable sawmills scattered throughout the forest. He argued that permanent mills used timber more efficiently and posed lower risk of accidental fires; towns provided better working conditions and housing than did logging camps. Without a permanent community, the forest cannot be properly managed. Promoting the interdependence of conservative forestry and stable communities became an oft-repeated Forest Service refrain.[31]

Supervisor Kelleter wrote that trees, like all agricultural crops, needed to be harvested at their peak and removed to make room for future crops. He sought to set prices on standing timber, known as stumpage, with reference to quality, accessibility to markets, and cost of removal.[32] But limiting timbering to mature or overmature trees or, as sometimes advocated, limiting annual cutting to annual stand growth turned out to be shortsighted. In fact, market demand for timber sometimes exceeded annual growth, and sometimes, supply of annual growth exceeded demand. To accommodate market fluctuations and, at the same time, conduct conservative forestry, the development and implementation of multi-year plans were needed, which is what Supervisor Duthie pioneered.

As a practical matter, Duthie divided the forest into working circles, so-called because timber was meant to be funneled into certain points for milling and shipment. Some working circles coincided with one or more watersheds, but mostly they were drawn in ways that ensured community stability. During the 1920s the Custer, Hill City, Rapid Creek, and Spring Creek working circles harbored the most timbering; by 1930 the entire Black Hills had been divided into ten working circles.[33]

Regarding timber sales, Duthie's plan reflected the principal steps outlined by Pinchot in the *Use of the National Forest Reserves*. First, a prospective purchaser of timber or a district ranger could recommend a timber sale site to the supervisor. If he agreed that a site should be timbered, he had to provide regional headquarters with reasons for his decision. To do so, a local forest officer needed to appraise the proposed site, for which the *Use of the National Forest Reserves* provided guidance: the officer should assess the "effect upon water-flow, possible profit in holding the timber for a future higher price, the need for the timber, the possibility or difficulty of getting it elsewhere, the reliability of the applicant, and the price which should be obtained."[34] Making such judgments became increasingly critical as larger operators made major investments in equipment and machinery to move deeper and deeper into the forest.

For each sale area, the Forest Service specified minimum diameters for cutting healthy, dead, and infested trees and specified the maximum allowable height for stumps. In addition, the Forest Service appraiser needed to recommend the best method of cutting, not necessarily the one requested by a prospective purchaser. Estimating that ponderosa pine in the Black Hills reached maturity at 16–17 inches diameter at breast height (dbh) at age 140, Duthie's plan allowed loggers to enter a given stand every thirty to forty years: on first entry, to remove mature and dead timber; on second entry, to remove trees that were large at the time of the first cut; on third entry, to remove trees ranging from 6 to 9 inches dbh at the time of first cut, plus any other mature or dead timber; and on fourth entry, to remove trees that were saplings at the time of the first cut. Cutting selectively through a series of entries, rather than cutting most or all trees at once, allowed smaller trees to develop under the shelter of remaining larger trees. The Forest Service's cutting method of choice, sometimes referred to as the selection system, in time evolved into a modified shelterwood system. The difference between the selection and shelterwood systems remained murky; under either system, some mature trees were left to provide shelter for younger trees. Duthie's plan did permit cutting most or all trees in stands where prior timbering records had shown rapid and successful regeneration, most notably on south slopes.[35]

Supervisor Duthie's tenure in the Black Hills coincided with the advent of the Warren-Lamb Lumber Company, based in Rapid City, a company sufficiently capitalized to move into un-logged forest areas—thereby extending the reach of conservative forestry, which, in turn, assisted the Forest Service with fire prevention and removal of infested trees. Warren-Lamb started in the 1910s, thrived during the 1920s, and survived through the 1930s and 1940s, thanks to its favored status with the Forest Service. Its operations compared with that of the current dominant operator suggest how the timber industry, on which the Forest Service

depends, has evolved in the face of improved science and technology and changing societal values.

When Lamphere-Heinrichs Lumber Company (the future Warren-Lamb Lumber
Company) began operations in the Black Hills, Homestake Mining Company was
still the largest timber and sawmill operator. Second in size, McLaughlin Tie and
Timber Company operated a permanent mill near Nahant, about 22 miles south
of Deadwood. In addition, the Forest Service dealt with roughly seventy-five small,
mostly family-operated portable sawmills—some a part of farm or ranch operations, some located around towns and along existing rail lines, and almost all func-
tioning only seasonally.[36]

In 1907 Wisconsin lumberman William Lamphere moved to Rapid City in
search of new timberlands. He entered into a business agreement with banker and
investor Henry W. Heinrichs and brought a sawmill from Wisconsin to Rapid City.
New to the Black Hills, his band saw, a horizontal metal blade with teeth along one
edge, could "rip-cut" large-diameter timber. With band saw, planers, and molders,
Lamphere-Heinrichs emerged as the only Black Hills mill to produce lumber that
competed in quality and finish with lumber imported from other states.[37]

During its second year of existence, Lamphere-Heinrichs started logging in the
Victoria Creek area, a few miles southwest of Rapid City. To transport timber out
of the hills, Lamphere-Heinrichs constructed a rail line narrower than the ordinary
narrow gauge and purchased steam-powered locomotives designed especially for
logging, as well as short flat cars to handle sharp curves. The rail line turned out to
be too narrow to balance loads, causing frequent derailments; and the locomotives
were not powerful enough to get over steep grades. Moreover, once out of the hills,
logs had to be trans-loaded onto a standard-gauge line for transportation to the mill
in Rapid City.

Following two major mill fires in 1914, C. C. Warren—in charge of sales for
Lamphere-Heinrichs—and Illinois investor Lyman Lamb bought a controlling
share in the company. They rebuilt the Rapid City mill and reset the Victoria Creek
rail line to the conventional narrow gauge. Warren and Lamb took control of the
company at a time of expanding demand for, and increasing availability of, timber,
as well as Forest Service incentives for cutting dead and diseased trees. As a well-
capitalized company, Warren-Lamb benefited from a new Forest Service requirement that successful timber bidders provide statements of their financial condition.

After exhausting the Victoria Creek area, Warren-Lamb moved its operations
west toward Deer Creek; in 1916 the company headed south into the Spring Creek
working circle. The Forest Service had agreed to make an extraordinary multi-year
sale of 145 million board feet to attract Warren-Lamb to that remote area. Smaller
operators could not afford to timber there; the Forest Service intended that

FIGURE 5.3. Shelterwood cut, 1951. Courtesy, USDA Forest Service, Black Hills National Forest, at http://www.ForestPhoto.com.

Warren-Lamb leave more accessible areas for those smaller operators. As further incentive to Warren-Lamb, the Forest Service made the sale at less than half the usual price and exempted the company from the requirement to collect cordwood. In general, smaller operators could use cordwood for their fuel needs; however, large operators found it impractical to dispose of cordwood.[38]

With its sizable capital, Warren-Lamb could take substantial business risks. Its most spectacular venture was construction of a 6-mile-long flume to move logs from the headwaters of Slate Creek down to the rail line along Rapid Creek. Construction consumed vast amounts of timber, thus necessitating the location of a sawmill near the headwaters of Slate Creek. The flume required uniform gradients and wide curves to keep water within the V-shaped wood structure and prevent logjams. To ensure sufficient water flow, the company built small storage reservoirs every 2 miles. Before completion, however, a lower section washed out, either because of a design error or a sudden downpour; in additional, the drought meant there was not enough water to maintain the storage reservoirs. Furthermore, the company had overestimated the amount of merchantable timber in the Slate Creek area, all of which contributed to its move to the Spring Creek area.

The Spring Creek timber sale represented an unprecedented effort by the Forest Service to increase the amount of commercial timber over the long term. The rationale for this approach came from research conducted during summer 1913 by Assistant Regional Forester Christopher M. Granger and Assistant Chief Forester William B. Greeley. They had prepared a timber marking plan specific to the Spring Creek area that presumed a 150-year rotation and 30-year cutting cycles. Underlying the plan, they classified stands into five age groups: (1) saplings 3–10 feet in height, (2) small pole-size trees 3–7 inches dbh, (3) larger pole-size trees 8–12 inches dbh, (4) middle-aged trees 12–18 inches dbh, and (5) mature trees greater than 18 inches dbh and decadent trees. Their plan called for loggers to remove all mature trees except for patches to ensure re-seeding and to thin crowded middle-aged and pole-size trees, leaving enough for a second cut in thirty years. In effect, Granger and Greeley proposed a selection system that, they argued, would allow operators to log quickly over large acreages of un-logged forest and exempt operators from having to cut smaller trees. According to Carl Newport, who wrote favorably about the timber industry, their marking plan demonstrated Forest Service willingness to accommodate the operators.[39]

To access the Spring Creek area, Warren-Lamb began work in late 1916 on a narrow-gauge rail line from Fairburn on the eastern edge of the Black Hills, where the company also built a sawmill. From Fairburn, rough lumber could be shipped to Rapid City by standard-gauge railroad. Operational by September 1917, the Fairburn mill could process an entire trainload of logs (twenty-four flat cars) each day. Meanwhile, at the timber-cutting site, mechanics (manual laborers, not technicians as we would use the term today) had jerry-built a gasoline-powered log loader, more efficient than a traditional horse-driven hoist, which enabled the Fairburn mill to operate at capacity.

As logging operations moved into increasingly difficult terrain, Warren-Lamb mechanics devised their own methods to move equipment in and get timber out. To reach Bear Gulch, separated by a steep hill from the valley of the rail line, mechanics built a counterbalancing hoist that worked somewhat like a cog railroad, using cables to move items up and over the hill. For those accustomed to seeing tracked vehicles with endless steel bands moving over rough terrain, it is difficult to imagine the work required to accomplish the same feat in the pre-caterpillar era; in the case of timbering, imagine the high cost of moving equipment and logs, especially considering the relatively brief period for any given cut.[40]

Although gasoline-powered trucks were available by the late 1910s, the lack of all-weather roads had precluded their use for timbering. The few roads that existed were little more than trails, impassable during and after summer rains as well as during frequent winter thaws when surfaces turned to mush over frozen ground. In the 1920s Warren-Lamb did start using gasoline-powered tractor trucks with front wheels and rear caterpillar tracks that could haul up to 10 tons, as well as gasoline-powered skidders to pull logs from where they were cut to loading docks. The use of trucks to transport logs from forest to mill expanded as the Forest Service developed its own forest road system; by 1930, log trucks had replaced narrow-gauge railroads.[41]

At the same time Warren-Lamb mechanized logging operations, it also modernized sawmill operations. By the late 1920s its Rapid City sawmill had earned the reputation as the most efficient sawmill in the Black Hills. To operate year-round at capacity, about 70,000 board feet per day, the company constructed a pond for the temporary storage of logs. During wintertime, pond water warmed by exhaust steam from the sawmill could defrost logs, making them easier to saw. From the log pond, logs moved mechanically to a supply deck, where they were measured for size and volume and loaded onto a steam-powered carriage, which moved each secured log through a primary or head saw, then turned the log for additional cuts by secondary saws and, finally, through basic edgers and trimmers before it was moved to the drying yard or to steam-heated kilns. Dried rough lumber was moved to the planing mill, "dressed" to a standard thickness, then edged and surfaced according to its intended use as a finished product.

With the invention of waterproof glue that did not require heating, Warren-Lamb added the manufacturing of plywood and cabinets to its staples of lumber, boxes, crates, and railroad grain doors. Overall, Warren-Lamb managed to reduce

FIGURE 5.4. Warren-Lamb sawmill and holding pond, 1939. Courtesy, USDA Forest Service, Black Hills National Forest, http://www.ForestPhoto.com.

sawmill waste from a national average of 47 percent per log to 35 percent. The company used mill residue to fuel its power needs, to convert sawdust into products such as composition flooring, and to sell pure sawdust for insulation and packing materials.[42]

In 1924 the Forest Service approved another multi-year sale, this time for Warren-Lamb to cut 10 million board feet annually for fifteen years within the Spring Creek working circle. Once again, the Forest Service offered standing timber at prices below those paid by smaller operators around Custer and Hill City. In response to criticism, the Forest Service argued that the Warren-Lamb sale area was overgrown, that timbering would encourage new growth, and that road building would provide access for smaller operators so they could bid against Warren-Lamb. The Forest Service indicated that at the end of fifteen years, cuts could be reduced to an annual sustained yield level of 4 million board feet. With some knowledge of prospective resignations and retirements at the company, the Forest Service anticipated that Warren-Lamb would likely close its operations by 1939.

Yet continuing confidence in Warren-Lamb's efficiency and effectiveness to assist in "cleaning" the forest and bringing about a balance of cutting and growth led the Forest Service in 1926 to award its single largest sale to date, another 62 million

FIGURE 5.5. Skidding and loading logs, 1939. Courtesy, USDA Forest Service, Black Hills National Forest, http://www.ForestPhoto.com.

board feet, in the Spring Creek area. In announcing that latest sale, Associate Chief Forester Edward E. Carter praised Warren-Lamb for assisting the Forest Service in carrying out its mission and for contributing to the stability of local communities.[43]

NOTES

1. *Custer Weekly Chronicle*, March 18, 1922; "George A. Duthie, Veteran Reforestation Expert to Retire," USDA Forest Service news release, Washington DC, June 20, 1949, USFS History Collection, Forest History Society, Durham, NC; see also "Annals of the Black Hills National Forests," typescript, 16–17, 1948 draft with 1967 addition, Black Hills National Forest supervisor's office, Custer, SD.

2. Quoted in *Custer Weekly Chronicle*, September 30, 1905.

3. Quoted in *Crook County Monitor*, March 15, 1907.

4. USDA Forest Service, Black Hills National Forest, *Black Hills National Forest 50th Anniversary* (Washington, DC: General Printing Office, 1948), 39–41; "Harney Forest History" (1933?), typescript, 3, cabinet 6, drawer 1, Black Hills National Forest Historical Collection, Leland D. Case Library for Western Historical Studies, Black Hills State University, Spearfish (hereafter BHSU Case Library).

5. *Custer Weekly Chronicle*, December 30, 1905, November 9, 1907.

6. Ibid., November 8 and 16, 1907, February 6, 1909.

7. George C. Smith to Edwin M. Hamilton, Sundance, November 30, 1907, box 1, folder 18, Black Hills National Forest, United States Forest Service Collection, Denver Public Library (hereafter DPL). Excerpts from the George Smith correspondence can be found in "Annals of the Black Hills National Forests," 42–47.

8. George C. Smith to John F. Smith, Sundance, October 23, 1907; George C. Smith to Edwin M. Hamilton, Sundance, November 23, 1907, both in box 1, folder 17, DPL.

9. George C. Smith to John F. Smith, Sundance, May 17, 1907, box 1, folder 18, DPL.

10. John F. Smith to George C. Smith, Deadwood, May 20, 1907, box 1, folder 3, DPL; same to same, July 3 and 30, 1907, box 1, folder 5, DPL.

11. George C. Smith to Gifford Pinchot, Sundance, September 13, 1907; Clyde Leavitt to George C. Smith, Washington, DC, September 23, 1907; John F. Smith to George C. Smith, Deadwood, September 30, 1907; all in box 1, folder 18, DPL.

12. George C. Smith to John F. Smith, Sundance, August 22, 1907, box 1, folder 17, DPL; John F. Smith to George C. Smith, Deadwood, August 24, 1907, and George C. Smith "to whom it may concern," Sundance, September 4, 1907, both in box 1, folder 6, DPL.

13. George C. Smith to John F. Smith, Sundance, August 22, 1907, and John F. Smith to George C. Smith, Deadwood, August 24, 1907, both in box 1, folder 2, DPL.

14. Quoted in "Annals of the Black Hills National Forests," 45.

15. Ibid., 44.

16. John F. Smith to George C. Smith, Deadwood, May 20 and 27, 1907, box 1, folder 3, DPL.

17. "Report of the Forester," in *USDA Annual Reports* (Washington, DC: US Department of Agriculture, 1905), 214; *Custer Weekly Chronicle*, July 20, 1907.

18. John Murdoch Jr. "Silvical Report on the Black Hills National Forest" (1908), and P. T. Smith, "Silvical Report" (1915), typescripts, in "Cumulative Silvical Report" (1934), Black Hills National Forest supervisor's office, Custer, SD.

19. *Yale Forest School News* 11, no. 2 (April 1923): 31; *Custer Weekly Chronicle*, February 6, 1909.

20. Paul D. Kelleter, "The National Forests of the Black Hills," *Pahasapa Quarterly* 2, no. 4 (June 1913): 10.

21. Gifford Pinchot, *The Use of the National Forest Reserves: Regulations and Instructions* (Washington, DC: US Department of Agriculture, 1905), 79.

22. Paul D. Kelleter, "Diaries," October 27–November 4, 1909, BHSU Case Library.

23. Pinchot, *Use of the National Forest Reserves*, 21.

24. *Black Hills National Forest 50th Anniversary*, 35–37; Pinchot quoted in Char Miller, *Gifford Pinchot and the Making of Modern Environmentalism* (Washington, DC: Island, 2001), 124.

25. "Albert F. Potter," *American Forestry* 16, no. 2 (February 1910): 107–8; Supervisor Imes quoted in "Harney National Forest History" (1922?), typescript, 1, cabinet 6, drawer 1, folder 2, section 7, BHSU Case Library.

26. "Harney National Forest History," 4–9, section 7.

27. *Custer Weekly Chronicle*, September 8, 1923, January 12, 1924, June 20, 1935.

28. Duthie news release.

29. George A. Duthie, "Plan for Handling the Timber Business of the Black Hills and Harney National Forest," 6, file cabinet 7, drawer 4, folder 36, BHSU Case Library.

30. George A. Duthie, "Timber, an Economic Resource of the Black Hills," *Black Hills Engineer* 16, no. 2 (March 1928): 101.

31. *Custer Weekly Chronicle*, March 18, 1922.

32. Kelleter, "National Forests of the Black Hills," 11–12.

33. Ibid., 16, 28; Carl A. Newport, *Forest Service Policies in Timber Management and Silviculture as They Affect the Lumber Industry: A Case Study of the Black Hills* (Pierre: South Dakota Department of Game, Fish, and Parks, 1956), 43–44.

34. Pinchot, *Use of the National Forest Reserves*, 43.

35. *Custer Weekly Chronicle*, March 29, 1924; Arthur F.C. Hoffman and Theodore Krueger, "Forestry in the Black Hills," in *USDA Yearbook* (Washington, DC: US Department of Agriculture, 1949), 323; Newport, *Forest Service Policies*, 36; cf. Charles E. Boldt and James L. Van Deusen, "Silviculture of Ponderosa Pine in the Black Hills: The State of Our Knowledge," USDA Forest Service Research Paper RM-124 (June 1974): 32–33.

36. *Custer Weekly Chronicle*, January 19, March 23, 1907.

37. Allyson Brooks, Brad Noisat, and Linda Sundstrom, "Logging," in *Black Hills National Forest Cultural Resources Overview,* ed. Lance Rom, Tim Church, and Michele Church (Custer: USDA Forest Service, Black Hills National Forest, 1996), 5b–6.

38. A. B. Hood, "Logging Operations in the Black Hills," *Black Hills Engineer* 16, no. 2 (March 1928): 120–21.

39. *Custer Weekly Chronicle*, July 26, 1913; Newport, *Forest Service Policies*, 37–38.

40. *Custer Weekly Chronicle*, October 14, 1916; Hood, "Logging Operations," 121–27.

41. E. W. Meeker, "Highways in the Black Hills," *Black Hills Engineer* 18, no. 2 (March 1930): 145; Hood, "Logging Operations in the Black Hills," 130; Mildred Fielder, *Railroads of the Black Hills* (Seattle: Superior, 1964), 85.

42. C. J. Warren, "The Manufacture of Black Hills Forest Products," *Black Hills Engineer* 16, no. 2 (March 1928): 136–44; Bancroft Gore, "Conserving Lumber Products by Fuel Economy," *Black Hills Engineer* 16, no. 2 (1928): 147, 158.

43. Newport, *Forest Service Policies*, 46–47; Duthie, "Timber," 106.

6

Peter Norbeck's Intrusion

Travel and Tourism

In the summer of 1905, Peter Norbeck and two friends made the first known automobile trip from the Missouri River to the Black Hills, no small feat considering that the men had to follow unmarked trails in their single-cylinder nine-horsepower Cadillac. By background a farmer from Redfield in northeastern South Dakota, Norbeck at the time owned and operated a highly successful water-well drilling business. While in the Black Hills, according to his biographer, Norbeck envisioned the establishment of a state game park in Custer County to augment the population of deer and reintroduce native game such as buffalo and elk. Norbeck's dream went beyond a hunter's paradise to encompass a forest-wide recreation destination for midwesterners.[1]

During his tenure (1908–21) as a state senator, lieutenant governor, and governor, Norbeck personally directed the founding and development of Custer State Park and supervised construction of a highway network within the national forests in the Black Hills that, in his mind, allowed the public to see and enjoy the most scenic part of the Black Hills. As US senator (1921–26), Norbeck helped recruit Gutzon Borglum to carve Mount Rushmore and convinced two presidents, Calvin Coolidge and Franklin D. Roosevelt, to budget federal funds for the project. Through his many efforts to establish tourism as a major industry, Norbeck contributed to the transformation of the Black Hills into what he called the "playground of all the people."[2] The impact on the forest and the Forest Service, though often indirect, would be profound.

DOI: 10.5876/9781607322993.c006

FIGURE 6.1. Devils Tower National Monument, 2010. Author photo.

Focused on timbering and well before the popularity of the automobile, the Forest Service understandably considered tourism a minor use of the forest. In the *Use of the National Forest Reserves,* Gifford Pinchot did provide for special occupancy privileges for hotels, summer residences, and similar establishments on forestlands. His successor, Henry Graves, obtained congressional approval to issue thirty-year fixed leases for up to 5 acres to any person or group wanting to build seasonal hotels, restaurants, stores, and homes on Forest Service land; his intent was "to enlarge the usefulness of the forests for recreative purposes." As far as is known, leasing for recreation did not occur in the Black Hills until the 1930s.[3]

Local business interests had taken advantage of President Theodore Roosevelt's conservation interests, getting Wind Cave designated a national park in 1903 and Jewel Cave a national monument in 1908. Not unlike the situation with Wind Cave, parties holding unproven mine claims had sought to open Jewel Cave as a tourist attraction and turn the surface area into a game preserve; but others wanted to keep the area for grazing and timbering. Nothing suggests that the early supervisors, John Fremont Smith and Edwin Hamilton, expressed any interest in deflecting their efforts away from timbering and grazing.

Meanwhile, for reasons more scientific than economic, President Roosevelt proclaimed Devils Tower near Hulett, Wyoming, the country's first national monument in September 1906, three months after passage of the Antiquities Act. That act authorized the president to declare as monuments objects of scientific interest, as well as prehistoric artifacts and ruins on federal lands; such monuments were "to be confined to the smallest area [1,347 acres in this case] compatible with the proper care and management of the objects to be protected." The president's proclamation recognized Devils Tower, rising 1,267 feet above the nearby Belle Fourche River, as "such an extraordinary example of the effect of erosion in the higher mountains as to be a natural wonder and object of historic and great scientific interest."[4] Devils Tower had become a tourist attraction by the 1930s and gained notoriety after Steven Spielberg's 1977 movie *Close Encounters of the Third Kind*. More recently, ethnographers have suggested that Devils Tower has been a sacred site for several tribes, most notably the Lakota Sioux, and that since its name was considered "culturally insensitive," it should be renamed "Bears Lodge," subject to approval by the tribes.[5]

Although the Forest Service put "business interests" first, it did not, as some suggested, entirely neglect the interests of recreationists. In 1913, Supervisor Paul Kelleter cited Forest Service cooperation with the Spearfish National Fish Hatchery in stocking trout in streams throughout the Black Hills. Management of national forests for economic uses rather than as natural preserves helped push conservationists to lobby for establishment of the National Park Service, which eventually led to the administrative transfer of Wind Cave, Devils Tower, and Jewel Cave to the Park Service. Suzanne Barta Julin, who has carefully studied the development of tourism in the Black Hills, suggested that failure by the Forest Service to promote Jewel Cave and other monuments within its boundaries as tourist sites encouraged the efforts by Peter Norbeck and local business interests to create Custer State Park.[6]

Norbeck's dream of a game preserve coincided with the State of South Dakota's attempt to exchange school sections within national forest boundaries for lands more accessible to economic development. As western states joined the Union, the federal government had granted township sections sixteen and thirty-six to the states for the support of schools and other public purposes. To administer these lands, the State of South Dakota had created the office of Commission of School and Public Lands, with income generated from those lands designated in support of schools. In 1906 Commissioner O. C. Dokken first approached the Forest Service about exchanging state sections within forest boundaries for federal lands outside those boundaries. Dokken had received numerous requests from loggers to cut on those sections, which would mean income for the state. Since those sections had yet to be surveyed, the Forest Service insisted that it alone manage timber sales but that proceeds from those sales go to the commissioner's office.[7]

The two parties created a special committee consisting of Commissioner E. Brinker, Dokken's successor; Supervisor Kelleter (chairman); and US marshal Seth Bullock to negotiate a land exchange. Following four years of survey work, the parties agreed to the exchange of all state sections within the forest for a 40,000-acre parcel east of Custer. On July 1, 1912, State Forester George W. Roskie took over management of that parcel, while the Commission of School and Public Lands took title to the land. Whereupon Peter Norbeck enlisted a fellow state senator, John F. Parks (R-Custer), to introduce a bill to designate the 40,000-acre parcel as a game preserve, to appropriate monies to cover the costs of fencing and the purchase of game animals, and to ban fishing and hunting until game populations became large enough to support hunting. The state senate unanimously passed the bill, but the state house of representatives failed to produce the two-thirds vote necessary for approval. When Norbeck and his allies agreed to supply the votes to pass a pending measure to ban the sale of alcoholic beverages statewide, the representatives passed the game preserve bill in exchange.[8]

With congressional passage of the Game Preserve Act in 1913, Norbeck took charge of fence construction to keep game animals inside the preserve while thirty inholders were forced to protect their homesteads by fencing out. With fencing completed in 1914, the Department of Game, Fish, and Parks purchased the first thirty-six buffalo and seventy elk. Before placing them inside the park, the state held a special one-day hunt "to exterminate as far as possible all predatory animals in the park, of which there are reported to be mountain lions, bobcats, wolves, and coyotes."[9] The rationale: predators caused loss of harvestable resources. Three years later, the state forester began selling timber, mostly to the Warren-Lamb Lumber Company. In contrast to the Forest Service, the state allowed virtually unregulated timbering, which aroused sufficient opposition from the general public to impose rules in what by then was the nation's largest state park.[10]

Meanwhile, the South Dakota and Wyoming state wildlife agencies had entered into cooperative agreements with the Forest Service for enforcement of game and fish laws. Within the forest boundaries, Forest Service personnel were supposed to report violations to state game wardens; in flagrant cases, however, the Forest Service could make arrests to prevent offenders from escaping. Game wardens, in turn, were expected to notify the Forest Service when they spotted fires and to assist in firefighting.[11]

As governor, Peter Norbeck continued his oversight of the game preserve. He convinced the state legislature to move the game preserve from under the jurisdiction of the Commission of School and Public Lands to that of the Department of Game, Fish, and Parks and to establish Custer State Park with its own board, consisting of the governor as chair and two directors. Norbeck named his brother Enoch the director representing "East River" and John A. Stanley, editor and publisher of the *Lead Daily Call*, director from "West River." In March 1919 the state legislature voted and Governor Norbeck signed legislation that empowered the

Custer State Park board with responsibility for all park management, including timber sales, with net proceeds going to the state's general fund; enabled the board to purchase land, both public and private, and, if warranted, to condemn private land under the principle of eminent domain; and appropriated monies for improvements and land acquisitions.[12]

At the same time, pressed by Norbeck, the state legislature passed a resolution requesting that the US government turn over an additional 30,000 acres, contiguous to the 40,000 acres already transferred, "in order that the natural beauty and majestic grandeur of the region [Harney Peak–Sylvan Lake area] may be preserved and handed down to posterity." President Wilson's secretary of agriculture, David F. Houston, declined outright South Dakota's request on the grounds that designating game management as a priority use was unnecessary because such protection already existed as part of conservative forestry.[13]

Governor Norbeck, however, wanted assurances that the state could fence in the additional acreage as long as it remained a game preserve. He traveled to Washington in December 1919 where, with support of the South Dakota congressional delegation, he drafted legislation to set aside 30,000 acres in the Harney Peak–Sylvan Lake area, to be named Custer State Park Game Sanctuary. Representative Harry L. Gandy (R-SD) sponsored the legislation, approved by Congress and signed by President Wilson on June 5, 1920. Under the Game Sanctuary Act, the Custer State Park board obtained custody of the additional land; the Forest Service retained title to that land. The South Dakota Department of Game, Fish, and Parks assumed game management; the Forest Service retained responsibility for timber sales and fire protection. In 1924 then-senator Norbeck successfully sponsored federal legislation to expand the game sanctuary from 30,000 to 46,000 acres. As testimony to his political clout, Norbeck also extracted from the federal government permission for the state to prescribe development of a scenic highways system and other improvements on Forest Service land.[14]

Peter Norbeck's passion for scenic highways was part of his dream to make the Black Hills a travel destination for the same "great multitude" Henry Ford had envisioned as customers for his Model T. As Norbeck wrote to fellow Custer State Park board director John Stanley, "Our tourists do not, as a rule belong to the wealthy class—not even the well-to-do class."[15]

Building roads to provide more access to timber and for fire fighting became an integral part of conservative forestry; connecting the communities of the Black Hills to one another and to the nation was a separate, though in time related, matter. Until 1911, road building in South Dakota had been the responsibility of counties and municipalities, which meant travelers depended mainly on unimproved tracks. Where local governments did not levy taxes for road construction, citizens could build their own roads—a genteel version of the medieval corvée labor on public roads in lieu of taxation. In a few cases, private parties had built toll roads that extended up to 4 miles beyond some town limits. Without set standards or qualified oversight, these efforts proved irregular at best.

The Lawrence County commissioners developed South Dakota's first countywide road system, even spilling into the Black Hills National Forest. Between 1911 and 1919, Lawrence County invested an unparalleled $500,000 in roads designed by engineers and constructed by highway contractors. The county purchased tractor graders for road maintenance, although many roads remained impassable during wet weather, mainly because of insufficient gravel.[16]

Beyond that, Lawrence County commissioner George A. Ayres, along with two representatives from "East River," organized the first South Dakota Good Roads convention, which took place at Deadwood in 1912. The Good Roads movement, started in the 1880s by bicyclists seeking equal status with horse-drawn vehicle users, turned into a nationwide lobbying effort in support of roads good enough for motorized vehicles. In addition to voting to pressure the South Dakota state legislature to appropriate funding for statewide highway construction, the Deadwood conventioneers pressed for completion through the Harney National Forest of the Hot Springs to Deadwood section of the Denver to Deadwood highway. They also endorsed the plan to build a highway from the Midwest to Yellowstone National Park, passing through the Black Hills. Seth Bullock, for one, had long sought to convince local business leaders and the various commercial clubs to join together in promoting the Black Hills as a summer destination. To eastern South Dakotans taking their vacations around Minnesota's 10,000 lakes, Bullock argued that the Black Hills were nearer and, best of all, mosquito free.[17]

By the time of the second annual Good Roads state convention at Deadwood in spring 1913, the east-west highway boosters were calling themselves the Chicago to Yellowstone Park Interstate Highway Association; they met concurrently with the newly organized Black Hills Automobile Dealers' Association. After hearing reports that key bridges had been constructed for the interstate highway during the past year, the conventioneers called for an advertisement campaign to attract tourists to the Black Hills.[18]

If Forest Service presence at the Deadwood conventions was limited or nonexistent, that was not the case when representatives of towns along the Hot Springs to Deadwood section of the Denver to Deadwood highway met at Custer in May 1913. Harney National Forest supervisor Richard Imes, as secretary of the local group, moderated the meeting. Participants decided that all those catering to tourists be urged to locate their businesses in the towns, along the designated highway route rather than on side streets, and that, between towns, the route needed first to be laid out "by eye," then surveyed by trained engineers to avoid having to relocate the route. Representatives pledged that each town would furnish a one-man team of horses to work thirty days on its section of the road; construction would be coordinated with Custer and Lawrence Counties and with the Forest Service for the Custer to Sylvan Lake section.[19]

That section was the first recorded case in the Black Hills in which the Forest Service used its funds, equipment, and workers on a highway that went through the forest. For summer 1913 Supervisor Imes assigned a forest ranger and a crew of thirty to replace the Custer to Sylvan Lake trail—which had grades up to 20 percent—with a road with no more than a 7 percent grade. Later, when Imes prepared to leave his position as supervisor, the local newspaper commended him for "converting the people to the opinion that their interests are better taken care of now than in the old days when everyone did as he pleased" because of his commitment to highway building and, in particular, for his leadership in completing the Hot Springs to Deadwood section.[20]

The Federal Aid Road Act of 1916 inaugurated federal financial assistance, initially on a fifty-fifty matching basis with the states. Thereafter, South Dakotans approved an amendment to their constitution enabling the state to construct and maintain "good roads" and to expend monies for the same upon a two-thirds vote of the legislature. Governor Norbeck proposed, and in 1917 the legislature approved, the plan for a statewide system of highways connecting all county seats and towns with populations over 750 and for a state highway commission chaired by the governor. With passage of additional legislation in 1919, South Dakota came into compliance with federal legislation, thereby qualifying for federal highway monies.[21]

Of particular use in the Black Hills, the Federal Aid Road Act had earmarked appropriations for road building within national forests; a rider to the Post Office Appropriations Act of 1919 set aside monies for the secretary of agriculture to use to make grants for road building within or near national forests. Of those monies, $93,000 went for completion of the Hot Springs to Deadwood section.[22] Such special appropriations for local improvements came in addition to the Forest Service's annual allocation of 25 percent of revenues from timber sales to affected counties for support of roads and schools, as per the Payment in Lieu of Taxes Act of May 23, 1908.

With the availability of federal highway funds and through his continuing capacity as a director of the Custer State Park board, Peter Norbeck guided the development of the scenic highway system. The story goes that, along with State Engineer Scovel Johnson, Norbeck walked and, where possible, rode horseback through the dense forest to lay out the Needles Highway—the 14 miles of present-day State Highway 87 from a point in the state park just east of Custer to Sylvan Lake, named for the fact that it winds around high granite outcroppings.

FIGURE 6.2. Sylvan Lake and hotel, 1920s. Courtesy, Black Hills National Forest Historical Collection, Leland D. Case Library for Western Historical Studies, Black Hills State University, Spearfish, SD.

Norbeck believed his route offered the touring public the easiest-to-access, safest, and most scenic views. His biographer relays an incident, reported by a member of the survey party, in which "the governor's trousers were badly torn and his legs were scratched and bleeding. It was not easy to push his 240 pounds over such a difficult route. As he sat on a log breathing heavily, he turned to Johnson and said: 'Scovel, can you build a road through there,' to which the engineer replied: 'If you can furnish me enough dynamite.' "[23]

Norbeck did find the monies for highway construction. By 1921 an east-west highway from Fairburn to Custer ran through Custer State Park and connected with the Needles Highway. With additional roadways surveyed or under construction, state park board director John Stanley noted that new highways would not only serve the traveling public but also enable Forest Service personnel and other firefighters to reach parts of the State Park Game Sanctuary that had been virtually inaccessible. Stanley could have added that as a result of Norbeck's efforts and passage of the Game Sanctuary Act, the State of South Dakota had coerced the federal government into paying the bills and, with the advent of more visitors, to improve Forest Service efforts to prevent and fight fires.[24]

FIGURE 6.3. Harney Peak lookout, 1921. Courtesy, Black Hills National Forest Historical Collection, Leland D. Case Library for Western Historical Studies, Black Hills State University, Spearfish.

Retrospectively, Supervisor Duthie credited Supervisor Bullock with introducing to the local public the notion that forest fires were not an inevitable evil, left to burn themselves out; if not always preventable, at least fires could be fought so as to greatly reduce losses.[25] Kelleter had likely been the first supervisor actively to campaign for public vigilance, with the operative slogan "Prevent Forest Fires—It Pays."[26]

Sometime in 1911, Supervisors Kelleter and Imes inaugurated the policy and practices of fire preparedness, sometimes called pre-suppression activities. They persuaded the Burlington Railroad to place strategically four gasoline-powered motor cars along the rail line between Custer and Edgemont. Each car could transport two firefighters and contained a full complement of fire-fighting tools. By 1914 the Forest Service had stationed one gasoline-powered "twin motorcycle" at Custer and one at Deadwood. The hope was that, with these vehicles, firefighters could reach some locations more quickly and with more equipment than they could using pack horses.[27]

Although community- and industry-sponsored fire lookouts already existed in other regions of the West, the 1910 season of catastrophic fires convinced the Forest Service to establish the first lookout in the Black Hills, on Harney Peak. At first, the lookout consisted of an alidade set on a wooden crate, for use by a ranger with compass and binoculars to calculate the position of a fire. Forester Graves and Region 2 inspector Smith Riley hiked up to the lookout in September 1911, its first season. In time, the makeshift arrangement was replaced by a plane-table, which consisted of a circular drawing board mounted on a tripod, legs set in concrete, with the alidade pivoted over the center of the drawing board. When he spotted a fire, the ranger could use a system of flashing mirrors to alert headquarters at Custer.[28] By 1915 the Forest Service maintained lookouts on Harney Peak and Custer Peak in the northern Black Hills; spotters used hand-cranked telephones to connect with ranger stations and headquarters over 100 miles of telephone lines. To augment Forest Service spotters, the postmaster general instructed rural carriers to report fires to the nearest ranger.[29]

Formal training in fire prevention as well as fire fighting began during the 1910s; in a further step toward preparedness, the agency supplied district rangers with sufficient tools and supplies to outfit ten to twenty-five firefighters, with additional materiel kept at forest headquarters. Beyond agency staff, the Forest Service sponsored training sessions for contract firefighters and employees of cooperating state agencies. The Weeks Act of 1911, better known for enabling the Forest Service to acquire forestlands in the eastern United States, provided financial assistance to states that established forest fire protection plans on private and state lands. The act represented a congressional step in bringing together federal and state forestry agencies, augmented by the Clarke-McNary Act of 1924 and, more recently, by the Healthy Forests Restoration Act of 2003.[30]

It was generally agreed that both the number and size of forest fires had gradually increased over the years, principally because of human carelessness. In the southern Black Hills during April 1913 alone, nearly 1,000 firefighters were dispersed to an unprecedented number of fires that engulfed 12,000 acres of public and 8,000 acres of private land. That brought forth a strong editorial opinion: "The man who will throw a lighted match into the grass needs a guardian, and the man who doesn't know any better than to try to burn up a worthless straw stack with the wind blowing a gale, should be consigned to an institute for the feeble. That is a very mild expression of our private opinion."[31]

Perhaps the least recognized fire-related task involved rangers apprehending arsonists and following through on their prosecution. A case in point: at 5:45 p.m. on August 26, 1924, Ranger Charles H. Fox, stationed at Hill City, received a call from the Harney Peak lookout. Two separate small plumes of smoke had been observed rising from the north end of nearby Elk Mountain; three or four minutes later, the lookout called about another plume a few hundred yards from the first two. By the time Ranger Fox arrived at the scene, three or four ranchers had contained the fires. The fact that the fires had occurred in a single line aroused suspicion. Fox found horse tracks, concluded that the rider had set the fires without getting off his horse, and followed the tracks to a nearby ranch, where they ended. He suspected a ranch hand named George Woodward who had helped put out the fires. Fox kept watch over the suspect during the night. After hearing conflicting stories from Woodward and conferring with ranchers gathered at the ranch, Fox decided to take the suspect to Custer, accompanied by one of the ranchers, so Supervisor John Conner could confirm that Fox had a case. With Conner's approval, the party returned to Hill City, picked up two more witnesses, traveled to Rapid City, and appeared before the assistant US attorney. During interrogation, Woodward admitted starting the fires and was entrusted to a federal marshal who brought him before a federal judge in Deadwood. Since Woodward could not post bond, he was jailed pending trial in federal court. Nothing more is known about the case.[32]

Maps of improved roads such as the ones Ranger Fox and his party took, combined with descriptions and scenic photographs, had become subjects of brochures and other materials distributed by local commercial clubs to promote the Black Hills. The war in Europe had deflected tourist travel to the West, but in summer 1921, nearly 100,000 visitors toured the Black Hills. "It lies within these hills," a booster wrote, "to become as attractive to the American tourist as the mountains of Switzerland, indirectly adding to his [and her] patriotism and love of country."[33]

Patriotism would serve as the popular screen for perhaps the most successful tourist venture in the United States prior to the opening of Disneyland. But Mount Rushmore was even more than that. As Suzanne Barta Julin insightfully noted, marvelous scenery, good roads, and publicity were not enough; "tourists needed to be served and entertained."[34] Peter Norbeck, among others, had understood that to attract the mass of middle- and working-class vacationers to the Black Hills, places had to be developed that offered excitement and entertainment for families, in addition to providing easy access to the scenery. That would be a lesson South Dakota promoters imposed on the Forest Service.

The idea of carving a monumental sculpture in the most scenic portion of the Black Hills came from Jonah Leroy "Doane" Robinson, secretary of the South Dakota Historical Society. Robinson had farmed, taught public school, and read law before he emigrated from Wisconsin to South Dakota. He opened a law office in Watertown but spent most of his time as a newspaper correspondent, columnist, magazine editor, and poet; he became a South Dakota history buff, a well-connected political figure, and an overall enthusiast for South Dakota.[35] In early 1924 Robinson addressed the Black Hills and Yellowstone Trail Association, a Good Roads group meeting in Huron, on historical monuments and marked historical sites as tourist attractions. During his speech, he unexpectedly proposed the creation of a "colossal monument" in the Black Hills, an idea favorably received by the delegates. Following a later telephone call to Robinson, an Associated Press reporter in Pierre wrote: "A definite project of converting a round of Black Hills Needles into massive and spectacular figures of sculpture, emblematic of the outstanding historical life of the state has been conceived by Doane Robinson, state historian. Mr. Robinson believes that such work would establish to South Dakota one of the most compelling tourist objectives in America."[36]

Robinson's idea engendered immediate opposition from individuals who feared the Needles would be defaced and the surrounding natural scenery violated. Senator Norbeck, whose early support Robinson had recruited, criticized the opposition as hypocritical, arguing that "a great deal of mutilation [throughout the forest] has been done the last forty years and the people out there seem perfectly willing some more shall be done, just so it is not called 'art.'"[37] As far as is known, the Forest Service expressed no opinion on the proposed project.

Meanwhile, Robinson had taken it upon himself to recruit a high-profile sculptor with strong financial backers. He found John Gutzon de la Mothe Borglum—son of Idaho polygamists, sometime Ku Klux Klansman, self-professed protégé of Auguste Rodin, and exploiter of famous wealthy people whom he sought as patrons of his colossal sculpture. Borglum was embroiled over his work-in-progress at Stone Mountain, Georgia, a colossal portrayal of General Robert E. Lee and the Confederacy, when he paid his first visit to the Black Hills in late summer 1924. He was received with enthusiasm and convinced Robinson that the subject matter of any proposed work should be national rather than limited to the state; Borglum reiterated an earlier pledge that he could raise the necessary monies from private nongovernmental sources, though he did not manage to raise one cent.[38]

Norbeck, Robinson, and Borglum agreed that since the proposed site was on national forest land, congressional action would be required. On February 16,

1925, Representative William Williamson (R-SD) introduced to the Committee on Public Lands a bill authorizing the creation of a national memorial in Harney National Forest to be administered by the Mount Harney Memorial Association, created and endorsed by the South Dakota legislature. Its mission: to select the name, exact location, and design of the colossal sculpture "in heroic figures commemorative of our national history and progress." The Committee on Public Lands added a phrase providing "that the Secretary of Agriculture find that the location of the site will not interfere with the administration of the Harney National Forest." The amendment suggested some uneasiness, if not outright opposition, among professionals within the US Department of Agriculture and the Forest Service, not unlike the opposition to creation of the Cheyenne Horticultural Field Station two years later, which evaporated in the face of congressional support from powerful local constituents.[39]

After the Mount Harney Memorial Association bill passed Congress, Doane Robinson appeared before the Joint Appropriations Committee of the South Dakota legislature, seeking support of a state bill to establish the Mount Harney Memorial Association with an initial appropriation of $10,000. The new governor, Carl Gunderson (R), remained uncommitted, in part because of his personal dislike of Senator Norbeck. He did sign the bill that authorized the association and declared that the monument would be state-owned, with no legal or financial risk to the State of South Dakota. In other words, Robinson, Norbeck, and Borglum needed to attract private monies.

Still, opposition to the project persisted. The Black Hills chapter of the General Federation of Women's Clubs went on record against the project, on grounds that it would destroy the natural landscape within the national forest; some local residents expressed fear that the influx of tourists would destroy their favorite fishing and hunting spots. Robinson and Borglum nonetheless pressed ahead with a dedication ceremony that took place on October 1, 1925, at the foot of Mount Rushmore (named after Charles A. Rushmore, attorney-businessman representing an early Black Hills tin-mining company). Both men sought to assure local residents that Borglum would not touch the Needles and to convince prospective funders of their seriousness.

Between October 1925 and May 1926, the Mount Harney Memorial Association raised $5,000, far short of the $50,000 Borglum had insisted he needed to start the project. The Homestake Mining Company, a prospective major donor, declined to contribute; the State Highway Commission deferred consideration of building a road to the monument site until the association had attracted at least $25,000 in pledges.[40] All of this led Senator Norbeck, pledges and promises to the contrary, to conclude that the only way for the project to proceed was with federal financial support. Through political skill and persistence, Norbeck secured the endorsement of President Calvin Coolidge and the financial support of the US Congress. In doing so, he would realize the fulfillment of his dream to turn the Black Hills into "the playground of all the people."

Despite initial reluctance, President and Mrs. Coolidge did yield to an aggressive campaign by Senator Norbeck and South Dakota political and business leaders for the president and his entourage to spend three months during summer 1927 at the Custer State Park Game Lodge. In advance of the trip, the state legislature met in special session to appropriate monies to reimburse the game lodge lessee for lost revenues; pressed by Norbeck and friends, the legislature further consolidated state park management and permanently allocated state revenues for park maintenance. In addition, the legislature appropriated funds to gravel the road between Custer and Hermosa, making it easier for the president to travel to and from his summer office in Rapid City. Other roads in the state park as well as in the Harney National Forest were improved and, in the case of Mount Lookout (renamed Mount Coolidge), completed for access to recreation areas. The state park board renamed Squaw Creek, the stream that flowed past the game lodge, Grace Coolidge Creek; and the Forest Service reserved some streams for presidential fishing.[41]

From the viewpoint of the promoters of tourism in the Black Hills, the high point of Coolidge's visit occurred on August 10, 1927, when, at the Mount Rushmore site, the president formally presented Gutzon Borglum with the drills needed to begin carving the national memorial. Cloaking his speech in patriotism, the president made the pitch for both federal and private financial support while deftly excusing South Dakotans from any financial obligation.[42]

After Coolidge returned to Washington, Senator Norbeck and the South Dakota congressional delegation pursued federal funding, succeeding in obtaining $250,000 in matching monies in February 1929. At the same time, they engineered the dissolution of the Mount Harney Memorial Association in favor of a seemingly more prestigious Mount Rushmore Memorial Commission, whose members would be appointed by the president. With private contributions lagging, the South Dakota delegation persuaded Congress to remove the matching requirement. Later, President Franklin D. Roosevelt supported another $200,000 in federal appropriations in appreciation of Norbeck's support for the New Deal. The president placed Mount Rushmore under supervision of the National Park Service and in 1938 supported another congressional appropriation. By the time Gutzon Borglum retired in 1941, the federal government had invested $836,000, or about 85 percent of total costs, in the memorial.[43]

As a result, South Dakota gained a premier tourist attraction at no cost to the state or its citizens, a reminder of Bernard de Voto's famous quip describing a

FIGURE 6.4. Gutzon Borglum (*center, wearing hat*), Doane Robinson (*second from left*), and supporters, Mount Rushmore, 1932. Courtesy, South Dakota State Historical Society, Pierre.

prevalent western attitude toward the federal government: "get out, and give us more money."[44] The Forest Service, meanwhile, found itself not only with a scenic highway system it had not requested but with a "competing" federal agency occupying 1,500 acres (today, 1,280 acres) within the National Forest's scenic core that, in time, would attract millions of visitors annually. The Mount Rushmore profile permeated virtually every business in the region, a symbol of the eventual economic preeminence of tourism over timbering.

NOTES

1. Gilbert C. Fite, *Peter Norbeck: Prairie Statesman* (Pierre: South Dakota State Historical Society Press, 2005 [1948]), 25.

2. "What President Saw in Hills," *Custer Weekly Chronicle*, October 6, 1927.

3. Ibid., April 3, 1915; Gifford Pinchot, *The Use of the National Forest Reserves: Regulations and Instructions* (Washington, DC: US Department of Agriculture, 1905), 49.

4. An Act for the Preservation of American Antiquities, Public Law 59–209, *US Statutes at Large* 34 (1906): 225; President Theodore Roosevelt's proclamation reprinted in *Crook County Monitor*, April 26, 1907.

5. Jeffrey R. Hanson and Sally Chirinos, "Ethnographic Overview and Assessment of Devils Tower National Monument, Wyoming," *Intermountain Region, National Park Service, Cultural Resource Selections D–36* (1997): xi–xiii, 13–17.

6. Paul D. Kelleter, "The National Forests of the Black Hills," *Pahasapa Quarterly* 2, no. 4 (June 1913): 12; cf. Samuel P. Hays, *The American People and the National Forests: The First Century of the U.S. Forest Service* (Pittsburgh: University of Pittsburgh Press, 2009), 13; Suzanne Barta Julin, *A Marvelous Hundred Square Miles: Black Hills Tourism, 1880–1941* (Pierre: South Dakota State Historical Society Press, 2009), 21–24.

7. *Custer Weekly Chronicle*, November 23, 1907, December 4, 1909.

8. Doane A. Robinson, *Doane Robinson's Encyclopedia of South Dakota* (Pierre: by the author, 1925), 76–77; "Annals of the Black Hills National Forests," typescript, 51, 1948 draft with 1967 addition, Black Hills National Forest supervisor's office, Custer, SD; *Custer Weekly Chronicle*, March 1, 1913.

9. George W. Roskie, "State Game Preserve," *Pahasapa Quarterly* 4, no. 3 (April 1915): 12–14; Fite, *Peter Norbeck*, 75; quotation in *Custer Weekly Chronicle,* November 28, 1914.

10. Harry R. Woodward, "Forest Management versus Recreation Management," *American Forests* 63 (January 1957): 51.

11. *Custer Weekly Chronicle*, May 8, 1915.

12. Julin, *Marvelous Hundred Square Miles*, 42–43.

13. "Master Plan for the Protection and Administration of the Norbeck Wildlife Preserve" (June 1927), 1, cabinet 1, drawer 4, Black Hills National Forest Historical Collection, Leland D. Case Library for Western Historical Studies, Black Hills State University, Spearfish, SD (hereafter BHSU Case Library).

14. Ibid., 1–7; Fite, *Peter Norbeck*, 76.

15. Quoted in Julin, *Marvelous Hundred Square Miles*, 60.

16. George V. Ayers, "Lawrence County Roads and How They Were Done," *Pahasapa Quarterly* 5, no. 1 (December 1915): 9; Frank S. Peck, "Roads: Past, Present, and Future," *Pahasapa Quarterly* 8, no. 3 (April 1919): 16–17.

17. *Custer Weekly Chronicle*, June 3, 1911.

18. Ibid., March 8, 1913.

19. Ibid., May 10, 1913.

20. Ibid., June 28, 1913, July 8, 1916.

21. Herbert S. Schell, *History of South Dakota*, 3rd ed. (Lincoln: University of Nebraska Press, 1975), 364.

22. *Custer Weekly Chronicle*, July 1, 1916, March 15, 1919.

23. Fite, *Peter Norbeck*, 76.

24. John A. Stanley, "South Dakota's State Park," *Pahasapa Quarterly* 10, no. 4 (June 1921): 183.

25. George A. Duthie, "The Origin of Deadwood's Name," *Black Hills Engineer* 11, no. 1 (January 1930): 9.

26. *Custer Weekly Chronicle*, August 2, 1913, August 22, 1929.

27. Ibid., May 20, 1911, February 21, 1914.

28. Ibid., September 6, 1911, June 3, 1982.

29. Kelleter, "National Forests of the Black Hills," 10; *Custer Weekly Chronicle*, June 8, 1912, May 31, 1913, July 24, 1915.

30. *Custer Weekly Chronicle,* March 20, 1915; "Harney National Forest History" (1922?), typescript, cabinet 6, drawer 1, folder 2, BHSU Case Library; An Act to Enable Any State to Cooperate with Any Other State or States . . ., Public Law 61–435 [Weeks Law,] *US Statutes at Large* 36 (1911): 961.

31. *Custer Weekly Chronicle*, April 19, 1913.

32. Ibid., August 30, 1924; Duthie, "Origin of Deadwood's Name," 11.

33. Arthur I. Johnson, "Scenic Highways," *Pahasapa Quarterly* 8, no. 3 (April 1915): 55.

34. Julin, *Marvelous Hundred Square Miles*, 38.

35. James R. Elkins, "Strangers to Us All: Lawyers and Poetry," West Virginia University, http://.myweb.wvnet.edu/~jelkins/lp-2001/robinson.html; accessed August 2010.

36. Quoted in Doane Robinson, "Inception and Development of the Rushmore Idea," *Black Hills Engineer* 18, no. 4 (November 1930): 334.

37. Quoted in Julin, *Marvelous Hundred Square Miles*, 90.

38. Soylent Communications, "John Gutzon de la Mothe Borglum," http://www.nndb .com/people/610/000166112/; accessed March 2011; Julin, *Marvelous Hundred Square Miles*, 86–87.

39. An Act to Authorize the Creation of a National Monument in the Harney National Forest, Public Law 68–589, *US Statutes at Large* 43 (1925): 1214; John F. Freeman, *High Plains Horticulture, a History* (Boulder: University Press of Colorado, 2008), 196–99.

40. Julin, *Marvelous Hundred Square Miles*, 91–94.

41. Ibid., 70–74; John Taliaferro, *Great White Fathers: The Story of the Obsessive Quest to Create Mount Rushmore* (New York: Public Affairs, 2002), 223.

42. Julin, *Marvelous Hundred Square Miles*, 97.

43. Fite, *Peter Norbeck*, 150, 199; Taliaferro, *Great White Fathers*, 271.

44. Quoted in Edward K. Muller, ed., *DeVoto's West: History, Conservation, and the Public Good* (Athens, OH: Swallow, 2005), 88.

7

Forestry for Community Stability and Economic Growth

In announcing the extension of grazing lease periods, circulated to local newspapers in March 1935, President Franklin D. Roosevelt's secretary of agriculture, Henry A. Wallace, included this statement: "The basic function of the National Forest system is to help bring stability and security to the social and economic structure of communities dependent upon its resources and to the nation as a whole. That is why National Forest resources are conserved through use rather than being withdrawn from use."[1] By giving conservative timbering a social as well as an economic purpose, Secretary Wallace placed the national forests firmly within the context of New Deal social policy.

The national forests of the Black Hills were among the first to benefit from federal legislation designed to stimulate the national economy. Over a period of ten years, an army of unemployed young men were put to work, at no cost to the US Forest Service. Not only did they greatly improve future stands of commercial timber, but they built the foundation for a vast expansion of forest use. In reminiscing about their work in the 1930s and 1940s, Supervisors Arthur Hoffman and Theodore Krueger wrote that "many people think more and oftener of the other uses that are made of the forest."[2] That would cause some anxiety within the agency during the postwar period, when the public sought more opportunities for recreation while successive national administrations called for more timbering. To confirm its commitment to make decisions from the standpoint of "the greatest good of the greatest number in the long run," the Forest Service sought, and received from Congress and the president, passage of the Multiple Use–Sustained Yield Act of 1960.

DOI: 10.5876/9781607322993.c007

When Secretary Wilson instructed Gifford Pinchot that the administration of each National Forest was best left largely in the hands of the local supervisor, he could not possibly have imagined the impact of the Great Depression and World War II on the national forest system. Arguably, the conditions that had attracted Pinchot to the Black Hills—vast timber potential and the existence of nearby communities—contributed to attracting the architects of the New Deal.

During the late 1920s, before the Great Depression, the overall population of the five South Dakota and two Wyoming counties that covered the Black Hills was 69,581, about the same as it had been in 1910 except for Rapid City, which had grown from 3,854, to 10,404 people. In the southern Black Hills, the inhabitants of Custer, Hill City, and Pringle depended almost entirely on the timber industry. Thirty sawmills employed about 1,000 people and produced about 15 million board feet of rough lumber annually, primarily for railroad ties. Harney National Forest had twelve full-time, year-round employees; during a brief period in the late 1920s, revenues from timber sales equaled expenditures for timber management, an unusual phenomenon that has occurred neither before nor since.[3]

During this period, the Forest Service raised the amount of timber allowed for cutting each year on both forests, from 20.1 million board feet to 41.3 million board feet. The actual amount cut in 1921 was 7 million board feet, 35 percent of the allowable cut; the annual cut in 1929 was 45.3 million board feet, 110 percent of the allowable cut.[4]

Virtually no recreational facilities existed within the national forests, but the state had built campgrounds and other facilities in Custer State Park and had purchased Sylvan Lake Resort. By 1929 the early municipal campgrounds with amenities such as running water, electric light, and water closets had given way to private auto courts, roadside eating places, and souvenir stands. Despite tourist development, the Black Hills in the late 1920s remained relatively free of the crass commercialism the editor of the *Sioux Falls Press* had observed in and around Estes Park, Colorado. Prices seemed much higher there and, in contrast to the Black Hills, billboards along the highways obstructed the scenery: "Trees, telephone poles and fence posts [were] littered with the signs of all descriptions." He continued, "The Black Hills people deserve credit . . . for the way in which they have maintained nature's playground and avoided the mistakes so frequently made in such places [as Estes Park]."[5]

Some credit for keeping the Black Hills beautiful should go to the Izaak Walton League, with the first South Dakota chapter organized in Rapid City in 1924—making it the first national conservation organization to become active in the Black Hills. Remarkably, the Custer newspaper encouraged all Black Hills residents to join an Izaak Walton chapter and editorialized that no place in the entire nation needed an Izaak Walton League more than the Black Hills, "where nature has been so lavish with her gifts—the forests, the streams, the fish, all kinds of animal life—all needing preservation for not only our own benefit and satisfaction, but for future generations to come."[6] The league's first publicized project occurred in 1929 when several chapters, joined by ranchers and businesspeople, successfully petitioned the Department of Game, Fish, and Parks to stop mine operators around Keystone from dumping tailings into Battle Creek, killing fish as far away as 16 miles downstream.[7] During the 1930s, league members volunteered for numerous beautification projects, including along the shores of the principal lakes constructed by the Civilian Conservation Corps, and raised monies to purchase the site for the dam that holds Sheridan Lake.

As happened elsewhere in the nation, the stock market crash of 1929 had an immediate impact on the Black Hills economy. In the Black Hills National Forest, the number of timber sales valued at over $500 each fell from twenty-four in 1929 to one in 1932; cutting declined from 45.3 million board feet in 1929 to 8.4 million board feet in 1932. In the Harney National Forest, cutting declined by 90 percent because the Burlington Railroad suspended purchases of timber for railroad ties and grain doors.[8] To make the situation worse, Supervisor John Conner described 1931 as the worst fire year since 1911, burning nearly 2,000 acres in the Harney National Forest. With livestock numbers greatly reduced, Conner authorized grazing permits for up to 15,000 sheep in summer 1932. Both national forests suspended the first half of grazing fees for that year, with payment due for the second half only after ranchers received payment for livestock shipped to market.[9]

Within eight months of taking office, President Herbert Hoover found himself focused on seeking ways to lead the country out of the Great Depression. By conviction a laissez-faire economist, Hoover favored voluntary action and cooperative approaches toward recovery. In November 1930 he appointed a Timber Conservation Board, privately funded, to recommend ways to address overproduction in the timber industry.[10] Underlying the board's recommendations, made to the president in June 1932, was a revised notion of conservative forestry (by then called sustainable yield forestry) advocated by the nationally recognized forester David T. Mason. While Pinchot and later Duthie had defined conservative forestry as cutting the greatest amount of timber consistent with long-term forest reproduction, Mason defined sustainable yield forestry in terms more strictly economic: cutting enough timber to meet the production capacity of local sawmills. Mason argued that forestry based on sawmill capacity rather than on the reproductive capacity of the forest provided the best way for forest managers, both in the private sector and in the Forest Service, to ensure the stability of the timber industry and that of nearby communities. Mason's argument was adapted by policy makers of the New Deal.[11]

Toward those ends, Chief Forester Robert Y. Stuart directed that timber sales valued at $500 or greater be suspended, except to supply the needs of existing sawmills when timber was not otherwise available. Stuart authorized extensions in time for timber contracts and reductions in volume for annual cuts to reduce financial burdens on smaller operators but retained pre-Depression prices for standing timber as another way to limit production. As a result, small operators in the Black Hills tended to cut only the best trees, while big operators reduced their overall cutting. Homestake Mining Company stopped buying federal timber, cutting only on its private holdings. In 1931 Representative William Williamson (R-SD) obtained $150,000 in federal funds to enable unemployed loggers to conduct pre-commercial thinning operations in the Black Hills.[12]

Given the reproductive rate of the ponderosa pine, pre-commercial thinning had long been deemed essential to economic forestry. Indeed, thinning as a means to open up dense stands and increase the supply of commercial timber over the long term had been used in European forests for several hundred years and reached the United States in the late 1880s. Although the record is obscure, thinning in the American West actually began on an experimental basis in the Black Hills around 1906. Again experimentally, in 1926 the Forest Service opened a stand near Sturgis, allowing stock farmers free use of timber marked for thinning; the farmers, however, had little use for the small trees. In 1931 the Homestake Mining Company started thinning operations, apparently on its own land but with the advice of the Forest Service. The company's aim was to increase the volume of commercial timber, keep workers gainfully occupied, and provide better fire protection to inholders. At the same time, near Deadwood, the Forest Service marked strips of stands for thinning and invited the public to cut in designated areas at no cost. In addition, Lawrence County used prison labor to cut cordwood from the thinning stands for free distribution to the poor.[13]

In support of unemployed or underemployed loggers and sawmill operators, Harney National Forest supervisor Conner and Black Hills National Forest supervisor Theodore Krueger (1930–39) testified before the South Dakota State Highway Commission in favor of using Black Hills timber for guardrails, bridges, and signposts. At the time, federal rules required that cedar posts from Michigan be used on all federally supported highways and that guardrails be treated with creosote, for which no plant existed in South Dakota. Although the result of their testimony is unknown, the federal government through the Economic Stabilization Act of 1931 did provide $800,000 for a period of five years (1932–37) to both national forests for employing workers in road construction, developing water, building employee housing, and improving recreational facilities.[14] In addition, the Knutson-Vandenberg Act of 1930 enabled the Forest Service to place a portion of timber sales

FIGURE 7.1. Planting crew at Custer camp burn site, 1930. Courtesy, USDA Forest Service, Black Hills National Forest, http://www.ForestPhoto.com.

receipts into a revolving fund to pay for reforestation and, generally, to protect and improve "the future productivity of the renewable resources of the forest lands on such sale areas."[15] As with many government programs, resources had to be used before they could be renewed; thus in times of low timber production, when subsidies were most needed, monies were least available.

Amid the gloom of economic depression, with considerable foresight some Black Hills forester—perhaps Conner himself—recommended and Arthur M. Hyde, President Hoover's secretary of agriculture, set aside the first Research Natural Area in the Black Hills. In designating 1,190 acres on upper Pine Creek, just northeast of Harney Peak, Secretary Hyde explained that the purpose was to preserve permanently an area of natural conditions "so that past and future generations can see it as it was when the Indians used the Black Hills for their hunting grounds." Perhaps more significant, he noted that the Research Natural Area "can also be used for comparison with research plots in cutover lands and will be increasingly valuable as time goes on." Such foresight would be of inestimable value to future forestry, though not always so acknowledged.[16]

With the failure of President Hoover's measured approach to economic recovery, Franklin D. Roosevelt won the 1932 election in a landslide. In proposing a "New

Deal for the American people," the president called for swift federal action to revitalize the economy. To begin with, he proposed, and Congress approved, the creation of federally financed job training and jobs for the unemployed. Perhaps the New Deal's most popular program, certainly the one with the greatest impact on the Black Hills, was the Civilian Conservation Corps (CCC).

Precedents for government-funded forest work programs had existed in Europe as well as in the United States, in Pennsylvania under Governor Pinchot and in New York under then-governor Roosevelt. By early 1933 the Forest Service under Chief Earle Clapp had drawn up *A National Plan for American Forests* (Copeland Report) that, among other matters, addressed the opportunity for reforestation through federal job creation.[17] It was no surprise, therefore, that the Emergency Conservation Work Act, signed by President Roosevelt on March 31, 1933, provided for a Civilian Conservation Corps to work on forestry and related projects. Within six weeks of the president's signature, the first of twenty-eight CCC camps in the Black Hills was established at the site of the logging camp used for Timber Case #1. Within that same six weeks, Black Hills National Forest supervisor Krueger and his assistant, Clarence C. Averill, completed the preparatory work—locating campsites, testing water, arranging logistics, and developing work plans in cooperation with the US Army officers tasked with managing the camps. The swiftness with which the Forest Service and the military organized the camps reflected the sense of national urgency; just as extraordinary, with neither federal precedent nor a routine to follow, these government officials effectively made up the rules as they carried out their assignments.[18]

The daily experiences of Civilian Conservation Corpsmen in the Black Hills have been recorded fully by former enrollees; their legacy has been celebrated by local history buffs and, recently, by the promotion of a CCC museum in Hill City.[19] During its existence, 1933–42, the CCC created temporary jobs in the Black Hills for more than 30,000 unemployed young men recruited through local welfare offices, instructed them in useful job skills and in subjects that allowed them to complete their secondary education, and provided them with healthcare. CCC projects also created work for people other than enrollees. During summer and fall 1933, six sawmills around Custer hired full-time workers to meet the demand for lumber to build barracks for the coming winter, replacing tents that housed 2,400 enrollees and staff; crew foremen, too, were selected from the local unemployed.[20]

The Civilian Conservation Corps was a godsend to the Forest Service, supplying workers to carry out highly labor-intensive activities. A 1996 "cultural resources overview" summarized the breadth of their activities: "Construction of bridges, fire towers, and service buildings; construction of truck trails, roads, foot trails, and landing fields; erosion control through check dams, terracing, and planting

FIGURE 7.2 Civilian Conservation Corps, Woodville Camp, 1934. Courtesy, Black Hills National Forest Historical Collection, Leland D. Case Library for Western Historical Studies, Black Hills State University, Spearfish.

protective vegetation; irrigation and drainage projects, including construction of dams, ditches, channeling and rip-rapping; planting trees and improving stands in forests; firefighting, fire prevention, and insect and disease control; construction of public camping and picnicking facilities; improvement of lakes and ponds; range improvements, including stock watering systems and predator eradication; stream improvement, fish stocking; surveying; mosquito control; and emergency work."[21]

Considering that the CCC started up quickly as an entirely new program, principal accomplishments during its first year of operations in the Black Hills were nothing short of extraordinary: its workers thinned 12,000 acres of ponderosa pine, out of which 28,000 cords of firewood were taken to railroad sidings for shipment to residents of drought-stricken areas of South Dakota; cut 2,000 acres of insect-infested timber; constructed or improved 278 miles of roads and truck trails; opened 122 miles of fire lines; increased grazing areas by hundreds of acres by constructing stock reservoirs, developing springs, and clearing stock driveways; established erosion controls over 50 acres; eradicated rodents from 3,000 acres; and spent 3,900 enrollee-days fighting forest fires.[22]

From the viewpoint of making the forests commercially more productive, the Civilian Conservation Corps enabled the Forest Service to inaugurate widespread thinning, especially where natural re-seeding had replaced stands destroyed by fire or illegal timbering. Altogether, the CCC thinned 204,500 acres, about 20 percent of the forests, the largest thinning project undertaken within the national forest system to that time. In an effort to open stands without harming remaining trees, the Forest Service established standards for the CCC laborers: leave 1,200 trees per acre, spaced about 6 feet apart, where the height of trees left after thinning would be 2–8 feet; leave 680 trees per acre, about 8 feet apart, where the height of remaining trees would be 8–15 feet; and leave 480 trees per acre, about 9½ feet apart, where the heights would be 15–30 feet.[23]

Each Civilian Conservation Corps work crew consisted of twenty-five to thirty-five young men and came under the supervision of a foreman with technical training. Each day the foreman laid out a one-tenth-acre plot in which trees were counted according to height categories and then calculations made as to what trees needed to be left, according to the established standards. Enrollees decided which specific trees to cut. Some natural replacement stands contained as many as 40,000 12–15-inch seedlings per acre; sometimes these volunteer seedlings were called dog-hairs, so dense that it was said dogs running through them would leave half of their hair behind. Thinning generally took place where tree heights ranged from 8 feet to 30 feet. To attain thinning according to the established standards, crews usually cut 10 percent less than ideal to compensate for possible losses from fire and disease.[24]

Thinning, however, was not an entirely unmixed blessing, evoking complaints from some ranchers. They criticized CCC crews for leaving slash on meadowlands, thus reducing the areas for grazing; in addition, by leaving slash, the crews created breeding grounds for insects that damaged trees and also made it more difficult to control ground fires. One might wonder whether underlying those complaints was rancher opposition to anyone intruding on stock leases. Nonetheless, the Forest Service took the problem seriously, working out compromise rules between complete slash removal, which would have been prohibitively expensive, and no slash removal, which might have caused other problems. Slash could remain no higher than 2 feet aboveground but had to be removed if located within 100 feet of roads, within 25 feet of trails, and on ridge-line firebreaks.[25]

Just as the Civilian Conservation Corps, and the monies that came with it, allowed the Forest Service to implement widespread thinning, so, too, did it enable the Forest Service to carry out the labor-intensive "out by 10:00 a.m." official policy of fire suppression. Developed as a result of large fires in the Pacific Northwest, the policy required immediate containment and control of every fire, regardless of cause; if that were impossible, then within the first work shift after detection; failing that, by 10:00 a.m. the next morning; or, failing even that, organizing operations to obtain control by 10:00 a.m. the following day, and so on. The hour of

10:00 a.m. was likely selected because controlling fires after that hour became far more difficult as a result of the heating of the day and wind.[26] In retrospect, an unintended consequence of the 10:00 a.m. policy was denser stands and excessive fuel buildup, in time causing more and larger fires and more insect epidemics; the policy was quietly abandoned in the 1980s.

Civilian Conservation Corps crews served as the Forest Service's principal fire-fighting units. During their first five years in the Black Hills, crews went on 652 fire-fighting missions, for a total of approximately 44,000 work days. Crews had trained to deploy from their camps or worksites within fifteen minutes of notification by telephone or radiophone. Upon arrival at a fire, the ranger or other Forest Service officer already on-site dispersed the first crew at critical points on the fire line until additional crews could start trenching the fire. Trenching meant clearing away needles and other debris down to mineral soils and back-burning, by setting small fires in front of a fire to burn back toward the main fire line, to produce a burned strip that prevented the main fire from moving ahead. Meanwhile, a couple of enrollees immediately established radio contact with the nearest lookout and, through the lookout, made telephone contact with the supervisor's office. Equipment and more crews were called in as needed so that, in a longer operation, the US Army brought in food, potable water, and sleeping bags as part of its responsibility for the care of the enrollees. In addition, the army sent medical personnel and an ambulance in case of emergency.[27]

While surface fires were relatively cool and easy to suppress, far more dangerous were the fires that swept through the tops of trees. The McVey fire (July 8–12, 1939), north of Hill City, was the largest fire fought with assistance of the CCC. Caused by lightning, the fire burned 20,759 acres, at one point occupied 1,755 firefighters along 47 miles of fire lines, and contributed to making 1939 the longest and most severe fire year in the Black Hills to that date. Shortly thereafter, the crews collected 8,000 bushels of pine cones, took them to a seed extraction facility at Custer, and later sowed seeds over burned areas. Since artificial reforestation was usually unnecessary in the Black Hills, seeds collected were shipped to the Nebraska National Forest's Bessey Nursery.[28]

Perhaps the CCC's most lasting legacy in the Black Hills concerned fire preparation projects such as new and improved roads, trails, firebreaks, small reservoirs, and lookout towers. The Harney Peak tower overshadowed all others and attracted the most visitors, 8,000 to 10,000 annually in the late 1930s. The CCC replaced the hut (built in 1919) with a 35-foot-high stone tower, described by the local press as a "stupendous undertaking" because every piece of building material had to be transported from the foot of the mountain 3 miles up a trail on specially built two-wheel carts, each pulled by a single horse.[29]

FIGURE 7.3. Cabin destroyed by McVey fire, 1939. Courtesy, USDA Forest Service, Black Hills National Forest, http://www.ForestPhoto.com.

From a story in a Civilian Conservation Corps camp newspaper, we learn that the normal fire watch day at Harney Peak lookout began at 5:15 a.m. with a fire check, followed by the raising of the flag, breakfast, and general cleanup. Hikers began arriving around 7:30 a.m.; lookouts considered early morning visitors the most interesting because they tended to be young and enthusiastic. At 8:30 a.m., lookouts called headquarters, making sure the phone line was in good order, sending the humidity reading for the previous day, and obtaining the correct time. Weather observations were taken daily at 7 a.m., noon, and 5 p.m., including cloud cover, temperature, humidity, wind velocity, and extent of visibility. Lookouts recorded all weather and smoke observations, telephone calls, and other highlights in a daily logbook.[30]

While the flow of visitors helped break up their routine, the lookouts kept to their principal task of watching for smoke, using their binoculars, knowing that every minute counted after a fire was spotted. When they sighted smoke, the lookouts referred to a map of the area mounted and correctly oriented on their plane-table. A pin marked the lookout, with a circle drawn around it and divided into 360 degrees. Attached to the pin was a pointer that could move around the pin to sight the direction of the fire by reading the bearing directly off the plane-table. Lookouts

FIGURE 7.4. Ranger in lookout tower, 1940s. Courtesy, Black Hills National Forest Collection, Leland D. Case Library for Western Historical Studies, Black Hills State University, Spearfish, SD.

then telephoned their sighting to headquarters. With readings from other lookout points, whenever possible, a fire could be definitively triangulated and the nearest fire personnel dispatched.

During periods of extreme fire danger, using CCC enrollees, the Forest Service set up checkpoints at principal national forest entrances, stopped motorists to warn them of the fire risks, and distributed pamphlets regarding fire safety. For the purpose of public education, the Forest Service placed its first "fire danger meter" in downtown Custer in 1938. The meter, which looked like a thermometer, was adjusted according to conditions reflecting dormant, low, moderate, high, or extreme fire danger.[31]

As an extension of its fire preparation work, the Civilian Conservation Corps built the roads, buildings, and recreational facilities that would make possible the expansion of recreational and related commercial activities within and around the national forests. Primarily to lessen flooding and soil erosion, the CCC built an 18-acre lake (Horse Thief) on Pine Creek, northeast of Harney Peak, and a 120-acre lake on Bismarck and French Creeks within Custer State Park. The most ambitious CCC watershed project, to dam Spring Creek and create the 340-acre Sheridan Lake, took two years to complete. With 6 miles of shoreline, Supervisor Krueger envisioned Sheridan Lake as the center of a multipurpose recreational area close to the population center of Rapid City.[32]

Except for fighting fires on private land within and around the national forests, Civilian Conservation Corps projects took place only on public lands. It is worth repeating that private land still occupied about 250,000 acres within forest boundaries. Chief Forester William B. Greeley (1920–28) had worked hard to make public-private cooperation on fire fighting part of what he described as "cooperative forestry," common management policies and practices regardless of forest ownership.[33] In the spirit of cooperative forestry, Greeley had helped secure passage of the Clarke-McNary Act of 1924, which enabled the Forest Service to distribute seedlings from federal nurseries to private parties at little or no cost and provide technical assistance to private owners of timber, much as Pinchot and Graves had done through the old Division of Forestry. By extending the scope of the Weeks Act of 1911, the Clarke-McNary Act allowed the Forest Service to purchase private lands around and within national forest boundaries. President Franklin Roosevelt executed boundary adjustments and land acquisitions for the national forest system. Near Hot Springs in the southern Black Hills, the president attached 22,000 acres of federal land to Harney National Forest.[34]

Then, in June 1933, President Roosevelt ordered the transfer of all national monuments from the Forest Service to the National Park Service, as part of the reorganization of federal agencies. Jewel Cave, considered something of a nuisance by the Forest Service, had remained mostly closed to the public until 1928, when Supervisor Conner negotiated an agreement for the Custer Commercial Club and the Newcastle [Wyoming] Lions Club to manage the site. Senator Norbeck strongly supported Conner's efforts and in 1931 secured a special federal appropriation to improve the Custer-Newcastle highway, the main access route to Jewel Cave.[35] Both the highway improvement and the transfer of Jewel Cave from Harney National Forest to Wind Cave National Park were celebrated at Jewel Cave on a Sunday afternoon in June 1934, with speeches and a barbecue attended by 1,500. Wind Cave National Park supervisor Edward D. Freeland announced that funds for modern facilities, including a small office building with staff quarters, had been requested from the Works Progress Administration and that a Civilian Conservation Corps crew assigned to Wind Cave would be moved to Jewel Cave.[36]

As noted earlier, President Roosevelt placed the Mount Rushmore National Memorial under the National Park Service in 1938. Relieved of fiscal responsibility for Mount Rushmore, though still positioned to reap its tourist benefits, South Dakota state leaders were emboldened to seek the transfer of Custer State Park and the game sanctuary to the National Park Service while again retaining its financial benefits. This time, however, Park Service director Arno B. Cammerer, who had not welcomed Mount Rushmore into his agency, succeeded in preventing acceptance of South Dakota's offer. According to a report prepared by National Park Service staff, Custer State Park and the game sanctuary did not qualify "because of the extensive changes in land forms through the construction of artificial lakes, the carving of figures on Mt. Rushmore, the existence of many roads and the mining and timbering operations."[37]

By 1939, however, the National Park Service possessed three sites within the boundaries of Harney National Forest: Wind Cave National Park, Jewel Cave National Monument, and Mount Rushmore National Memorial. In addition, the CCC had completed construction of the Iron Mountain Road, a 16-mile stretch through the national forest (today, US Highway 16-A), which Senator Norbeck had proposed as a picturesque approach to Mount Rushmore; tunnels were placed in such a way as to frame the presidential faces for travelers coming from the southeast. Again, the national forest provided the gateways for tourists traveling to National Park Service sites and to an increasing number of commercial facilities within and around national forest boundaries but without the authority to manage such development. With perhaps a bit of irony, Forest Service crews continue to thin trees along the approach to Mount Rushmore that is now called the Peter Norbeck Scenic Byway.

To promote the region as a tourist destination, business leaders, mostly from Rapid City, established the Black Hills and Badlands Association in 1939. The association sought to mitigate competition among communities for tourist dollars, to maintain some standards in the quality of commercial facilities and services catering to tourists, and to take advantage of the infrastructure built by the Civilian Conservation Corps. To allay fears that its interest was to promote only Rapid City, the association moved its headquarters twenty-five miles northwest to Sturgis.[38]

While often unpleasant and not particularly useful, competition between communities such as Deadwood and Sturgis remained a reality. Most notably, in August 1938 Sturgis motorcycle shop owner Clarence Hoel, together with the local Jackpine Gypsies motorcycle club, organized the first motorcycle rally at the fairgrounds in Sturgis, meant as a competitive alternative to Deadwood's annual "Days of '76" rodeo. Eighty people attended that first rally, compared to the 500,000 riders who would invade the Black Hills in August 2000. They were perhaps not what Peter

Norbeck had in mind when he envisioned "the playground for all the people," but successive Sturgis rallies certainly contributed to commercial development within the region and to increased travel through the national forest.[39]

Yet timbering remained the preeminent activity. Both Clarence C. Averill, Black Hills National Forest supervisor (1939–41), and Elva A. Snow, Harney National Forest supervisor (1935–42), embraced New Deal social policy to the extent that their more politic superiors had to decline some of their suggestions. Just prior to his appointment as supervisor but already on staff as assistant supervisor, Averill had been charged with preparing a plan for logging on those portions of working circles that supplied timber to the Warren-Lamb sawmill in Rapid City. Recall that the Forest Service had guaranteed a fifteen-year supply of timber and continued to favor Warren-Lamb as a reliable operator, abiding by the rules and obtaining efficient use of timber. Because of the variety of its products, Warren-Lamb employed more workers per volume of timber than smaller operators; by contracting for timber from smaller logging operators and for rough lumber from smaller sawmills, it kept those smaller operators in business.

Under Averill's plan, the Forest Service promised to sell 100 million board feet of timber spread throughout four working circles over ten years to Warren-Lamb and another 40 million board feet to smaller companies dependent on Warren-Lamb. In addition, the plan called for Warren-Lamb to supply logs to local farmers and ranchers and to give local residents employment priority. As it completed the 1939 contract, Warren-Lamb reduced operations, closing the last facility—a molding plant in Rapid City—after it was damaged by the great flood of 1972.[40]

For the northern Black Hills, Averill prepared a logging plan with similar objectives but different specifics. Because the Homestake Mining Company had consolidated its mill operations in Nemo and Moskee into a single sawmill at Spearfish, the company received approval to cut on one working circle and to hire beyond the Spearfish working circle. Acting chief forester C. E. Richards suggested that it might be "better sociology and better economics" for Homestake to purchase most of its logs from smaller operators, but Averill still preferred the large operator to the smaller operators.[41] Homestake hired year-round employees, paid them nearly twice as much as did the smaller operators, and provided hospitalization and pension benefits. Smaller operators hired mostly seasonal labor and provided them with deplorable camp conditions.

Supervisor Averill wanted operators timbering on private land to adhere to minimum forestry standards as a prerequisite for bidding on public timber, a laudable proposal in the spirit of cooperative forestry, but Washington rejected it on grounds that it might hinder competitive bidding. Instead, Richards suggested that Averill simply withhold putting up for sale timber sought by an operator with a poor record on private land or placing that timber on the market only after the operator pledged to improve logging practices.[42]

As the economy began to improve, with a corresponding increase in demand for lumber, Supervisor Snow decided that it would be prudent to place cutting quotas on individual operators. He explained that the Custer working circle was being overcut and ventured the opinion that, sometime in the future, timbering in the Harney National Forest might have to stop altogether—a prospect damaging to all parties, especially to loggers who had developed a constant pace of operations. To lessen that prospect, Snow prepared tentative annual quotas for all operators, based on their average cutting over the prior five years, and offered to make adjustments upward if operators agreed to cut damaged trees.[43]

Snow's plan was voluntary in the sense that an operator from the outside could still outbid an established operator, which happened on at least one occasion. Some argued that the uncertainty brought on by competition discouraged established operators from making capital investments. In response, Snow sought approval for a number of administrative changes in favor of established operators, such as raising the earnest money required of bidders, requiring bonding, and selling timber to established operators without going through a competitive bidding process. The Forest Service rejected Snow's proposals, but Carl Newport made the point that Snow's suggestions illustrated the extent to which an engaged forest supervisor pursued alternatives for the sake of local economic and community stability. Newport also noted that an unanticipated result of the quota list was an attempt by established operators informally to divvy up stands for sale prior to actual sales, seeking to preempt competitive bidding with the express purpose of controlling the price of lumber.[44]

The entrance of the United States into World War II altered Averill's plans. The US Congress gave the president broad authority to expedite the war effort; the president, in turn, authorized the Forest Service to suspend competitive bidding after giving seven days' advance notice. In April 1943 Black Hills National Forest supervisor Arthur F.C. Hoffman (1941–48) sold 15 million board feet to the Homestake Mining Company without competitive bidding so the company could timber easily accessible stands to supply its Spearfish mill and save on fuel. At the same time, the federal Office of Price Administration imposed price ceilings on the sale of standing timber, based on appraisals plus a profit allowance; it had already imposed price ceilings on lumber. Because of wartime shortages of labor, critical parts, and supplies, forest supervisors could hold the line on cutting.[45]

Shortly after the attack on Pearl Harbor, a Japanese submarine off the California coast fired shells that landed near Los Padres National Forest, which drove the Forest Service to inaugurate a nationwide forest fire prevention campaign. The

FIGURE 7.5. Smokey Bear poster, 1950s. Courtesy, Black Hills National Forest Collection, Leland D. Case Library for Western Historical Studies, Black Hills State University, Spearfish, SD.

Walt Disney Company volunteered Bambi as the campaign's symbol; after a year's trial, the Forest Service and the Advertising Council decided in favor of Smokey Bear, in honor of a popular New York City assistant fire chief named Smokey Joe Martin. Adding a note of sentimentality to the campaign, in 1950 firefighters cleaning up a major fire in the Lincoln National Forest in New Mexico found a 5-pound black bear cub with singed paws clinging to a blackened tree. They rescued the cub and sent it to the National Zoo in Washington, DC, where for fifteen years the cub served as the living symbol of the fire prevention campaign. Beyond that, the Smokey Bear campaign had a significant, perhaps unintended long-term impact on the Forest Service. Historian Samuel Hays has expressed the insight that, over time, Smokey Bear and his "friends" expanded the American public's view of the forest and its values and encouraged citizens to take a closer look at the management of the national forests.[46]

During the postwar period, meanwhile, successive national administrations pressed for the very highest levels of production on public lands. With the lifting of price controls, the price of lumber from the Black Hills rose by 25 percent; the price of standing timber rose from seven dollars per 1,000 board feet in 1945 to thirteen dollars per 1,000 board feet in 1952. Some timber operators in the Black Hills complained that the Forest Service had raised its appraisals; but Carl Newport, a timber industry advocate, found that average bids for timber sales actually exceeded appraised values. In addition, to compensate for market fluctuations, he noted that the Forest Service had instituted a procedure for adjusting prices over the period of long-term sales.[47]

With economic diversification and expansion occurring during and after the war, timber no longer remained the predominant industry in the Black Hills, except around Custer, Hill City, and Pringle. Homestake Mining Company remained a major employer around Deadwood, but Warren-Lamb Lumber Company had pretty much ceased operations, in part because of competition from more nimble operators such as the Minnesota-based Buckingham Trucking Company. To avoid sending empty trucks eastbound from Rapid City, Buckingham purchased rough lumber from small operators, collected and stored that lumber in its concentration yard, and shipped from that facility as trucks became available and demand warranted.[48]

Beginning with the administration of President Harry S. Truman, postwar appropriations greatly increased for construction of US Forest Service roads, specifically to access more timber more efficiently. At the same time, better roads attracted recreational visitors, not all of whom either understood or valued the utility of timber production. More roads left some longtime residents with the feeling that their backyards were being destroyed. Gustav A. Pearson, the longtime director of Fort Valley, the oldest Forest Service experimental forest in the United States, recalled visiting the Black Hills in the mid-1930s and at that early date listening to residents "deplore forest destruction and in many instances [they] would go so far as to [want to] prohibit any cutting whatsoever."[49]

Such was not the opinion expressed by Ezra T. Benson, secretary of agriculture under President Dwight D. Eisenhower. In a speech to the American Forestry Association in October 1953, Benson explained that forest conservation meant managing resources for use, and forest preservation meant no management and no usefulness; the former was productive and desirable, the latter unproductive and undesirable.[50] Benson advocated the most intensive timbering possible, raising the upper limits on what could be cut in the short term, though still in balance with growth over the long term. By short term he meant the amount of timber the Forest Service allowed to be cut in a given year; long term or "sustained yield" meant the amount of timber that could be cut without depleting the overall timber stand. The Eisenhower administration and the timber industry viewed "allowable cut" as the minimum cut required to achieve the "sustained yield" quotas set by the Forest

Service. The Forest Service viewed "allowable cut" as the upper limit of logging permitted annually.[51]

With the intent to improve efficiency and reduce government spending, the Eisenhower administration welcomed the chance to consolidate the two Black Hills national forests. Responsibility for executing that consolidation rested with Jack C. Kern (1953–55), the supervisor of Harney National Forest. He had arrived from San Francisco, where he had served as chief of operations for Region 5. Conveniently, the supervisor's position in the Black Hills National Forest had been vacant since the departure of Supervisor Averill in fall 1952.[52]

Apparently, talks of consolidation had been taking place for some time and gained some urgency with the pending transfer of public grasslands in southwestern South Dakota to the US Forest Service. Under the New Deal, the federal government had purchased these sub-marginal farmlands to help resettle impoverished farm families. President Eisenhower approved the administrative merger of the grasslands to the national forest system and the consolidation of the two national forests on February 1, 1954. Regional Forester Donald E. Clark reiterated to the local press that the main purpose of consolidation was to save money and gain efficiency, as well as to enable the Forest Service to conduct day-to-day relations with forest users and permittees on a decentralized basis through district rangers and their staffs. Reminiscent of Gifford Pinchot's approach perhaps, this was definitely a favor to the timber industry.[53]

The consolidation of the two forests took place during a time of decline in lumber demand and a parallel decline in timbering, from 55.7 million board feet in 1951 to 24.9 million board feet in 1955. Once again, the industry blamed the Forest Service for precipitating the decline by keeping appraisals high and imposing too many rules. Accompanied by Senator Francis H. Case (R-SD), a former Black Hills journalist, the timber operators confronted Supervisor Kern with their complaints. In response, Kern invited them on a tour to observe Forest Service markers estimating the value of standing timber and measuring the volume of logs cut so they could see for themselves the care taken in making appraisals. Whether the operators accepted Kern's invitation remains obscure.[54]

As demand for lumber increased, the Forest Service found itself seeking more timber stands to cut. With numerous inactive mining claims throughout the forest, the Forest Service favored the separation of surface from subsurface rights so that, presumably, more land could be available for timbering as well as grazing. Passage of the Multiple Use Mining Act of 1955 enabled the Forest Service to assess the validity of claims but only those made after passage of the act and, in the case of unpatented claims, to initiate legal action to reclaim surface rights.[55] As for mining, considerable postwar exploration and extraction of defense-related minerals such as beryllium occurred in the Black Hills but marginally affected the Forest Service, which could only control surface access throughout the forest.

In line with Eisenhower administration policy favoring intensive timbering, Senator Karl E. Mundt (R-SD), a member of the Senate Appropriations Committee, obtained funding for the establishment of the Rocky Mountain Research Center— "dedicated to more proficient and profitable forest management"—to be located on the campus of the South Dakota School of Mines and Technology in Rapid City. Since the Forest Service regional research station in Fort Collins, Colorado, already served the research needs of the Black Hills, one could reasonably conclude that the Rocky Mountain Research Center came into existence not as a result of systematic analysis by the Forest Service or anyone else but by a single act of pork-barreling sponsored by one senator on behalf of a constituency.[56]

Considerable experimentation took place during the late 1950s on the use of chemicals to combat forest diseases and on new techniques to assist with fire suppression. Firefighters in California had been using helicopters since the late 1940s. Studies suggested that helicopters would work well in the Black Hills because of the many open spaces for landing in the forest. In June 1959 the Forest Service contracted for the first helicopter, stationed at Hill City, to transport firefighters and supplies, as well as to drop water. During that same summer, again for the first time in the Black Hills, the Forest Service used a modified B-24 bomber to spread fire retardant, a mixture of clay-like bentonite and water.[57]

In conjunction with other federal agencies, the Rocky Mountain Research Center did try to assist the timber industry in developing capacity for manufacturing wood products locally. Speaking to the Custer Chamber of Commerce, Harney National Forest supervisor Marion J. Webber (1944–53) lamented the fact that approximately half of all timber cut in the Black Hills went to waste because of the lack of facilities to manufacture marketable products.[58] Some of the smaller sawmills had yet to convert their operations to meet grading standards set by the Western Pine Association. Compliance with those standards would have made it easier to competitively manufacture products that required uniformity, such as door stock, moldings, and ammunition boxes for the military.[59]

In addition to cutting for lumber, during the 1950s paper companies from the upper Midwest began to purchase timber. Among the first, the Nekoosa-Edwards Paper Company contracted for timber, mostly from private land west of Hermosa. Clearing timber not usable for lumber helped stock growers by increasing forage areas, improving road access for winter feeding, and making land more fire-resistant. In 1960 the Green Bay Pulp and Paper Company purchased wood chips from a new manufacturing facility near Custer. The plant received sawmill waste, took it through a cutting chamber by conveyor, moved the resulting chips over a screen to get rid of impurities, and loaded the cleaned chips directly into railroad boxcars for shipment to paper mills.[60]

During the postwar years, the problem of overgrazing led hunters and other outdoor enthusiasts to request remediation. The Granger-Thye Act of 1950 had reaffirmed the role of local committees made up of grazing permittees to advise the Forest Service on fees and permits, but the act also reemphasized the agency's authority to use income from grazing fees for a variety of range improvements, some resented by stock growers.[61] Supervisor Webber had sought to persuade permittees that they would gain nothing in the long run if range conditions deteriorated beyond the point of annual restoration. He had received complaints from hunters worried about declines in forage for big game and warned stock growers that their failure to conserve forage could bring calls for complete removal of livestock from all national forestlands. Some grazing permittees grumbled that hunters and recreationists were putting the well-being of wildlife over subsistence of working people.[62]

To cope with dramatic increases in recreational use nationwide, the Forest Service secured a special congressional appropriation in 1957 to launch Operation Outdoors, a five-year project to improve existing recreational facilities and construct new ones. The Forest Service patterned its project after the National Park Service's Mission 66, established with the goal of improving visitor facilities and building new ones by the organization's fiftieth anniversary in 1966. Unlike Mission 66, Operation Outdoors did not include the use of the right of eminent domain to purchase inholdings, which, especially for the Black Hills, meant a lost opportunity to cope with what would become an ever more complicated task. The impact of Operation Outdoors on the Black Hills remained inconsequential.

While the Forest Service sought to address varied, often conflicting demands on forest resources, Custer State Park inaugurated a management plan designed so that recreational use and timbering complemented each other. Recall that the first state park plan, adopted in 1927, was meant to halt unregulated and unsustainable timbering. For the next twenty years, park management consisted of fire fighting and disease control. At the same time, the federal government, through the Civilian Conservation Corps, built recreational infrastructure: picnic grounds and campgrounds, outdoor theaters and other tourist facilities, roads, and dams that created three lakes. In 1945 the state legislature dissolved the three-member state park board and placed management responsibility with the state forester, head of the Division of Forestry in the Department of Game, Fish, and Parks. Two years later the legislature passed a state park plan submitted by State Forester Harry R. Woodward Jr. that divided the park into management zones by topography and principal function: timbering, recreation, and natural or no cutting.[63]

Considering that the initial intent of the state park was to attract tourist dollars, Woodward's commentary on the 1947 plan and its first years of implementation seemed remarkably balanced and prescient. Woodward affirmed that the best method to manage the forest for recreation was through conservative or sustained-yield forestry; failure to cut the equivalent of annual growth would result in forest fires, as well as insect and disease epidemics "that will take their toll without benefitting anyone."[64] He acknowledged that the public generally viewed loggers as devastators and offered park tours to show visitors that such an impression was false. To be sure, some loggers look for shortcuts—especially on land they do not own—which is why the public land manager must impose and enforce rules: construct logging roads for permanence; burn slash along roads and in draws, and scatter slash on slopes and ridges; skid only with horses to prevent damage to soil and young trees; and cut all standing dead trees to reduce the incidence of lightning-caused fires. Woodward was convinced that public opinion would ensure the "golden mean" between cutting and no cutting. His confidence in the public may strike some as idealistic and naive. But by recognizing changing public attitudes toward the use of the forest, Woodward drew up a blueprint for accommodating multiple uses years before the Forest Service did.[65]

Developing and implementing a plan for a relatively small area, about 48,000 acres, with virtually no inholders and no communities within its boundaries was relatively uncomplicated. The Forest Service had a far more complex task, not simply because of the immense geographic spread but also because of an ingrained loyalty within the agency to timber as the dominant forest use. Also, timbering was the major reason for congressional fiscal support for the agency. It was through Congress, then, that the Forest Service sought to reassert its commitment to timber while at the same time seeking to appease the growing number of recreationists and those who loved Smokey Bear's friends. To the original purposes of managing the reserves for timber and water, the Multiple Use–Sustained Yield Act of 1960 specified outdoor recreation, range, wildlife, and fish and deemed wilderness as consistent with its purposes. The act defined the term *multiple use* as "the management of all the various renewable surface resources of the national forests so that they are utilized in the combination that will best meet the needs of the American people" and the term *sustained yield* as "the achievement and maintenance in perpetuity of a high level annual or regular periodic output of the various renewable resources of the national forests without impairment of the productivity of the land." In sum, the act acknowledged the possibility of limiting timbering and, at the same time, cutting as much as possible.[66]

Forest Service advocates argued that the Multiple Use–Sustained Yield Act simply confirmed Gifford Pinchot's intent for the agency and put it to paper.

Historian Paul W. Hirt has suggested that the act was the last major piece of federal legislation asserting the Forest Service's "full discretionary control over national forest management."[67] Prior to the 1960s, Forest Service officials managed the forests with advice from livestock growers and loggers, but otherwise there was no direct public involvement; the agency was left alone to manage the forests. Beginning in the 1960s, some within the Forest Service would recognize that following the postwar emphasis on timbering, the time had come to rebalance it with other uses. Toward that end, Congress and the president would seek to ensure broad and direct public involvement in the planning and monitoring of Forest Service operations.

NOTES

1. Reprinted in *Custer County Chronicle*, March 5, 1936.

2. Arthur F.C. Hoffman and Theodore Krueger, "Forestry in the Black Hills," in *USDA Yearbook* (Washington, DC: US Department of Agriculture, 1949), 325.

3. *Custer Weekly Chronicle*, January 24, 1925, August 14, 1930; Gustav A. Pearson and Raymond E. Marsh, "Timber Growing and Logging Practices in the Southwest and the Black Hills Region," *USDA Technical Bulletin* 480 (October 1935): 76.

4. Carl A. Newport, *Forest Service Policies in Timber Management and Silviculture as They Affect the Lumber Industry: A Case Study of the Black Hills* (Pierre: South Dakota Department of Game, Fish, and Parks, 1956), 42–43, 96.

5. Reprinted in the *Deadwood Pioneer-Times*, August 6, 1926.

6. *Custer Weekly Chronicle*, February 6, 1926.

7. Ibid., March 28, 1929.

8. Newport, *Forest Service Policies*, 48; *Custer Weekly Chronicle*, January 15, 1931.

9. *Custer Weekly Chronicle*, December 31, 1931, March 17 and 24, 1932.

10. Kendrick A. Clements, "Herbert Hoover and Conservation, 1921–33," *American Historical Review* 89, no. l (February 1984): 67, 75–76.

11. B. Thomas Parry, Henry J. Vaux, and Nicholas Dennis, "Changing Conceptions of Sustained-Yield Policy on the National Forests," in *Community Stability in Forest-Based Economies,* ed. Dennis C. LeMaster and John H. Beuter, Proceedings of a conference in Portland, Oregon, November 16–18, 1987 (Portland, OR: Timber, 1989), 25–26. A graduate of the Yale School of Forestry and a former professor of forestry at the University of California, Mason served as the first manager of the Western Pine Association, formed in 1931 to develop and maintain uniform grade standards for lumber and advocate on behalf of large timber operators. Today, it is known as the Western Wood Products Association.

12. *Custer Weekly Chronicle*, June 4, September 3, 1931; Newport, *Forest Service Policies*, 49–51.

13. Jacob J. Roeser Jr., "The Role of Timber Stand Improvements in the Black Hills," *Black Hills Engineer* 24, no. 1 (December 1937): 49–50. Roeser was a forest assistant in the Harney National Forest.

14. *Custer Weekly Chronicle*, April 21, July 7, 1932.

15. An Act Authorizing the Secretary of Agriculture to Enlarge Tree Planting Operations on National Forests, Public Law 71–319 [Knutson-Vandenberg Act], *US Statutes at Large* 46 (1930): 527.

16. Quoted in "Report of Black Hills Commission" (1988), typescript, 3–4, Black Hills National Forest supervisor's office, Custer, SD (hereafter BHNF).

17. Char Miller, *Gifford Pinchot and the Making of Modern Environmentalism* (Washington, DC: Island, 2001), 318.

18. Theodore Krueger, "The CCC in the Black Hills and Harney National Forests," *Black Hills Engineer* 24, no. 1 (December 1937): 14.

19. See C. N. Alleger, ed., *Civilian Conservation Corps, South Dakota District History* (Rapid City: Johnston and Bordewyk, ca. 1935; Lyle A. Derscheid, *The Civilian Conservation Corps in South Dakota, 1933–1942* (Brookings: South Dakota State University Foundation Press, 1986).

20. *Custer Weekly Chronicle*, August 24, 1933.

21. Jessie Sundstrom and Linea Sundstrom, "The Civilian Conservation Corps," in *Black Hills National Forest Cultural Resources Overview*, ed. Lance Rom, Tim Church, and Michele Church (Custer: USDA Forest Service, Black Hills National Forest, 1996), 4C 1–2.

22. *Custer County Chronicle*, April 5, 1934.

23. Roeser, "Role of Timber," 52.

24. Ibid., 48 53.

25. *Custer County Chronicle*, July 5, 1934; Theodore Krueger, "Practices and Problems in the Disposal of Brush Resulting from Thinnings in Ponderosa Pine in the Black Hills National Forest," *Journal of Forestry* 32, no. 7 (October 1934): 758–59.

26. Ferdinand A. Silcox to regional foresters, May 25, 1935, cited in Stewart Lundgren, "The National Fire Management Analysis System (NFMAS) Past 2000: A New Horizon," USDA Forest Service General Technical Report PSW-GTR–173 (Albany, CA: USDA Forest Service, Pacific Southwest Research Station, 1999), 71; see also Stephen J. Pyne, *Fire in America: A Cultural History of Wildland and Rural Fire* (Seattle: University of Washington Press, 1997 [1982]), 272–87.

27. Clarence C. Averill, "The Civilian Conservation Corps as a Fire Suppression Organization," *Black Hills Engineer* 24, no. 1 (December 1937): 38–45. At the time, Averill was assistant forest supervisor, Black Hills National Forest.

28. *Custer County Chronicle*, March 9, September 14, 1939, April 23, 1959; "Annals of the Black Hills National Forests," typescript, 36, 1948 draft with 1967 addition, BHNF.

29. From *Mornin' After*, reprinted in *Custer County Chronicle*, July 25, 1935.

30. Ibid., January 4, 1940.

31. Pearson and Marsh, "Timber Growing," 38; *Custer County Chronicle*, July 9, 1936, July 22, 1937, June 23, 1938.

32. *Custer County Chronicle*, June 15, 1933, January 23, 1936; Alison T. Otis, William D. Honey, Thomas C. Hogg, and Kimberly K. Lakin, *The Forest Service and the Civilian Conservation Corps, 1933–1942* (Washington, DC: USDA Forest Service, 1986), 24.

33. Pyne, *Fire in America*, 270.

34. *Custer County Chronicle*, November 22, 1934.

35. Suzanne Barta Julin, *A Marvelous Hundred Square Miles: Black Hills Tourism, 1880–1941* (Pierre: South Dakota State Historical Society Press, 2009), 65–67, 106–8, 111–13.

36. *Custer County Chronicle*, June 7 and 21, 1934.

37. Quoted in Julin, *Marvelous Hundred Square Miles*, 133.

38. Ibid., 165–67.

39. Carleton L. Bonilla, "A South Dakota Rendezvous: The Sturgis Motorcycle Rally and Races," *South Dakota History* 28 (Fall 1998): 124; John Taliaferro, *Great White Fathers: The Story of the Obsessive Quest to Create Mount Rushmore* (New York: Public Affairs, 2002), 12–13.

40. Brooks, Noisat, and Sundstrom, "Logging," 5b 7–8; Paul V. Miller (retired archaeologist), Custer, discussion with author, July 2011.

41. C. E. Richards, review of "Administrative Timber Plan for the Bearlodge, Northeast, and Spearfish Working Circles, Black Hills National Forest, February 20, 1940," 1, Washington, DC, March 13, 1940, copy, BHNF.

42. Ibid.; Newport, *Forest Service Policies*, 56–58.

43. Newport, *Forest Service Policies*, 58–64.

44. Ibid.

45. Ibid., 66–72.

46. Samuel P. Hays, *The American People and the National Forests: The First Century of the U.S. Forest Service* (Pittsburgh: University of Pittsburgh Press, 2009), 102.

47. Newport, *Forest Service Policies*, 83–84.

48. Ibid., 76–77, 83–84.

49. Pearson and Marsh, "Timber Growing," 11.

50. Cited in Paul W. Hirt, *A Conspiracy of Optimism: Management of the National Forests since World War Two* (Lincoln: University of Nebraska Press, 1994), 107, 132.

51. For discussion of these definitions, see Nancy Langston, *Forest Dreams, Forest Nightmares: The Paradox of Old Growth in the Inland West* (Seattle: University of Washington Press, 1995), 168.

52. *Custer County Chronicle*, March 5, 1953, August 11, 1955.

53. Ibid., January 14, 1954.

54. Ibid., December 25, 1953.

55. Ibid., July 19, 1956.

56. Ibid., July 14, 1955.

57. Ibid., May 15, 1958, June 11, September 10, 1959.

58. Ibid., April 23, 1953.

59. Newport, *Forest Service Policies*, 86.

60. *Custer County Chronicle*, January 29, 1959, August 4, 1960.

61. An Act to Facilitate and Simplify the Work of the Forest Service, Public Law 81–478, *US Statutes at Large* 64 (1950): 82–88.

62. Edward P. Cliff, regional forester, to Marion J. Webber, Denver, January 3, 1950, and "Range Management, 1952," draft, both in cabinet 7, drawer 4, folder 2, Black Hills National Forest Historical Collection, Leland. D. Case Library for Western Historical Studies, Black Hills State University, Spearfish, SD.

63. Harry R. Woodward Jr., "Forest Management versus Recreation Management," *American Forests* 63 (January 1957): 33, 52.

64. Ibid., 53.

65. Ibid., 32–33.

66. Multiple Use–Sustained Yield Act, Public Law 86–517, *US Statutes at Large* 74 (1960): 215.

67. Hirt, *Conspiracy of Optimism*, 190.

8

Advent of Public Participation

In the summer of 1966, Wallace Lloyd, recreation specialist for the Black Hills National Forest, told a group in Rapid City that the Forest Service was in the early stages of considering a large-scale recreation development on and around Harney Peak. The Forest Service envisioned construction of a paved road to within one-third of a mile of the summit, a large parking lot, an aerial tramway reaching nearly to the summit, and a visitor center in place of the lookout tower. The Forest Service contemplated constructing picnic and camping facilities nearby, as well as rebuilding two access roads. Accordingly, the Forest Service estimated that annual visits to Harney Peak would increase incrementally, from 14,000 to 500,000; Lloyd stressed, however, that the area's wilderness aspect would be retained, mainly by screening the new road and the tramway cut so that, from the summit, visitors would see only the forest.[1]

The proposal to develop the Harney Peak area can be viewed as belated recognition by the Forest Service of Peter Norbeck's premise that scenery alone did not attract family vacationers, but it failed to take into account voices in favor of preserving the natural beauty of special places. In fact, a small, unorganized group of local nature lovers managed to harness enough public sentiment to block the proposed development; that action was the first, but by no means the last, by a voluntary group to successfully challenge the Forest Service on its management of the Black Hills.

Beginning in the late 1960s and continuing into the first decade of the twenty-first century, varied users with differing views about the value of the national forests

DOI: 10.5876/9781607322993.c008

caused the agency essentially to operate in reactive ways. In its defense, the Forest Service invoked the Multiple Use–Sustained Yield Act of 1960, in its words, to practice "the harmonious and coordinated management of the various resources, each with the other, without impairment of the productivity of the land, with consideration being given to the relative values of the various resources, and not necessarily the combination of uses that will give the greatest dollar return or the greatest unit output."[2] The Forest Service did change its procedures, though initially at least it did not alter the belief that it knew best how to manage the forests or that timber remained the dominant forest use.

Indeed, the 1961 Black Hills National Forest timber management plan stated as management's primary purpose the maximum sustained yield of timber "in harmony with other forest uses."[3] With the goal of doubling the annual allowable cut, the plan called for reducing cutting cycles from thirty-five to twenty years and, in certain cases, to ten years; accelerating thinning activities and removing round-wood (small-diameter trees usable for posts, poles, and pulp) within the acreages thinned by the Civilian Conservation Corps; preventing insect infestations from reaching epidemic levels by using chemical sprays; keeping fire damage below 1,000 acres annually, the average annual loss over the prior twenty years; reforesting 30,000 acres of burned areas; and explaining the conservative necessity of timbering to the public. In addition, the Forest Service solicited new operators to cut saw-timber (generally, 9 inches in diameter at breast height [dbh] or greater) in the Limestone and Rochford areas of the northern Black Hills and sought to attract a pulp mill or another industry to absorb the increased cutting of round-wood. While noting that round-wood production had tripled since the 1940s, the Forest Service claimed that even more could be cut by exterminating porcupines, either by hunting or poisoning, and that porcupines had damaged an estimated 10 percent of post- and pole-sized trees.

To simplify administration, the Forest Service replaced working circles with management units laid out roughly to coincide with ranger districts, by then reduced to eleven. To improve access to timber, the agency planned to more than double the miles of official roads, from 2,304 to 5,366. Most roads were classified as primitive or unimproved, sufficient for handling logging trucks; the plan called for more than quadrupling improved roads, from 209 miles to 880 miles. More improved roads also meant better access for recreationists, for which the Forest Service required loggers to remove slash along improved roads and around areas of high public use rather than simply to cut and scatter slash. For aesthetic reasons, the 1961 plan required that, on a case-by-case basis, the forest supervisor approve construction of any roads crossing parklands or meadowlands and to authorize any clear-cutting.[4]

To accommodate the traveling public, the Forest Service sought to maintain "healthy stands of pleasing appearance" along and around roads, streams, lakesides, and other recreation sites. The revised timber management plan (1963) prescribed for areas of "high esthetic value" a more intensive three-cut entrance into sale stands: removing poor-quality and older trees and opening stands to encourage younger trees to grow.[5] In Forest Service parlance, the public wanted to see clean, well-groomed forests.

Beyond areas of scenic value, the revised plan set forth a new criterion for estimating optimal timber density, with a view to managing stands accordingly. Rather than base such estimates on tree heights, as was traditional, foresters came to understand that a more reliable criterion depended upon estimating the cross-sectional area of all trees on a given acre, measured at breast height and expressed in square feet. Based on silvicultural studies, the revised plan defined optimal density as 80 square feet, or basal 80, which translated roughly to 410 trees per acre, each 6 inches in diameter, or 230 trees, each 8 inches in diameter.[6]

In an effort to create more space for growing commercial timber, the plan called for removal of more than 3,000 acres of aspen, though recognizing that earlier efforts, using mechanical and chemical means, had generally failed to eradicate those trees. Through several extensions of the 1963 plan, the Forest Service sought to increase timbering, although actual timbering remained below expectations. Some blamed the Forest Service for keeping appraisals high on standing timber and for levying additional fees on sales of stands. Others pointed out that lumber of comparable quality shipped from the Pacific Northwest to the Black Hills could be sold more cheaply than local lumber.[7]

Nonetheless, the volume of cutting on federal lands in the Black Hills had accelerated over the long term. Roughly 1 billion board feet of timber were cut during the first fifty years (1898–1947), a second billion during the next twenty-one years, and a third billion during the decade 1968–79. At the same time, estimates of growing stock—the volume of wood in live trees of merchantable species—increased from 1.5 billion board feet in 1898 to 4.5 billion board feet in 1977. Although better information gathering can explain part of that increase, much had to do with the extraordinary reproductive capacity of the forest. Seemingly counterintuitive, with more cutting there was more timber to cut.[8]

Forest supervisors also sought ways to cope with dramatic increases in recreational use, from an estimated 1 million visits in 1953 to 3 million visits in 1962. Supervisor Theodore A. Schlapfer (1963–65) used funding from President Lyndon B. Johnson's "War on Poverty" to expand recreational facilities. Despite local public opposition, Schlapfer attracted a job-training program to a former Civilian Conservation Corps camp (today, the Boxelder Job Corps Center). As part of their training, participants helped maintain and improve forest roads, trails, and other facilities. Schlapfer supervised a major cleanup project to remove dead trees and debris along highways from Rapid City into the national forest. In the viewpoint of local businesses, however, improving national forest facilities was not enough to attract tourists.[9]

This is why, in early 1962, the Custer Chamber of Commerce sought and received bids for an aerial tramway to carry people from downtown to Big Rock Mountain. Perhaps the most ambitious, and definitely the most outlandish, proposal came from developer Byron T. Brown. Declaring that he had attracted financial backing from a group of out-of-state investors, Brown proposed to build what he called the world's first self-propelled "aerial bus system"—a pumpkin-shaped gondola designed to transport twenty-five passengers—and construct a twenty-six-mile loop over the Black Hills National Forest, from Custer to Mount Rushmore to Custer State Park and back to Custer. To assure local support, Brown requested a municipal election. By a ten-to-one margin, Custer voters approved leasing twelve undeveloped blocks in the northwest part of town and granted Brown a twenty-year franchise in expectation of substantial income to the municipality and, indirectly, to local businesses.

For three summers the aerial tramway operated from a city block to the top of Big Rock Mountain, a distance of a few hundred yards. As it experienced more and more technical difficulties and mechanical failures, local enthusiasm for the project waned; in turn, the developer tried without success to collect damages from suppliers for allegedly faulty equipment. The project ceased operations in 1966, with the gondola removed two years later when the Forest Service began contemplating the Harney Peak development, also featuring an aerial tramway.[10]

With every good intention to serve the public, Supervisor Kenneth C. Scholz (1965–72) underestimated the growing sentiment in favor of protecting the natural beauty of special places. Such sentiment had surfaced from time to time in the Black Hills, most notably when the Mount Rushmore project first came under consideration; but organized opponents to development on public lands had taken root in California and on the East Coast, which produced a series of landmark congressional acts, promulgated during the 1960s, that constrained the Forest Service and other federal agencies from managing their affairs with relative autonomy.

All subsequent Forest Service decision making would occur within the context of these landmark acts. First in time, the Wilderness Act of 1964 designated over 9 million acres of federal lands as permanently off-limits to development, allowed for setting aside additional federal lands as wilderness, declared it to be national policy that those lands be preserved and protected in their natural condition, and outlined how those lands were to be managed. In contrast to areas "where man and his own works dominate," the act defined wilderness "as an area where the earth and its community of life are untrammeled by man, where man himself is a visitor who does not remain."[11] Except for grazing and mining claims, the Forest Service could no longer exercise its own managerial discretion over the wilderness portion of land under its jurisdiction. In the Black Hills, that would not occur until establishment of the Black Elk Wilderness, although Forest Service discretion regarding the game sanctuary (renamed Norbeck Wildlife Preserve in 1949) had been limited since 1920.

Next, the Endangered Species Preservation Act of 1966, revised and expanded in 1973 as the Endangered Species Act, directed the secretary of the interior—through the Fish and Wildlife Service and the National Oceanic and Atmospheric Administration—to protect species from extinction by listing such species, purchasing critical habitat, and directing federal land agencies and urging non-federal agencies to preserve such habitat on their lands. This act stated the national policy that all species had aesthetic and scientific value and that any development activity had to be tempered by conservation.[12] Potentially the most prescriptive of the federal laws regarding human activity on public lands, this act affected forestry in the Black Hills beginning in the late 1980s.

The National Environmental Policy Act of 1969 (which took effect on January 1, 1970) was a lofty and far-reaching statement on the interrelationship between people and nature; it called on each citizen to help ensure "safe, healthful, productive, and aesthetically and culturally pleasing surroundings." In time, the act would force the agency to abandon its primarily silvicultural and engineering approach in favor of an interdisciplinary approach to forest management and to solicit public comments and suggestions prior to making major decisions.[13]

Sometime in late 1968, the Forest Service had begun to consider the desirability and practicability of developing the Harney Peak area. When it learned of the proposal in early 1969, the Black Hills chapter of the Society of American Foresters opposed making the jeep trail up Harney Peak into a road, having resolved that motor vehicle traffic "be limited to that necessary for the protections and administration of the area." The foresters favored the development of "good hiking trails and facilities" but wanted "use [to] be limited so as to cause the least interference with the aesthetic, geologic, forest and wildlife values"; they recommended only noncommercial timbering to make the forest look cleaner and be better protected from fire.[14] Their resolutions in favor of preservation appeared in sharp contrast to the traditional view of foresters, though in fairness the topography around Harney Peak did not lend itself to commercial timbering.

By early 1970, enough rumors about Forest Service plans had circulated to warrant a visit to Custer by Assistant Regional Forester David S. Nordwall. He confirmed that a private party had proposed constructing an aerial tramway to Harney

Peak and that the proposal was under careful review. Reflecting national policy, he stated that "the Forest Service does not intend to make any snap judgments" on the proposal because "we recognize this is an extremely sensitive area in terms of aesthetics, public interest, mountain goat habitat and general ecology." Nordwall's mention of "ecology" may have been the first time the Forest Service used that term publicly specifically with regard to the Black Hills. Nordwall noted that the Forest Service had contracted with a landscape architect to conduct an ecological study and with a forest recreation specialist to apply a computerized technique to measure the potential visual impact of the proposed aerial tramway. Both experts were working through the Forest Service's Pacific Southwest Forest and Range Experiment Station. Nordwall gave assurances that their analyses of environmental impacts would be considered in conjunction with an assessment of the need for easier public access and more public facilities in the area.[15]

To obtain public comments, Supervisor Scholz called a meeting for May 12, 1970, in Rapid City. In his announcement, he acknowledged that interest in the proposed development and protection of the natural environment was running high: "I'm counting on public participation and want to utilize this interest in making any decisions concerning the mountain."[16] About two dozen people participated in the meeting. Hoadley Dean, president of the Western South Dakota Development Corporation, spoke favorably, explaining what the proposed development would mean for the area's economy.[17] According to the editor of the *Custer County Chronicle*, proponents of development seemed to be middle-aged while opponents, in the majority, seemed either young or old: "This is perhaps because the young are inclined to be idealists, the old are inclined to be sentimental, while the middle-aged are inclined to be more materialistic." The editor continued: "Some who opposed have been called 'selfish' in that they do not want this wilderness area clogged by people who are more interested in circuses than in natural beauty. While the writer can no longer be classified as 'young' and is not ready to be called 'old,' we feel that we must go along with these groups in opposing the project, not only from an idealistic and sentimental standpoint, but we might even claim to be a bit 'selfish' about Harney."[18]

As a result of press reports announcing Scholz's meeting, a young collection agency clerk named Samuel N. Clauson called on a handful of outdoor lovers who banded together as the Committee for the Preservation of Harney Peak. Clauson had no prior experience as a community organizer, but in short order he became known as a leading proponent of preserving and protecting the Black Hills National Forest. Born into a farm family in eastern South Dakota, he had enlisted in the military after high school, served his first stint as a member of a missile-launch crew attached to Ellsworth Air Force Base near Rapid City, and returned to Rapid

City after completing his tour of duty. He had become attached to the Black Hills because of the dry climate and opportunities for hunting.

In a spontaneous sort of way, Clauson and members of his informal committee chipped in to place a paid advertisement in the Rapid City newspapers, asking readers to express their opposition to the proposed development by completing a coupon and sending it to Supervisor Scholz. Shortly thereafter, Clauson received a call from Scholz. "He was very gracious," Clauson recalled, "and told me that he had received a pile of coupons, that we had made our point, and that the Forest Service had decided to drop the project."[19]

In celebrating their success, members of the Committee for the Preservation of Harney Peak determined that they had other outdoorsy interests in the Black Hills and decided to remain together through some form of formal organizational structure. Norman E. Nelson, a science teacher at Douglas High School on Ellsworth Air Force Base, suggested affiliation with the Rocky Mountain chapter of the Sierra Club. A native of Deadwood with degrees in biology from Carleton College and the University of South Dakota, Nelson was more a nature lover than a hunter or hiker, spending summer weekends at the family cabin in the Norbeck Wildlife Preserve. He was a lifetime member of the Sierra Club. Until Nelson suggested affiliation, Clauson recalled that he and the other committee members had thought of the Sierra Club as a strictly West Coast organization. Nonetheless, he and Nelson received permission to establish a Black Hills subchapter of the Rocky Mountain chapter. The Black Hills group never consisted of more than a half-dozen activist members; through the 1990s, their mission to preserve the Black Hills seemed to reflect their appreciation of nature more than any science-based interest in preserving biological diversity.[20]

Contemporary with the advent of public participation in decision making, federal agencies found themselves in the position of having to confront far less pleasant public manifestations on public lands that spilled over to adjacent communities. In addition to having to cope with plain lawlessness or with what some described as "carefree hell-raising," the Forest Service in particular had deemed it necessary to prepare for an influx of so-called hippies searching for harmony with nature, among other things. Supervisor Scholz met several times with municipal and county officials at Custer in spring 1969 and discussed the Forest Service's experience with hippies in Colorado, which he knew firsthand; he cautioned against generalizing because "under the beards and long hair," hippies ranged from quiet, peaceful people such as doctors and lawyers to criminals who broke into summer homes of forest inholders. He suggested that the main source of potential violence came not from hippies but from "vigilante action by local residents against the hippie element."[21]

While a hippie invasion of the Black Hills National Forest never materialized, the National Park Service, and later the US Forest Service, had to cope with a different sort of intrusion that added an unpleasant and inconvenient element to public land management. On August 24, 1970, about 20 Lakota Sioux arrived at Mount Rushmore to protest against the federal government for transferring a 100,000-acre former gunnery range on the Pine Ridge Reservation to the Badlands National Monument rather than to their reservation. By Saturday, August 29, the demonstration had grown to about 150 and been taken over by the American Indian Movement, viewed locally as a radical group in the manner of the Black Panthers. That evening a group of about 25, led by Dennis Banks, Clyde Bellecourt, and Russell Means—all American Indian Movement members from Minnesota, though Means had been born on the Pine Ridge Reservation—tried to reach the presidential faces on Mount Rushmore but only managed to "occupy" a place about 100 yards behind the faces. By then, their rhetoric had shifted to a protest against the federal government's violation of the 1868 Treaty of Fort Laramie, the subsequent desecration of the Black Hills, and the government's failure to compensate the tribes for the land as well as for the revenues generated from that land. Through the exercise of remarkable restraint, the National Park Service simply watched and waited the group out.[22]

Two years later about 40 Lakota Sioux, including Bellecourt and Means, returned to the "Indian camp" behind the presidential faces armed with cans of red paint, baseball bats, and ax handles. Tipped off to the likelihood of violence, National Park Service law enforcement officers, backed by 50 National Guard members, arrested the group for trespassing. "Perhaps the most noteworthy aspect of the day's drama," commented journalist John Taliaferro, "was that the Park Service never closed Rushmore to tourists, not even for an hour."[23]

Violence precipitated by the American Indian Movement did occur in the town of Custer, making local, federal, state, and county public authorities more leery about negotiating with the Lakota Sioux and their advocates. On February 6, 1973, about 250 Indians led by Dennis Banks and Russell Means arrived at the Custer County Courthouse to celebrate a "National Indian Day of Rights" and protest the charge of second-degree manslaughter rather than murder against a Caucasian man accused of fatally stabbing a twenty-year-old tribal member outside a bar in Buffalo Gap. An earlier threat of violence by Banks mobilized law enforcement authorities to appear in full strength and attracted local and national media. For the sake of security, officers allowed only four protestors at a time into the courthouse to meet with the state's prosecuting attorney, Hobart Gates. When Gates declined to increase bail or change his charge of the accused, Means angrily left the prosecutor's office to address supporters outside. When he returned, he warned that protestors would storm the building within forty-five minutes if their demands were not met, but the protestors did not wait. They pillaged the courthouse, set it on fire, damaged neighboring buildings, and destroyed several vehicles. Within three hours the authorities had restored order, but the American Indian Movement–inspired tumult would not soon be forgotten.[24]

In 1979 Lakota Sioux spiritual leaders applied for a special use permit to establish a religious camp on 100 acres of forest service land about 3 miles northeast of Custer. Their application went to Supervisor James F. Mathers (1977–87), who had earned the reputation as "kind of a tyrant" in his prior position as supervisor of the Rio Grande National Forest and became known in the Black Hills for his unrefined, buck-stops-here, confrontational approach.[25]

To Mathers, local residents expressed fear of property damage and violence. Their attorney argued against granting the permit for environmental reasons and because access to the site would go across their private properties. Mathers denied the permit on the grounds that it would conflict with a grazing permit that had been in effect for twenty-two years and offered tribal leaders a temporary lease on another site. Rejecting Mathers's offer, the tribal leaders appealed to the chief forester, without success. Apparently, nothing further was heard on this particular case, though two years later Mathers confronted another case.[26]

In April 1981 a group of Lakota Sioux from the Pine Ridge Reservation set up camp near Victoria Lake, about 12 miles southwest of Rapid City, without notifying the Forest Service. Calling it Yellow Thunder Camp, the group applied to the Forest Service for a special use permit to establish a permanent "religious, cultural, and educational community" on 800 acres. Supervisor Mathers denied the application and gave camp occupants two weeks to leave. When they failed to do so, the federal government filed an action seeking to eject them. The occupants, including Russell and William Means of the American Indian Movement, filed a counteraction. Combined into one case, the matter went to federal trial, which took place intermittently over a period of three years ending in December 1988. Although the occupants had been allowed to remain until legal proceedings ended, they abandoned camp well before that date. In finding that the Forest Service had acted properly concerning Yellow Thunder Camp, the court presumed no special rights to the Lakota Sioux. Its decision provided personal satisfaction to an embattled supervisor and suggested that there were limits to accommodation.[27]

Such matters deflected Forest Service personnel and resources from timber management. Although the technique of clear-cutting had been used sparingly in the Black Hills National Forest, immoderate clear-cutting elsewhere brought on more prescriptive federal legislation. In November 1973 small-game hunters who used the Monongahela National Forest in eastern West Virginia decided that the Forest

Service had not responded satisfactorily to their complaints about clear-cutting, which they alleged had destroyed wildlife habitat. Some of these hunters belonged to the Izaak Walton League and persuaded the league to file suit in federal district court on their behalf. Judge Robert E. Maxwell agreed with the league's argument that the Forest Service had violated the Forest Management Act of 1897: only "dead, matured, or large growth trees," each appraised and marked before being sold, could be cut. Judge Maxwell's ruling was upheld by the federal appeals court in August 1975; Forest Service chief John R. McGuire promptly ordered a halt to all timber sales within the four states under that court's jurisdiction.

Fearing that the Monongahela case could serve as a precedent to stop timbering in all national forests, Congress approved, and President Gerald R. Ford signed, legislation that repealed portions of the Forest Management Act; the National Forest Management Act of 1976 permitted clear-cutting under guidelines prepared as a result of lengthy hearings held before the Senate Subcommittee on Public Lands, chaired by Senator Frank F. Church (D-ID). Essentially, the National Forest Management Act reaffirmed the policy of securing maximum production without degrading the forests. The act prescribed taking an interdisciplinary rather than a strictly silvicultural approach to forest planning, engaging outside scientists to ensure the execution of such an approach, and making further allowances for public participation. Once the Forest Service issued the regulations to carry out the act, leading national conservation groups, including the Sierra Club, prepared a handbook titled *A Conservationist's Guide to National Forest Planning* on how to use administrative procedures set forth in the act to advance their agendas.[28]

For its part, the Black Hills timber industry had warned of dire economic consequences. By narrowly interpreting the Forest Management Act, Judge Maxwell had effectively banned the thinning and cutting of small-diameter trees, activities that engaged more than half of the Black Hills timber workforce and represented about half of the total tree volume cut. Larger sawmills would have to close, counties would receive less "in lieu" income, and the Forest Service would be forced to reduce budgets for such items as road maintenance and, by reducing staff, have fewer personnel to fight forest fires. As it turned out, the annual amount of timber sold and cut annually between 1973 and 1979 increased by roughly 20 percent.[29]

Under pressure to accommodate members of the public who valued the forest for other than commercial timbering, Supervisor David S. Johns (1972–74) brought in two Forest Service silviculturists to review timbering practices and recommend changes: Charles E. Boldt and his associate, James L. Van Deusen, employed by the Rocky Mountain Forest and Range Experiment Station in Fort Collins, Colorado, but assigned to the Forest Service research unit (formerly known as the Rocky Mountain Research Center) in Rapid City. At the time, Boldt also served as administrator of the Black Hills Experimental Forest, a 3,438-acre plot northwest of Rapid City, established in 1961. Written as a guide for practicing foresters, Boldt and Van Deusen's "Silviculture of Ponderosa Pine in the Black Hills" would be used as the foundation for the 1977 timber management plan. Periodic revisions of their paper illustrated the incremental Forest Service acceptance of what is now called ecosystem management.[30]

While Boldt and Van Deusen reiterated that Black Hills timber stands were ideally suited as agricultural crops, they also made clear that "the day has passed when silviculture in the Black Hills can be aimed solely or even primarily at improved timber production." The challenge for foresters, they continued, "is to develop a much wider range of cultural [cultivation] options so that silvicultural practices can simultaneously serve the needs of various combinations of integrated forest uses." Keep focusing on timbering, but use "esthetic" and "environmentally safe" cutting methods.[31]

Starting with a description of forest conditions, Boldt devised an inventory system that divided the forest into classes of stands according to the quality of vegetative cover, productivity of growing stock, and suitability for management. Recall that, in preparing the first forest inventory, Henry Graves had looked strictly at individual trees, classifying them by diameter, height, and limb clearance and recording their topographic location, soil conditions, and forest density. In the 1930s, Forest Service entomologist E. M. Hornibrook had developed an inventory system for calculating annual allowable cuts. He divided the ponderosa pine into four groups by height, subdividing them according to their relative crown vigor. Boldt found Hornibrook's classification inapplicable to the entire forest and revised it based on soils and topographic research by Clifford A. Myers, Boldt's predecessor as administrator of the experimental forest.[32]

Boldt found that most ponderosa pine stands fell within one of two classes. The first was two-aged stands, which occupied more than half of the forest. These two-storied stands consisted of a few mature or overly mature trees rising above the many young trees growing too densely to be useful as saw-timber. He recommended removal of the old trees and pre-commercial thinning of the young trees. The second class consisted of even-aged or one-storied stands, which occupied somewhat less than half of the forest; at least 75 percent of trees in these stands fell within a twenty-year age range. If properly stocked, this second class could grow until maturity; if not properly stocked, Boldt recommended an intermediate cut for posts and poles or, if stagnant or diseased, complete removal followed by restoration.[33]

Boldt and Van Deusen concluded: "Final harvest is inevitable—no forest stand can be perpetuated forever. If not harvested by man, it will eventually be harvested by nature." By harvesting, they meant a cutting or a series of cuttings that resulted in the complete removal of mature stands.[34] Given the prolific reproduction of the ponderosa pine, Boldt and Van Deusen concluded that any cutting method could be used in the Black Hills. Because of the history of human activity in the forest, they found it inconceivable that any stand should be left unmanaged and recommended development of "a refined model of the forest production system, capable of simulating the behavior of the intensively cultured stands of the future."[35]

While the Forest Service pursued ways to accommodate multiple users within the context of timber management, the small band of outdoors lovers that had halted the Harney Peak development decided to concentrate their efforts on preserving the wilderness character of the Norbeck Wildlife Preserve. In spring 1974 the Black Hills Group of the Sierra Club announced a partnership with the Wilderness Society for the purpose of securing formal wilderness status for 18,000 acres including and surrounding Harney Peak. Samuel Clauson deplored damage in the area caused by four-wheelers, motorcyclists, and other motorized users and criticized what he called Forest Service "trail maintenance by bulldozer." While the groups pursued wilderness status, Clauson asked Supervisor Johns to close the Norbeck Wildlife Preserve to all motorized use, except for emergency fire and beetle control. Forest Service officers had argued consistently that the Harney Peak area did not qualify for wilderness designation because of its small size and the presence of human disturbances. This time, however, Johns designated Harney Peak and immediate surroundings a "special interest scenic area." Clauson commended the supervisor's action as an excellent interim approach but urged the Forest Service to go further by creating a protective buffer zone around the scenic area.[36]

Supervisor Johns knew the Black Hills well, having served years earlier as the first ranger on the consolidated Elk Mountain District (Newcastle, WY). In spring 1974 he and his staff began developing the first travel management plan for the Black Hills National Forest, precipitated by President Richard M. Nixon's executive order, dated February 8, 1972, that federal agencies establish policies and procedures for off-road vehicles on all public lands. The rapid increase in such travel had become a national issue, especially in the Black Hills where the topography made it easy for off-roaders to travel almost everywhere, creating more miles of cross-country tracks than there were of official Forest Service roads and trails.[37]

In the spirit of federal legislation mandating public participation, Supervisor Johns established an ad hoc advisory committee to help formulate a travel plan. He appointed the science teacher Norman Nelson representative of the Black Hills Group of the Sierra Club and Sam Clauson, longtime member of the Izaak Walton League, to represent that organization. Recognizing that the overwhelming majority of committee members opposed road closures and road-less areas,

Nelson pleaded with Johns not to make decisions by headcount. "I sincerely believe," Nelson wrote, "that there is actually only one basic question to be asked in devising a travel plan/off-road vehicle policy: what is best for the land itself."[38] He complained that the Forest Service sought to balance user interests rather than to do what was intrinsically best for the forest.

Calling himself "perhaps a quibbler," Nelson suggested that the Forest Service and the Sierra Club were using the same keywords but giving them different meanings: "As the Forest Service uses the term, 'management' seems to be limited to timber harvest and other manipulative actions: those areas which are planned to be left roadless are spoken of as 'not managed.' I would submit to you that the designation and maintenance of an area as roadless or scenic or wild or what-have-you is as much 'management' of that land as would be the decision to clear-cut it."[39]

In arguing that the Forest Service had failed to comply with President Nixon's order to establish an off-road vehicle policy and that development of such a policy necessarily preceded the development and implementation of a travel plan, Clauson and Nelson proposed that the Forest Service divide the forest into three travel "use zones": (1) 80 percent of the land for off-road travel restricted to secondary roads and other designated roads; (2) 10 percent of the land, off-road unrestricted access; and (3) 10 percent, no motorized vehicles. The Forest Service instead, on August 27, 1974, decided to issue broad "guidelines" as the basis for developing a travel management plan.[40] The next day the Forest Service found a lawsuit at its doorstep, beginning a period of confrontation between the agency and its critics. By 1974 those critics were less spontaneous local citizen activists and more organized representatives of regional and national groups.

As Clauson tells the story, members of the Black Hills Group of the Sierra Club somehow had missed reading the announcement of imminent timbering in the Norbeck Wildlife Preserve. With no time to apply for Sierra Club Foundation funding of their legal action, Clauson and three members of his executive committee pooled their personal finances to hire attorney John D. Wagner. The attorney succeeded in obtaining a temporary restraining order from federal district court on the very day timbering began. Luckily for the group, Judge Andrew W. Bogue appreciated the urgency of their case.[41]

Sam N. Clauson, et al., vs. [Secretary of Agriculture] Earl Butz, et al., filed in United States District Court for the District of South Dakota, Western Division, on August 28, 1974, represented the first legal action to stop timbering in the Black Hills National Forest. In granting the restraining order, Judge Bogue set a hearing date for September 9. At immediate issue was construction or reconstruction to 14-foot and graveled standards of roads in the Iron Creek–Camp Remington area, adjacent to the special-interest scenic area Supervisor Johns had designated.

In defending the decision to seek legal action, Clauson explained that his group had hoped that Johns would allow temporary repair of an existing road to permit removal of timber and then permanently close the area to all vehicular traffic.[42]

The underlying reason for filing the lawsuit appeared to be to obtain wilderness designation. Attorney Wagner had offered a litany of complaints: the Forest Service had failed to prepare an environmental impact statement prior to approval of the Norbeck Wildlife Preserve management plan in August 1973; failed to consult with the South Dakota Department of Game, Fish, and Parks, as required by the National Environmental Protection Act (1970); failed to manage the wildlife preserve, as mandated by the Game Sanctuary Act; and violated the Multiple Use–Sustained Yield Act by not taking into account the multiple resource values. The Black Hills Group asked that the Forest Service be enjoined from carrying out any development in Norbeck until the agency completed the required environmental analysis and, as a consequence, made adjustments to the Norbeck Wildlife Preserve management plan.[43]

Within one month of hearing the case, Judge Bogue arranged a settlement that appeared to support Clauson and the Sierra Club. The Forest Service agreed to conduct an environmental analysis in consultation with the Black Hills Group and its chosen science consultants and to prepare an environmental impact statement for the Norbeck Wildlife Preserve. In the interim, the Forest Service agreed to halt road construction and other management activities except control of beetle epidemics, in which case the Forest Service needed court approval of how and where it would use existing roads in their current conditions. The court would monitor adherence to the agreement until completion of the environmental analysis and approval of the revised Norbeck management plan.[44]

Shortly after settlement of *Clauson v. Butz*, Supervisor James C. Overbay (1975–77) succeeded Supervisor Johns. Overbay represented a new stock of forest supervisors, better versed on multiple uses and in managing public participation in forest planning. Overbay developed the framework and oversaw drafting of the 1977 timber management plan, for which he, his district rangers, and field specialists met on innumerable occasions with constituents, both individuals and groups. Even if required by federal law, their unprecedented openness to public participation was generally welcomed.[45]

Aimed at creating a forest more varied in tree ages, stand sizes, and tree species, the 1977 plan was the first accompanied by formal environmental impact analyses. Based heavily on Boldt's research, the plan set forth the main purposes of timbering: (1) controlling the mountain pine beetle epidemic; (2) improving non-timber forest values, especially scenery, recreation, and wildlife; and (3) building more roads and regulating motorized traffic. Without the third objective, the South Dakota

Department of Game, Fish, and Parks would have initiated legal action on behalf of wildlife protection.[46] The plan identified 84 percent of the forest, or 1.1 million of 1.3 million acres, as suitable for timbering; designated 39,000 acres annually over ten years for thinning and harvesting; and reduced the minimum diameter for commercial timber from 10 inches to 8 inches diameter at breast height (dbh) as a way to encourage loggers to cut smaller trees.[47]

On behalf of the timber industry, Peter Field, a University of California forestry graduate and owner of Cambria Forest Industries, the principal sawmill at Newcastle, Wyoming, welcomed plans to lower road standards and obliterate some roads as "a boon to both loggers and naturalists." Lower standards would lower road-building costs without limiting access, and temporary roads would serve loggers just as well as permanent ones.[48] Carl Newport, then representing the Federal Timber Purchasers Association, suggested that it would be more accurate to state that the Forest Service planned to close some roads and restore the land to a "productive condition." He noted that timbering still remained below the forest's capacity to grow, leaving the Forest Service "with the happy circumstance of deciding, not whether to, but how to increase the [annual] allowable harvest, how to encourage its full utilization and how best to sustain that level forever." His main concern, which he believed had yet to be addressed, was that the Forest Service would encourage operators to expand their businesses but at some future date might be compelled to reduce levels of timbering, catching operators short. The manager of the Custer Lumber Company expressed the fear that the Forest Service, though planning to increase timbering, would not receive the budget needed to prepare additional sales, support pre-commercial thinning, and pay for the construction of more roads—thereby leaving the timber industry in a position of unexpected difficulty.[49]

The plan received mixed reviews from other forest users. Stock growers represented by the Spearfish Grazing Association complained that the Forest Service failed to protect meadowlands from encroachment by ponderosa pine or to eradicate noxious weeds that took over timber cuts, both of which reduced the amount of forage. The Forest Service responded that lack of funds prevented it from conducting remediation.[50] Norm Nelson, on behalf of the Sierra Club, commended the Forest Service for attempting to create a more open forest with a greater mix of species without the appearance of a "tree farm." He agreed that large parts of the forest were overstocked with ponderosa pine, which he ascribed to decades of fire suppression and other Forest Service activities that, in retrospect, had been well-intentioned, though based on false assumptions.[51]

As a result of the planning process Congress had imposed on public land agencies, critics of the Forest Service found ways to question not only specific topical aspects of the management plans but also how well the agency followed the procedures outlined by legislation. With regard to the 1977 plan, Tim Maloney of the Wilderness Society found the Forest Service's description of the process "so confused and entangled in bureaucratic disarrangement as to lead an observer to question its worth." Maloney criticized the use of qualitative rather than quantitative measures of potential environmental impacts, accused the Forest Service of using a timber-only rather than a multiple-use definition of forest health, and expressed dismay at the absence of specifics to monitor implementation of the plan. He perceived a "trust us attitude" conveyed by the Forest Service, which he found contrary to the official policy of welcoming public participation.[52] Challenging the Forest Service for failure to follow its own procedures became a favored tactic to slow down or stop the implementation of approved forest plans.

Supervisor Overbay was succeeded in the Black Hills by Supervisor James Mathers who, as noted earlier, held the reputation of having a more traditional, non-consultative style. Almost immediately, Mathers became engaged in controversy regarding Forest Service roads. Under the 1977 plan, the Forest Service had determined to gate certain Forest Service roads for administrative use only; to obliterate certain other official roads, especially along streams and through draws; and to obliterate still other roads and tracks created by off-road vehicle users. At the same time, the plan called for rebuilding some existing roads and constructing new ones.

After learning of proposed new road construction through the national forest to reach timber in the Hay Draw area, about 10 miles southwest of Custer, inholders Larry and Linda Ventling offered as an alternative an easement on an existing road through a draw on their property, eliminating the need to construct 8 miles of new road around their ranch. Supervisor Mathers declined their offer on grounds that the Ventlings had agreed to allow Forest Service personnel and timber contractors to use their road but not the general public. Mathers viewed such a restriction as a violation of Forest Service policies and proceeded to award the Hay Draw timber sale. In April 1979, when the new road stood at 60 percent completion, the Ventlings, supported by the South Dakota Wildlife Federation and the National Wildlife Federation, obtained a temporary restraining order against further road construction. The order came from the same judge who had presided over *Clauson v. Butz* five years earlier. This time, however, Judge Bogue determined that the Forest Service had complied with all substantive and procedural requirements and denied the request for a permanent injunction. The Ventlings sought relief through the appeals courts but were turned down.[53]

Meanwhile, their case had stirred up local anger and resentment against the Forest Service. At a public meeting in Custer on November 23, 1978, Larry Ventling presented Mathers with a petition signed by 200 individuals opposed to all new road construction in the Black Hills National Forest. He argued with Mathers for an hour, criticizing him for, among other things, listening to his soils engineer rather than to people who had lived in the Black Hills all their lives. For his verbal attack on Mathers, Ventling received loud applause and then walked out of the meeting followed by about half of the attendees. His attorney, Edward Carpenter, remained, stating that his client wanted timber management, too. "What we don't want," he said, "is the Black Hills turned into a super campground for people from Denver." Mathers responded, seemingly exasperated, that for years the State Department of Game, Fish, and Parks had urged the Forest Service not to build roads in draws, and "now you [audience] tell me you want me to leave them there."[54]

Recognizing public opposition, Mathers observed, "Whether I build a work road or a permanent road, I still have the opening through the trees to contend with." To which Sam Clauson retorted: "You missed one alternative. Don't build any roads!" Mathers explained that he was required to make decisions based on Forest Service general policies and on forest-specific management plans regardless of whether his decisions met with popular approval. As the meeting concluded, he did volunteer: "I think the folks here tonight sent me a message. It's that we're replacing some roads and they are saying they don't need to be replaced. We will look into that."[55]

In a paid advertisement that appeared in the same newspaper as the report on the public meeting, Hot Springs–area rancher Frederick J. Stephan excoriated "Forest Service Bureaucrats" for stating "quite clearly that the people of the Black Hills do not have now and never will have a final decision-making voice in the management of these public lands"; Stephan called the Forest Service's attitude and practice "arbitrary, illegal, and definitely anti-democratic." He urged readers to "forget having any more 'meetings'" and instead to "complain loudly and often" to the media and beseech the congressional delegation to stop the "dangerous power" of the Forest Service.[56]

N. G. Pederson of Custer wrote in response, "It is you, Mr. Stephan, who is dangerous . . . with your loud mouth, big money, and scare tactics." Pederson admonished Stephan that "the Forest Service has a tough job trying to make everyone happy. But ads like yours make no one happy."[57] To Stephan's point about citizens having no voice in decision making, *Custer County Chronicle* editor Reda Hansen expressed the view that "we longtime Black Hills residents have a tendency to think we not only own but should have special privileges in using 'our' forest." She reminded readers that, indeed, "we do share our ownership with our fellow citizens of the United States even though they are not here twelve months of the year." Yes, the Forest Service had made mistakes, but it deserved credit for giving everyone a chance to speak: "Let's give Forest Service officials a hand, instead of a boot, at

FIGURE 8.1. Baneberry in Black Elk Wilderness, 2012. Courtesy, Cheryl Mayer, USDA Forest Service, Black Hills National Forest, http://www.ForestPhotol.com.

future meetings and come with constructive comments. One thing is certain—the public meeting is here to stay and it will be better if all of us make it work with wholehearted, positive participation."[58]

In a series of public meetings held in early 1979 in each of the ranger districts, by then consolidated to seven, Supervisor Mathers and his staff solicited suggestions on how best to achieve a net reduction in the number of miles of roads, as set forth in the 1977 plan. They failed, however, to explain that while 900 miles of Forest Service roads would be either closed or gated, the actual number of miles of open roads would increase temporarily to accommodate timber sales. That lack of clarity stirred doubts about the credibility of Forest Service numbers. After Paul Riley, outdoor editor of the *Rapid City Journal*, exposed discrepancies, the Black Hills Group of the Sierra Club unsuccessfully petitioned Secretary of Agriculture Robert S. Bergland to impose a moratorium on new road construction, pending agreement on how to further reduce the number of Forest Service road miles. State Game, Fish, and Parks officials asked Mathers to postpone implementation of the road plan, but he declined the request on the grounds that, after years of talking, it was time for action.[59]

As if he were not embattled enough, Supervisor Mathers received instructions from Washington to seek public comment about nominating road-less areas for possible inclusion in the National Wilderness Preservation System. His staff had identified four road-less areas: Beaver Park south of Sturgis, Inyan Kara south of Sundance, Sand Creek east of Sundance, and Norbeck Wildlife Preserve. Mathers recommended only the Beaver Park area, arguing that Norbeck had already been recognized as a wilderness of sorts. After South Dakota governor William J. Janklow and the South Dakota congressional delegation endorsed Norbeck, Secretary Bergland announced Norbeck as the only road-less area to be recommended for wilderness.[60]

On September 18, 1979, Senators Thomas A. Daschle (D-SD) and George McGovern (D-SD) and Representative James Abdnor (R-SD) introduced legislation to set aside 10,300 acres within the Norbeck Wildlife Preserve as the Black Elk Wilderness. Apparently, Senator McGovern came up with the name to honor the Oglala Sioux holy man made famous through John G. Neihardt's 1930s bestseller, *Black Elk Speaks*. According to legend, Black Elk was standing on Harney Peak when, at age seven, he received his famous vision about the world. Part of a bill to establish wilderness areas in four other states, the Black Elk legislation passed without controversy and was signed by President Jimmy Carter on January 3, 1980.[61] Establishment of the Black Elk Wilderness can be viewed either as a defeat for the Forest Service, which had lost control over part of its own land, or as a victory for public participation in setting forest policies. In either case, the fact of wilderness designation can be viewed as part of a general reassessment of forest uses and forest values that had begun in the 1960s.

NOTES

1. *Custer County Chronicle*, July 28, 1966.

2. Multiple Use–Sustained Yield Act, Public Law 86-517, *US Statutes at Large* 74 (1960): 215.

3. USDA Forest Service, "General Timber Management Statement, Black Hills National Forest, 1961," 14, mimeograph, Black Hills National Forest supervisor's office, Custer, SD (hereafter BHNF).

4. Ibid., 13–14, 17–27.

5. USDA Forest Service, "Timber Management Plan, Black Hills Working Circle, July 1, 1963–June 30, 1973," 4, mimeograph, BHNF.

6. Ibid.; Clifford A. Myers and James L. Van Deusen, "Growth of Immature Stands of Ponderosa Pine in the Black Hills," Rocky Mountain Forest and Ranger Experiment Station Paper 61 (July 1961): 6.

7. "Timber Management Statement, 1961," 18; "Timber Management Plan, 1963–1973," 11; *Custer County Chronicle*, July 12, 1962.

8. Blaine Cook (forest silviculturist and timber planner, Black Hills National Forest), discussion with author, October 2010.

9. *Custer County Chronicle*, April 27, 1961, April 4, 1963, September 9, 1965; Lawrence Rakestraw and Mary Rakestraw, *History of the Willamette National Forest* (Eugene, OR: USDA Forest Service, 1991), at http://www.foresthistory.org/ASPNET/Publications/region /6/willamette/chap6.htm; accessed July 24, 2011; Brian G. Krick, "Mountain Farmers: Supervisors of the Black Hills National Forest, 1898–1995 (MA thesis, University of South Dakota, Vermillion, 2001), 49.

10. *Custer County Chronicle*, March 1 and 29, 1962, December 19, 1968, November 14, 1984.

11. Wilderness Act, Public Law 88–577, *US Statutes at Large* 78 (1964): 890–91.

12. Endangered Species Act, Public Law 92–205, *US Statutes at Large* 87 (1973): 884–903.

13. National Environmental Protection Act, Public Law 91–190, *US Statutes at Large* 83 (1970): 852–56.

14. *Custer County Chronicle*, March 27, 1969.

15. Ibid., February 19, 1970.

16. Ibid., May 7, 1970.

17. Ibid., May 14, 1970.

18. Ibid., May 21, 1970.

19. Samuel N. Clauson, discussion with author, November 2010.

20. Ibid.; Norman Eugene Nelson obituary, April 15, 2009, copy, Clauson personal communication, Clauson's possession.

21. *Custer County Chronicle*, May 1, 1969.

22. John Taliaferro, *Great White Fathers: The Story of the Obsessive Quest to Create Mount Rushmore* (New York: Public Affairs, 2002), 348–51.

23. Ibid., 357.

24. *Custer County Chronicle*, February 1, 8, and 15, 1973.

25. Transcript of interview with Wendy Milner Herrett by Jacqueline S. Reinier, Salem, Oregon, June 13–15, 2000, US Forest Service Collection, Forest History Society, http://www .foresthistory.org/Research/Herrett%20final.pdf; accessed April 4, 2011.

26. *Custer County Chronicle*, April 26, June 7, December 27, 1979.

27. Ibid., June 11, August 27, 1981.

28. National Forest Management Act, Public Law 94–588, *US Statutes at Large* 90 (1976): 2957–58; Samuel P. Hays, *Wars in the Woods: The Rise of Ecological Forestry in America* (Pittsburgh: University of Pittsburgh Press, 2007), 16–19; W. Rupert Cutler, ed., *A Conservationist's Guide to National Forest Planning* (Washington, DC: Wilderness Society, 1981).

29. *Hill City Prevailer*, March 18, 1977, reprinted in *Custer County Chronicle*, April 8, 1978; Blaine Cook, discussion with author, November 2009.

30. Charles E. Boldt and James L. Van Deusen, "Silviculture of Ponderosa Pine in the Black Hills: The Status of Our Knowledge," USDA Forest Service Research Paper RM–124 (June 1974).

31. Ibid., 43.

32. E. M. Hornibrook, "A Modified Tree Classification for Use in Growth Studies and Timber Marking in Black Hills Ponderosa Pine," *Journal of Forestry* 37, no. 6 (June 1939): 486–88; see also Clifford A. Myers and James L. Van Deusen, "Site Index of Ponderosa Pine in the Black Hills from Soil and Topography," *Journal of Forestry* 58, no. 7 (July 1960): 548–55.

33. Boldt and Van Deusen, "Silviculture of Ponderosa Pine," 23–26.

34. Ibid., 32–33.

35. Ibid., 43.

36. "More Protection Sought for Harney Peak Area," *Rapid City Journal*, April 30, 1974, 2.

37. David S. Johns to district rangers, Custer, January 10, 1974, copy, Clauson personal communication.

38. Norman E. Nelson to US Forest Service travel plan team, Rapid City, June 2, 1974, copy, Clauson personal communication.

39. Ibid.

40. Samuel N. Clauson to US Forest Service travel plan team, Rapid City, June 5, 1974, copy, Clauson personal files; proposed "Black Hills National Forest Travel Guidelines," August 27, 1974, copy, Clauson personal files.

41. Clauson, discussion with author, November 2010.

42. *Rapid City Guide*, September 5, 1974, 5.

43. *Rapid City Journal*, September 9, 1974, copy, Clauson personal files.

44. Minutes, Black Hills Group, Rocky Mountain Chapter, Sierra Club, October 17, 1975, copy, Clauson personal files; Stipulation CIV 74–5043, *Clausen v. Butz*, United States District Court for the District of South Dakota, Western Division, October 14, 1974, copy, Clauson personal communication; John D. Wagner statement, September 26, 1974, copy, Clauson personal communication.

45. *Custer County Chronicle*, September 25, 1975; USDA Forest Service, *Final Environmental Statement for Timber Management Plan for the Black Hills National Forest* (Custer, SD: US Forest Service, March 1977), 179–80.

46. "Timber Management Plan of 1977," 9–10, 24.

47. *Custer County Chronicle*, April 15, 1976; "Timber Management Plan of 1977," 7.

48. *Final Environmental Statement* [1977], 134.

49. Carl A. Newport to Paul Ehinger, Hines Lumber Company, Portland, Oregon, June 9, 1976, in ibid., 205; Walter W. Black to James C. Overbay, Custer, South Dakota, June 11, 1976, in ibid., 154.

50. Wesley W. Thompson to James C. Overbay, Spearfish, South Dakota, June 1, 1976, in ibid., 117.

51. Norman E. Nelson to Craig W. Rupp [regional forester], Rapid City, South Dakota, June 5, 1976, in ibid., 136.

52. Tim Maloney to Craig W. Rupp, Denver, Colorado, May 24, 1956, in ibid., 108–14.

53. *Larry Ventling and Linda Ventling v. [Secretary of Agriculture] Bob Bergland*, decision memorandum, September 29, 1979, copy, at http://www.leagle.com/decision/197965 3479Supp174_1630.xml/VENTLING%20v.%20BERGLAND; accessed December 2010.

54. *Custer County Chronicle*, November 23, 1978.

55. Ibid.

56. Ibid., November 30, 1978.

57. N. G. Pederson to Editor, ibid.

58. Editorial, ibid., December 7, 1978.

59. *Custer County Chronicle*, February 22, March 8, 1979.

60. Ibid., January 11, April 19, 1979; see also Robert Wellman Campbell, "Wishlist: Wilderness Endgame in the Black Hills National Forest," *Great Plains Quarterly* 30, no. 4 (Fall 2010): 289–98.

61. An Act to Designate Certain National Forest System Lands . . . for Inclusion in the National Wilderness Preservation System, Public Law 96–560, section 103, *US Statutes at Large* 94 (1980): 3268.

9

Perils of Accommodation

In an editorial titled "Forest Service Deserves Better Treatment from Black Hills Citizens," *Custer County Chronicle*'s Reda Hansen lamented the angry public comments that, she believed, had gone far beyond the issue of that new road near the Ventling ranch: ranchers deplored roads crossing their properties, inholders protested timbering near their houses, hikers complained about damaged trails, loggers objected to clearing slash, off-road vehicle enthusiasts opposed road closures, skeptics argued that such roads would not remain closed, and hunters complained about disturbances to wildlife. "Now, all [Supervisor James] Mathers and his staff have to do," she wrote, "is determine how the forests are going to be used for logging, recreation vehicles, conservationists, ranchers, cabin owners, hikers, hunters, and tourists."[1]

That is precisely what Mathers and his staff sought to accomplish by preparing, writing, and implementing the 1983 *Land and Resource Management Plan*.[2] Long regarded as the first managed national forest in the nation, the Black Hills National Forest now gained the reputation as the first national forest in the nation to complete a comprehensive management plan. Arguably, preparing and writing plans is easier and less contentious than executing them or measuring their results. Nonetheless, this plan indicated the public's ever-increasing interest in the multiplicity of forest values and forest uses and the efforts of the Forest Service to reconcile those uses to the principal task of managing for commercial timbering.

The sheer volume and specificity of work mandated by the US Congress to prepare forest plans, not to mention their implementation, led to necessary growth in

DOI: 10.5876/9781607322993.c009

the number of staff, temporarily located in office space throughout Custer. Since the 1960s, the Forest Service had expressed the wish to move the supervisor's office to Rapid City to gain more office and warehouse space, but Custer business leaders secured congressional support to keep forest headquarters in their community. Senators George McGovern (D-SD) and Karl Mundt (R-SD) successfully obtained planning monies, followed by earmarks set aside for construction of a new headquarters complex. Located at the north edge of Custer, it was dedicated in 1980.[3]

Bipartisan support for the new headquarters obscured differences in approach by successive national administrations that, in turn, affected management of the national forests. In the wake of passage of the Wilderness Act, road-less area reviews and evaluations began during President Lyndon Johnson's term and resumed during President Jimmy Carter's term. Four sites in the Black Hills were inventoried as road-less areas, though none were recommended at the time for wilderness designation. Beginning in 1982, the administration of President Ronald Reagan reversed course by requiring federal agencies to inventory and classify all federal land for possible disposal, with proceeds from sales intended to help retire the national debt. In the Black Hills, prospective lands for sale included cabin sites and small plots of land surrounded by private property through which there was no public access. Supervisor Mathers expressed the view that only a few acres would fall into the category of further study for possible disposal.[4]

In 1986 the Forest Service announced its intention to dispose of approximately 25 acres, including 1,000 feet along Rapid Creek near Hisega, an early group of cabins about 6 miles west of Rapid City. By selling the acreage to established local property owners, the Forest Service meant to shed itself of maintenance costs and retain perpetual easement for public access. Because of the historic popularity of the area and latent suspicion of the Forest Service, public opposition materialized immediately, taken up by the congressional delegation under pressure from two recreational fishing groups and the South Dakota Department of Game, Fish, and Parks. Senator Thomas Daschle and Supervisor Mathers organized a meeting to hear public comments in February 1987; a few weeks later, Mathers announced that the Forest Service had dropped plans to dispose of that acreage.[5]

The Reagan administration also favored user fees. With relatively little opposition, the Black Hills National Forest had assessed fees for some recreation areas since the mid-1960s, but such was not the case for collecting firewood. In November 1986 Mathers announced that the Forest Service would begin charging a flat fee for up to five cords of firewood. He saw permitting as a way to manage the increasing demand for firewood. Fee income would be used to pay for noncommercial thinning (cuttings available for firewood), to help patrol the forest against theft of trees, and to restore areas damaged by illegal activities. Once again, Senator Daschle sided with the opposition, arguing that fees would cause hardship to low-income families, revenues would be diverted to unrelated programs, and permitting would be unenforceable since cutting on private and state land required no permits. Again, the Forest Service withdrew its plan.[6]

Whether measuring in cords of firewood, board feet of timber, animal units of forage, acre-feet of water, or numbers of recreational visitor days, the Forest Service had consistently emphasized production—that is, outputs. Thus the change in title, from *Timber Management Plan* to *Land and Resource Management Plan*, reflected a new policy that "no resource output is emphasized to the extent that standards for another resource are violated."[7] The 1983 plan appeared far more compatible with the Multiple Use–Sustained Yield Act than had earlier plans.

Although we have long abandoned the expectation that our government documents be literary masterpieces, it remains unfortunate that so often those documents lack clarity and, perhaps unavoidably, readability. Forest plans offer no exception, even though their intended audiences, in addition to agency staff, include current and prospective forest users and the general public. To meet requirements set forth by Congress in the National Forest Management Act of 1976, the Black Hills National Forest *Land and Resource Management Plan,* with its accompanying environmental impact statement, took up more than 500 pages, not including appendixes and maps.

It would be fair to state that the amount of time and effort invested in the preparation of the 1983 forest plan was immense, and it was eminently understandable that timber operators would feel restrained by what they perceived to be bureaucratic roadblocks and that citizen groups would view the plan as government double-speak. Longtime Forest Service employees, especially district rangers and silviculturists, used the term *analysis paralysis* to describe the operational condition of their agency since the early 1980s. The exponential increase in planning documents, related research reports, procedural manuals, and subsequent legal briefs lends credence to that term.

In April 1979 Supervisor Mathers had announced the Forest Service's decision to prepare a new plan—two years after approval of the last timber management plan. Headed by Mathers, the new planning team consisted of more than forty members, all either current or former Forest Service employees: roughly one-third from forest headquarters, one-third from district ranger offices, and one-third from outside the Black Hills National Forest. By 1979 headquarters staff—in addition to administrative officers, support staff, silviculturists, and engineers—included the so-called ologists: archaeologists, biologists, hydrologists, landscape architects, as well as wildlife, recreation, and other specialists.[8] Members of the planning team represented the various types of forest resources and uses; although comprehensive,

FIGURE 9.1. "Ologist" in the field: archaeological research, 1999. Courtesy, Gary Chancey, USDA Forest Service, Black Hills National Forest, http://www.ForestPhoto.com.

the plan suggested less focus on a shared purpose than on accommodating the particular specialties of individual team members.

If team members shared anything, it was the computer software the Forest Service had begun to use as its principal planning tool, determining how best to manage specific forest units for desired outputs. Universally acknowledged as difficult to operate, even by experienced users, FORPLAN could handle an enormous amount of information and thus generate a large number of alternative management practices and activities. Like most computer programs, FORPLAN allowed users to define characteristics and boundaries and thereby justify preconceived (often "political") notions of preferred results. It is generally acknowledged that FORPLAN emphasized timber production, which is why a different software planning tool eventually came into use that was more compatible with multiple uses.[9]

From individuals and organizations, the Forest Service received more than 150 written comments on the plan's supplementary environmental analyses. During the three-month period of public comment, members of the planning team held thirty-two public meetings attended by 250 individuals. In addition, team members traveled to the Pine Ridge Reservation to solicit comments from tribal leaders. After the public comment period ended, team members took more time with special-interest groups, seeking to resolve disagreements over specific issues prior to publication of the draft plan and thus reduce the chances of opposition through the courts.[10]

Once quoted as saying "you can argue with me all you want and you won't change my mind,"[11] Supervisor Mathers acknowledged that comments from the public "showed a remarkable range of interests and contained a number of good suggestions for improving the plan."[12] Still, some critics complained that the Forest Service had structured opportunities for public participation in such a way as to minimize the number of comments. In his defense, Mathers noted correctly that development of forest plans rested on four legs: federal law, technical information, professional judgment, and public opinion—with the last coming into play only when there was ambivalence over the meaning of any of the first three. The Forest Service welcomed factual corrections but did not count votes; the majority of public comments expressed personal preferences, the most difficult to reconcile with the first three legs.[13]

Everyone agreed that the ultimate goal was to create and maintain a healthy forest. To some, that meant restoring the forest to pre-settlement conditions, even if they were uncertain what those conditions might have been or whether they could be replicated. To others, obtaining a healthy forest meant leaving the forest to heal itself. The Forest Service argued that the forest, irrevocably changed by humans, required "vegetative manipulation" to regain and maintain a condition of health and that timbering remained the most effective vehicle to achieve that goal. Moreover, timbering supported local employment and provided revenue to local governments.[14]

Between 1930 and 1980, the population of the Black Hills area had doubled, to 136,000, as a result of the development of Rapid City as a regional center, the expansion of tourism in the Black Hills, and energy development in the nearby Powder River Basin. Although scenery and recreational opportunities had helped attract many new residents, the Forest Service referred to local opinion surveys in which the public, if faced with a choice, favored economic growth over environmental protection.[15] Yet the most frequent topics of concern expressed by the public during the planning period had to do with livestock grazing, wildlife habitat, clear-cutting, road closures, logging on steep slopes, and control of surface mining operations—all of which suggested a degree of interest in environmental protection.[16]

Furthermore, federal law required that special attention in planning be given to the protection of threatened or endangered species. Through environmental analysis, scientists had concluded that at one time the peregrine falcon had nested in the Black Hills, but no nesting pairs were found; the bald eagle wintered but did not nest in the Black Hills; and the black-footed ferret may have inhabited a single prairie dog colony. As to threatened or endangered plant species, researchers had found none.[17]

Consistent with the notion of multiple uses, the 1983 plan identified seven forest resources—minerals, timber, water, range, recreation, fish and wildlife, wilderness—and four "support elements" required to maximize resource outputs: good soils, disease control, fire protection, and a road network. As to minerals, the General Mining Act of 1872 had granted prospectors and miners the right to enter public lands to search for and extract minerals. Because the Forest Service held jurisdiction only over the surface, it could recommend actions to manage access but could not deny subsurface mine permits. By the early 1980s virtually all subsurface mining in the Black Hills had ceased, leaving the Forest Service with the challenge of ensuring rehabilitation of disturbed areas. As to surface mines, the Forest Service could withdraw mine permits if adjacent forest resources became adversely affected; apparently, that never happened in the Black Hills. Insignificant revenues accrued to the Forest Service from mine operations.[18]

Timbering continued to provide the single largest piece of revenue, supporting about 25 percent of the total operating budget; timber management consumed more than half of the budget. Forest Service financial statements, as well as the agency's accounting system, invited diverse interpretations, making it difficult to attribute which expenses properly belonged to timber management; they also stirred up controversy over below-cost timber sales when costs for preparing sales, constructing roads, and rehabilitating stands exceeded cash revenues from those sales. A 1983 Forest Service cash flow study concluded that the Black Hills National Forest had the greatest negative cash flow of any US national forest but pointed out that costs needed to be compared with all public benefits resulting from timbering, not simply balanced against cash revenues from timber sales. Such reasoning, in vogue at least since the 1960s, led Senator William Proxmire (D-WI) to famously muse, "The Forest Service never met a number it could not twist."[19]

In 1983 the Forest Service listed 1,071,960 acres, or 87 percent, of a total of 1,235,780 acres as suitable for timbering and estimated that 380,000 acres, or 36 percent, needed to be thinned. That estimate presumed the generally accepted growing stock level of 80 square feet of basal area per acre. While the 1977 timber management plan had identified an accumulation of 25,623 acres for pre-commercial thinning, by 1983 the accumulation had increased to nearly 120,000 acres. To catch up, the 1983 plan called for 200,000 acres to be thinned during the period 1983–92.[20]

Under the new plan, the Forest Service projected optimal cutting of commercial timber at 420 million cubic feet for the decade, which amounted to about 180 million board feet per year; but it set a sale limit of 380 million cubic feet, or about 160 million board feet per year, presumably to account for losses caused by fire and insect epidemics. The Forest Service set the annual allowable sale quantity at 34.2 million cubic feet (148.3 million board feet), only slightly higher than the 1977 plan though less than the estimated local mill capacity of 177 million board feet.[21] First used in the National Forest Management Act of 1976, the term *allowable sale quantity*, like the previous term *allowable cut*, would be interpreted in markedly different ways, ranging from a legal obligation or "duty" to cut a certain amount, generally favored by the timber industry, to a "ceiling" beyond which nothing more could be cut, favored by other interests. In addition, Congress continued to set timber "targets" as part of the Forest Service's annual budget. All of this left the agency's silviculturists in the unenviable position of making management recommendations fraught with political, economic, and ecological implications.[22]

Recall that, next to the conservative use of timber, watershed protection was the principal reason for creating the forest reserves. No major river begins in the Black Hills, but the national forest lands did produce usable water for the region. The 1983 plan sought to increase water yields by up to 20 percent to meet expected growth in demand for domestic as well as commercial and, to a lesser extent, industrial uses. As a way to increase yields, the plan did project some small clear-cuts, "two to seven tree heights in size and oriented so the winds will deposit snow in the openings." After trees took over those sites, similar clear-cuts would be made elsewhere. The Forest Service estimated that for the year 1980, surface water from the Black Hills amounted to roughly 225,000 acre-feet, some of which ended up in the Angostura (Cheyenne River) and Belle Fourche Reservoirs.[23]

As to use of rangelands, some stock farms still existed in and around the Black Hills. For the 1980 season, the Forest Service had issued 303 permits for 29,600 head of cattle and 300 sheep to graze on 119 different allotments. That added up to about 128,000 animal unit months (AUMs), compared with 154,000 AUMs in 1950 and 281,400 AUMs in 1930. The 1983 plan identified enough suitable forage to support 478,600 AUMs and estimated that thinning would improve grass and forb growth. Only 7,000 acres of meadows and grasslands were identified as in poor or very poor condition, for which the agency recommended fewer cattle and fencing water sources.[24]

Supervisor Mathers did not please the Black Hills Grazing Advisory Board when he notified ranchers that the Forest Service would likely require that all livestock on forest land be ear-tagged. He noted that his rangers had found seven cases of stray or illegally placed livestock in 1978; that number had increased to sixty in 1982. At the time, the only way the Forest Service could check on permitted numbers was for ranchers to round up their cattle for counting. In January 1983 about seventy-five ranchers met with Forest Service staff in Custer, where they voiced their objection to the cost of tags, the time required to affix them, and their fear that the tagging process would cause the animals to lose weight and thereby reduce profits. Arguing that cattle strayed because recreationists left gates open, one rancher urged the Forest Service to "go after them. Put a tag in their ear." Fearing imposition of a "national mandate," another rancher urged the Forest Service to handle the issue locally. Since some ranchers already used tags and to address some of their objections, Supervisor Mathers agreed to allow all ranchers to use their own color-coded tags.[25]

At the time Mathers reached an accommodation with ranchers, the number of recreational users of the Black Hills National Forest had increased to an estimated 2 million recreation visitor days, of which about half represented travelers driving through the national forest. Once again, as a measure of output, one recreation visitor day represented one visitor for twelve hours or twelve visitors for one hour or an equivalent combination, continuous or intermittent. The Forest Service extrapolated its estimates from visitors passing through turnstiles at Mount Rushmore National Memorial (1.3 million in 1980), Wind Cave National Park, Devils Tower and Jewel Cave National Monuments, and Custer State Park.[26]

Of 70 developed recreation sites within the national forest in the early 1980s, most were picnic grounds and campgrounds (627 units). In addition, there were 64 campgrounds (5,036 units) on private land, as well as campgrounds at Custer State Park (480 units) and Wind Cave National Park (100 units), for a total of 6,243 units, enough for 25,000 campers. The greatest density of developed sites occurred around the artificial lakes in the national forest and included beaches for swimmers and boat ramps. Indeed, the use of developed sites substantially exceeded their "total maximum managed capacity" of 380,000 recreation visitor days annually. Local Forest Service planners saw no possibility of meeting the Region 2 objective of more than doubling use of developed sites by 1995. Beyond developed sites, planners somehow estimated the potential for increases in dispersed recreation to 113 million recreation visitor days, a fantastic number considering escalating conflicts between motorized and non-motorized recreationists and increasing concern for protection of fish and wildlife.[27]

With more hunting pressure, the South Dakota and Wyoming wildlife agencies persuaded the Forest Service to expand the capacity of critical winter range for deer, from about 40,000 head to 65,000 head; a summer 1980 census had estimated that there were 62,000 deer in the Black Hills. To improve wildlife habitat, the 1983 plan called for cutting mature aspen-birch stands to effect regeneration, continuing pre-commercial thinning, and allowing limited clear-cutting. In addition, the Forest Service sought to ensure that 2,000 dead trees be left standing for every 1,000 acres, that livestock be fenced out of certain riparian areas, and that damaged stream banks be stabilized with walls of loose stone, or riprap.[28]

Perhaps the least understood aspect of wildlife habitat concerned "old-growth" stands. The Forest Service aimed to maintain old-growth conditions on 5 percent of ponderosa pine and 75 percent of oak stands. Silviculturists generally viewed old-growth stands as consisting of trees that were large for their species and locations, often over-mature or decadent, combined with trees of a variety of sizes, numerous large snags, and layers of forest canopy. Old-growth stands were often confused with never-timbered stands, characteristic of wilderness; thus silviculturists preferred the term *late successional*, meaning fully grown, mature trees.[29]

While projecting that the demand for wilderness experiences would far exceed what the Black Elk Wilderness could provide, the 1983 plan omitted recommendations for wilderness expansion on the grounds that the land surrounding Black Elk Wilderness did not meet the criteria for wilderness classification; neither did any other part of the forest. The Forest Service provided itself with some flexibility, however, by deciding to postpone management activities within the four areas previously identified as road-less, pending congressional action or the Forest Service's own reassessment.[30]

To improve the soil, reduce insect epidemics, and generally enhance the support elements that made possible the utmost use of forest resources, the 1983 plan allowed for controlled or prescribed burning. The deliberate use of fire as a management tool had been advocated by professionals in the Forest Service since the 1950s. They favored reducing the risk of catastrophic fires by mimicking what they considered normal fire routine. Beginning in the Southwest, some rangers wanted to allow lightning-caused fires to burn to reduce fuel accumulations; forest supervisors declined their requests as contrary to the out by 10:00 a.m. policy that called for the immediate control of all wildfires.[31] In the late 1970s, after the Forest Service abandoned that policy, Supervisor Mathers and his staff did experiment with letting certain wildfires burn that posed no threat to life or property and no unacceptable loss of forest resources.[32]

FIGURE 9.2. Prescribed burn, 2012. Courtesy, Beth Doten, USDA Forest Service, Black Hills National Forest, http://www.ForestPhoto.com.

The first prescribed burn occurred in fall 1978 on 480 acres in the Pleasant Valley, south of Custer. The aim was to improve livestock forage by eliminating young ponderosa pine encroaching on meadows and grasslands. In early 1979 the group followed with additional burns set in 1–10-acre plots over 200 acres in that same area, this time to increase winter forage for wildlife; in winter 1982–83 they burned another 1,200 acres to lower risks of wildfires near homes, create nutrient-rich seedbeds for quicker regeneration, and improve appearances along roads and around recreation areas.[33]

Prescribed burns, however, proved to be major operations, costly in personnel as well as in supplies and equipment. On February 23, 1983, the Forest Service scheduled a burn over 438 acres southwest of Pringle. Two weeks prior to that date, agency staff had notified area ranchers, homeowners, local law enforcement officials, and the news media. Staff set up a temporary weather station to take climatological readings to aid in determining the best combination of tactics to conduct the burn safely and successfully. On the appointed day, a burn crew did a small test burn, determined that fires needed to be set from south to north, and continued in a line to ignite groundcover and saplings, using kerosene drip torches. Another crew stood by with shovels and pumper trucks in case flames went high enough to endanger power lines or far enough to reach private land. The entire Forest Service operation lasted about four hours.[34]

In the 1983 plan, the Forest Service projected that 765 acres would burn annually on average, requiring an annual fire-fighting budget of $763,000 (about $1.8 million in 2010 dollars). The projection seemed to be based on averaging acres burned over the preceding ten to twelve years and did not account for the agency's increasingly critical role in protecting inholdings. Much of the private land immediately adjacent to the national forest contained buildings and other high-value properties. In early 1984 Supervisor Mathers established the Black Hills Forest Fire Advisory Group, consisting of two representatives from each county volunteer fire department (except Crook County), one representative from the South Dakota Division of Forestry (Department of Game, Fish, and Parks), and one representative from the Forest Service. The group's primary reason-for-being was to critique fire fighting over the prior year in an effort to make improvements for the coming year. At the time, no one could have imagined the dramatic increase in catastrophic fires and insect epidemics beginning in the late 1990s.[35]

To be sure, the Forest Service aimed to reach fires quickly and to contain them to fewer than 10 acres, except in the Black Elk Wilderness and Inyan Kara areas where fires were left to burn. As preventative measures, the Forest Service required loggers to cut up and scatter slash in low-risk, low-value areas and completely remove slash in high-risk, high-value areas. In addition, the agency sought to maintain firebreaks wide enough to keep fires below specified heat intensity levels, measured in BTUs. Managing fire, like all other forest activities, depended on a network of firebreaks and roads that provided access to all except the most remote areas.[36]

In preparation for the 1983 plan, the Forest Service estimated the total number of road miles within the national forest at between 6,000 and 8,000. Of that number, the agency counted 3,576 miles as official Forest Development Roads, of which about one-third were classified as arterial, usable by automobiles and logging trucks; one-third as year-round service roads for logging and pickup trucks; and most of the remaining roads as usable by logging and pickup trucks during dry seasons only. Because of ever-expanding residential development on private property within national forest boundaries, many arterial roads carried primarily non-forest traffic and served as mail and school bus routes. The Forest Service attempted, without success, to shift jurisdiction over those roads to the counties, which already maintained about 700 miles of county roads within the national forest boundary. In response to public pressure, the 1983 plan called for reduction in overall Forest Service road mileage by about 20 percent, even though the agency at the time planned to build new roads.[37] By seeking to accommodate most forest users most

FIGURE 9.3. Fighting forest fire, 1976. Courtesy, USDA Forest Service, Black Hills National Forest, http://www.ForestPhoto.com.

of the time, the agency still came under criticism from four-wheelers who wanted unimproved roads to remain unimproved, wildlife enthusiasts who sought more road closures, loggers who requested permission to operate larger trucks carrying heavier loads, and inholders who demanded direct rights-of-way over national forest lands—but only for themselves.

NOTES

1. *Custer County Chronicle*, December 7, 1978.

2. USDA Forest Service, Black Hills National Forest, *Land and Resource Management Plan, Black Hills National Forest* (Custer, SD: US Forest Service, 1983) (hereafter *1983 Plan*).

3. Ibid., April 7 and 28, September 5, 1966, February 12, 1970, June 26, 1980.

4. Ibid., December 16, 1982, March 24, 1983.

5. Ibid., January 28, February 11, March 4, 1987.

6. Ibid., April 22, 1965, November 26, December 31, 1986.

7. *1983 Plan*, II: 27.

8. USDA Forest Service, Black Hills National Forest, *Final Environmental Impact Statement for the Black Hills National Forest Land and Resources Management Plan* (Custer, SD: US Forest Service, 1983) (hereafter *1983 FEIS*), V: 1–8.

9. Roger A. Sedjo, "FORPLAN: An Evaluation of a Forest Planning Tool—a Summary," in Thomas W. Hoekstra, A. A. Dyer, and Dennis LeMaster, eds., FORPLAN: *An Evaluation of a Forest Planning Tool*, Rocky Mountain Forest and Range Experiment Station General Technical Report RM–140 (April 1987): 161–62.

10. *1983 FEIS*, VI: 1.

11. *Custer County Chronicle*, May 13, 1982.

12. Ibid., March 4, 1982.

13. *1983 FEIS*, VI: 2, 15.

14. *1983 Plan*, i–ii. See also Nancy Langston, *Forest Dreams, Forest Nightmares: The Paradox of Old Growth in the Inland West* (Seattle: University of Washington Press, 1995), 278–80.

15. *1983 Plan*, II: 6.

16. *Custer County Chronicle*, March 4, 1982.

17. *1983 Plan*, II: 3.

18. Ibid., 31.

19. Quoted in Paul W. Hirt, *A Conspiracy of Optimism: Management of the National Forests since World War II* (Lincoln: University of Nebraska Press, 1994), 281. See also Randal O'Toole, *Reforming the Forest Service* (Washington, DC: Island, 1988), 33–34.

20. *1983 FEIS*, III: 9, 30, 32, appendix Q: 4.i.

21. *1983 Plan*, II: 16, III: 6.

22. Greg Brown, Jay O'Laughlin, and Charles C. Harris, "Allowable Sale Quantity (ASQ) of Timber as a Focal Point in National Forest Management," *Natural Resources Journal* 33 (Summer 1993): 573.

23. *1983 Plan*, II: 29 (source of quotes); *1983 FEIS*, III: 25–27.

24. *1983 Plan*, II: 15; *1983 FEIS*, III: 28–29. In 1978, federal land managers introduced the animal unit month as a measure of carrying capacity. One AUM represents the amount of forage required by a 1,000-pound cow or equivalent for one month.

25. *Custer County Chronicle*, February 3 (source of the quotation), March 10, 1983.

26. *1983 Plan*, II: 20; http://www.nps.gov/moru/parkmgmt/statistics.htm; accessed December 23, 2010; Richard L. Hudson (recreation program manager, Black Hills National Forest), personal communication, January 2011.

27. *1983 FEIS*, III: 49–51.

28. Ibid., xx; *1983 Plan*, II: 17, 19, 30.

29. *1983 Plan*, II: 17, 19, 30; *1983 FEIS*, xx; Merrill R. Kaufmann, William H. Moir, and William W. Covington, "Old-Growth Forests: What Do We Know about Their Ecology and Their Management in the Southwest and Rocky Mountain Regions," in Merrill R.

Kaufmann, William H. Moir, and Richard L. Bassett, eds., *Old-Growth Forests in the Southwest and Rocky Mountain Regions: Proceedings of a Workshop,* USDA Forest Service General Technical Report GTR-RM–213 (1992): 4–5.

   30. *1983 Plan*, II: 20, 36.

   31. Jay H. Cravens, "Who Is the Guilty Party?" Canadian Institute of Forestry/ Society of American Foresters Convention, Edmonton, Alberta, October 5, 2004, typescript, 1.

   32. *Custer County Chronicle*, October 12, 1978.

   33. Ibid., September 28, 1978, March 1, 1979, September 30, 1982.

   34. Ibid., March 3, 1983.

   35. *1983 Plan*, II: 23, appendix I: 1; *Custer County Chronicle*, April 5, 1984.

   36. *1983 FEIS*, III: 56–57.

   37. Ibid., 59; *1983 Plan*, II: 24.

10

Forestry and Forest Industry

In making his case for a constant supply of federal timber, Jim D. Neiman of Hulett reminded members of a congressional subcommittee in 2009 that the timber industry was indispensable to achieving Forest Service planning goals. With specific reference to intermingling land ownership in the Black Hills, he made the additional argument that by obtaining 75 percent of its saw-timber from the Black Hills National Forest, Neiman Enterprises could use economy of scale to manage smaller stands for private landowners, an argument Gifford Pinchot would have appreciated. Neiman also envisioned changes in forestry as the result of better science and broader public understanding of forest values.[1]

Within the decade before Neiman's testimony, the Black Hills National Forest had experienced the most catastrophic fires in its history. Not surprisingly, Neiman expressed the view that compared to the costs of fire fighting and stand restoration, "preventative management is a bargain." He gave the example of a recent timber sale near Rapid City specifically meant to reduce fire risks, estimating the net cost to the Forest Service at $260 per acre compared to $900 per acre for fire fighting and stand restoration for a recent 4,000-acre wildfire.[2]

Changes in habits of mind within the timber industry, or at least changes in its political strategy, had not occurred quickly. Following passage of prescriptive federal legislation in the 1960s and 1970s and in the wake of burgeoning public support for non-timbering interests, the local timber industry formally organized. Meeting at the cabin of Peter Field, a Newcastle sawmill operator, owners

DOI: 10.5876/9781607322993.c010

established the Black Hills Forest Resource Association, electing Field as the first president and hiring Lloyd Stahl, longtime timber industry advocate, as the first paid employee.[3]

Stahl represented association members in direct talks with Forest Service staff and spoke on their behalf at public meetings. Shortly after his arrival in the Black Hills, such an event took place in Hill City attended by about 100 people, including South Dakota governor William J. Janklow and the congressional delegation. Stahl blamed local Forest Service rules and regulations for the timber industry's inability to compete successfully against operators from other regions of the nation. In particular, Stahl criticized Supervisor James Mathers for his decision to lower weight limits on logging trucks and accused him of sending an "army of administrators" to prowl Forest Service roads in search of violators. Mathers defended his position, arguing that Forest Service roads had not been built to accommodate heavier trucks and that lower limits would decrease road maintenance costs; road budgets had been cut as part of an economizing effort. The Black Hills Forest Resource Association failed in its efforts to get the chief forester to override Mathers's decision on truck weights.[4]

Stahl acknowledged that recent losses of paper companies as pulpwood customers, combined with declines in housing construction, had dealt severe blows to his industry. He criticized the Forest Service for exacerbating the situation by keeping prices of standing timber inordinately high to cover, in his opinion, the unnecessary costs of supporting environmental staff positions such as wildlife biologists, soil specialists, and archaeologists. The South Dakota congressional delegation gave the impression that it agreed with Stahl's analysis.[5]

As the post–World War II boom ebbed, the timber industry had experienced the consolidation and closing of smaller sawmills. Those operators who remained made major investments in new technology to adjust to workforce changes and remain competitive. By the 1960s, the Warren-Lamb Lumber Company had ceased timber operations. Homestake Mining Company operated its Spearfish sawmill at near capacity by purchasing rough lumber from three smaller operators: Patrick McLaughlin of Spearfish, James. S. Neiman of Hulett, and Walter Nicholson of Sundance. These independent operators provided Homestake with larger logs than the company could cut on its own property. As the need for mine timbers declined, the company became less dependent on forest products and transferred its entire timber operation to a separately managed subsidiary, Homestake Forest Products Company. In 1980 a devastating fire at the Spearfish sawmill took the lives of two employees and destroyed the entire facility. That fire, combined with persistent efforts to unionize mill workers, convinced the Homestake governing board to leave the timber business.[6]

In 1981 Pope and Talbot, Inc., headquartered in Portland, Oregon, purchased Homestake Forest Products Company, including the right to timber approximately 60,000 acres of Homestake's property in South Dakota and Wyoming. Started in eastern Maine in 1849 by brothers William and Frederick Talbot and their friend Andrew Pope, the company became a major, publicly traded forest products company, operating sawmills in British Columbia, Oregon, and South Dakota. By purchasing Peter Field's sawmill at Newcastle, Pope and Talbot became the largest sawmill operator in the Black Hills.

Within a year, Pope and Talbot completed construction of a state-of-the-art sawmill on the former Homestake site at Spearfish, with the capacity to produce 130 million board feet per year—in comparison to the Warren-Lamb Company sawmill in Rapid City that, in its heyday, could produce 30 million board feet per year. Despite vast improvements in sawmill technology since William Lamphere introduced the ripsaw to the Black Hills in 1907, the major stages in sawmill operations remained the same. James D. Rarick, manager of the Spearfish sawmill, described those stages for the Forest Service: logs were brought from the forest by truck and deposited in the collection yard; logs were first placed on the log deck, the platform where they were sorted by size and end use, and then de-barked, which was done to reduce wear on saws and to leave the ultimate saw waste (sawdust) pure enough to be sold as pulp. Also, bark served as fuel for steam boilers that heated both sawmill buildings and drying kilns. As logs moved by conveyor into the actual mill, they were scanned by lasers for readings of diameter, taper, shape, and length—enabling a single human operator to position head-saws for maximum utilization of logs. The logs continued on conveyors to be cut by band-saws into boards 1 or 2 inches thick. Next, the boards moved through another laser scanner, which calculated maximum widths (between 4 inches and 12 inches) for cutting by circular saws, before the boards proceeded, again by conveyor, through edgers and trimmers.[7]

After milling, boards continued by conveyor, were sorted by dimensions, and then were deposited into the appropriate bins. Workers placed strips of wood ("stickers") between the stacked boards to allow for ventilation during the drying process and moved the boards by forklift to drying kilns. After drying under controlled temperature conditions, the boards went through a planer for surface smoothing, after which workers marked each piece of finished lumber with a grade according to the standards established by the Western Wood Products Association. The boards were then prepared for shipment. The entire process took about three days: fifteen minutes in the sawmill, two days in drying kilns, and a day for finishing.[8]

By the time the new Spearfish sawmill went into operation, only three major mills remained in the Black Hills: Pope and Talbot in Spearfish, Edward Hines

Lumber Company in Hill City, and Neiman Sawmill, Inc., in Hulett. Because timbering had become such a high-volume, low-margin business, Lloyd Stahl of the Black Hills Forest Resource Association pressed the Forest Service to sell more timber or, at the very least, to provide assurances that the annual allowable sales would remain constant. Once again, the industry interpreted the total amount of timber to be cut under the 1983 forest plan, equivalent to 158.8 million board feet annually, as the amount required to be cut and accused the Forest Service of violating its own plan by setting the annual allowable sale quantity at 127 million board feet. Supervisor Mathers responded that market trends simply did not justify higher sales or lower appraisals and reminded Stahl that recent cutting levels had stayed well below annual allowable sale levels.[9]

Of the three major operators, only Neiman remained locally owned and would be the only operator to survive. By 2010 Neiman Enterprises had bought both the former Hines mill in Hill City and the Pope and Talbot mill in Spearfish and was purchasing 90–95 percent of all federal timber in the Black Hills. That represented a far greater portion of the total timber than the amounts purchased by Homestake, Warren-Lamb, or Pope and Talbot and represented an opportunity as well as a challenge for the Forest Service.

Historically, Americans dislike monopolies; accordingly, federal laws exist to prevent restraint of trade and other anticompetitive activities. Antitrust laws, however, exempt monopolies or quasi-monopolies fairly achieved by means of "superior skill, foresight, and industry," in the words of the late justice Learned Hand. There was no question that quasi-monopoly status would put Neiman Enterprises in a favorable bargaining position, though competitors in other parts of the country, market conditions, and other factors would provide some restraints.

The Neiman story began during the depths of the Great Depression, when Albert C. Neiman left the Sandhills of Nebraska and resettled with his family along Skull Creek between Upton and Sundance. Neiman had found an abandoned steam-powered portable sawmill that he used to start his business, then he moved it to a more accessible site near Upton and enclosed his sawmill in a wooden structure. His facility burned in 1939, after which Neiman purchased a ranch near Hulett for its timber stands and set up another portable sawmill. In 1945 his youngest son, Jim S., dropped out of ninth grade to work full-time for his father. Jim married Sally Ann Bush, fourth-generation member of a local ranch family, and in time started his own sawmill, selling rough lumber to the Homestake Mining Company. His sawmill, too, burned down. As Jim tells the story, he was left with an outstanding bank loan and "a pile of ashes." His banker trusted him enough so that, the evening after the fire, Jim drove to an auction in Montana, where he purchased enough equipment to start over. He built a new facility, on the present site just outside the town of Hulett, with the capacity to produce between 20,000 and 25,000 board feet per day, or about 8 million board feet per year.

In 1974 Jim lost his contract with Homestake Forest Products and decided to refit his sawmill to produce planed lumber for sale to retailers. "Instead of selling lumber the day I sawed it," Jim reminisced, "I had to sticker the lumber and let it air dry which, in the winter, takes up to five months."[10] That was the year his oldest son, Jim D., graduated with a degree in agricultural economics from the University of Wyoming and decided to enter the family business rather than pursue a graduate degree. Over a period of many years, Jim D. took on more and more executive responsibilities, helping to modernize, expand, and diversify the family enterprise into a forest products company that surpassed in efficiency and capacity any sawmill operation that had existed in the Black Hills.

In the transition from producing rough lumber to finished lumber, Neiman Enterprises incrementally purchased a used planer and trimmer, installed their first dry kiln and a steam boiler heated by wood waste, purchased a second kiln and an automatic lumber stacker, enclosed parts of their Hulett sawmill and installed a steam-heat system so work could continue during winter months and machinery could operate with less maintenance, and purchased equipment to package planer shavings and grind other wood waste into saleable by-products. By the late 1980s, with further automation, their sawmill capacity increased from 8 million to 40 million board feet annually.[11]

That capacity increased to 175–190 million board feet annually after Neiman Enterprises purchased the Hill City sawmill in 1998 and the Spearfish sawmill in 2008. Altogether, by 2010 the sawmills were receiving about 480,000 board feet, or 120 truckloads, of logs per day. Under the Forest Service system of checks and balances, logs were weighed when they entered the mills, with a formula used to translate log weight into cubic feet, which was compared with the cubic foot estimates by the Forest Service appraisers who prepared the timber sales. If actual weights proved greater than estimated weights, the timber operator gained; if estimated weights were greater than actual weights, the timber had become more costly to the operator.

As with many other enterprises, profits in timbering depended on continual technological advances and increased efficiencies. By 2010, 1,000 board feet of logs produced roughly 1,700 board feet of lumber, compared with 1,000 board feet in 1905; and more than 60 percent of log volume became lumber, compared to with 35 percent in 1905.[12] Neiman sawmills produced uniform-grade lumber for wholesale and retail markets and shop-grade lumber for window and door manufacturers. Of the remaining 40 percent of log volume not used as lumber, Neiman Enterprises sold wood chips (about 32 percent) and sawdust (about 8 percent) for engineered

FIGURE 10.1. View of Hulett sawmill from control cab, where operator uses a computer to get the most lumber from each log, 2013. Courtesy, Marcus Neiman, Neiman Enterprises.

products such as particle board and plywood, as well as for pulp, and packaged by-products for uses such as decorative bark, animal bedding, and wood pellets.

Beyond automation, technology had contributed to other efficiencies. Even saw blades had changed markedly. In 1905, a primary saw blade measured 0.250 inch in width; in 2010, primary saws were as narrow as 0.125 inch. For every 1/10,000th-inch reduction in the width of a primary saw blade, Neiman Enterprises could produce an additional 2 million board feet of lumber annually.[13]

The practice of burning wood waste to fuel drying kilns and other sawmill operations had occurred for some time; converting such waste into a source of renewable energy was a much more recent phenomenon. Following the 1973 oil embargo, discussions about experiments for producing fuel from wood waste took place, but no projects materialized. In 2002 the Forest Service supported a study commissioned by Neiman Enterprises to assess the economic and technical feasibility of constructing a biomass-fired electrical generation facility next to either the Hulett or Hill City sawmill. The idea was to use sawmill residue, forest slash, and beetle-infested timber to produce electricity while, at the same time, assisting the Forest Service in meeting its management goal of reducing the risk of catastrophic wildfires. The study concluded that economic prospects were poor as a result of depressed market conditions and a seemingly unfavorable regulatory climate; the idea was dropped.[14]

In 2005 the State of South Dakota, with support from the US Department of Energy through the Western Governors Association, sought to determine the feasibility of heating schools and other public facilities in the Black Hills. Although the study showed that heating with wood pellets would cost less than half as much as heating with fossil fuels, monies needed to fund the initial cost of conversion generally proved unavailable.[15] That same year the US Department of Agriculture (USDA) awarded $250,000 each to Baker Timber Products of Rockerville and Bearlodge Forest Products of Hulett for equipment to prepare and move woody biomass to a demonstration facility under construction at Upton.[16] The purpose of that plant was to produce ethyl alcohol from cellulose, the structural part of the cell walls of plants, and to mix cellulosic ethanol with conventional gasoline fuel. KL Energy Corporation opened the plant in 2007 but soon changed from using local biomass to importing less expensive sugarcane residue. In 2009 the USDA approved the facility for its Biomass Crop Assistance Program, making it eligible for federal subsidies to purchase biomass and thus more likely to use local wood waste.[17]

In purchasing the Spearfish sawmill, Neiman Enterprises entered its first venture into renewable fuels through Heartland Wood Pellets, the mill subsidiary that produced premium pellets for residential stoves—premium because those pellets contained less than 8 percent moisture content and less than 1 percent ash content. Also in 2008 Jim Neiman began discussions with a multinational renewable energy firm about constructing and operating a woody biomass–fed facility to generate electricity and steam for heat and power. The idea was to locate the plant next to the Spearfish sawmill so it could produce enough energy to supply the mill and the campus of nearby Black Hills State University. Almost immediately, the prospective partners discovered that the federal definition of biomass specifically excluded fiber from "mature" stands on federal lands, designed to protect against competition pulp and paper companies that own private forests. Without federal renewable energy subsidies, the project was not feasible.[18]

Advances in logging technology in the Black Hills lagged behind advances at the sawmills. In part, that was a result of the contract and subcontract nature of logging in which small, often undercapitalized independent businesses did the cutting and transporting. For traditional cut-to-length logging, basic equipment consisted of chainsaws, skidders, logging trucks (some with loading cranes), and cant hooks for positioning logs. By the early 1990s, however, the Forest Service had begun to require that most trees be cut and removed in their entirety, which required highly

FIGURE 10.2. Single-grip harvester thinning timber stand, Norbeck Wildlife Preserve, 2004. Courtesy, © Karen Wattenmaker Photography, http://www.ForestPhoto.com.

maneuverable, costly new machinery. That made it increasingly difficult for the few remaining small operators to bid successfully on national forest timber sales, leaving them to compete for logging on private lands. Unquestionably, whole-tree logging reduced accumulations of slash better than did cut-to-length logging but only when used in conjunction with chipping at landing sites. Absent chipping, tens of thousands of slash piles were burned annually. By 2010 whole-tree logging accounted for 80 percent of all logging in the Black Hills.

In recognition of the collateral damage that could be done by conventional cut-to-length logging, the 1983 forest plan had set forth rules on placing skid tracks, felling trees close to skid tracks, and cleaning up and restoring sites. Even the most conscientious loggers, however, incurred some damage to the forest. Partly on the recommendations of its own scientists and partly in reaction to growing public criticism, the Forest Service began to support more basic research into the nature of the forest as a whole.[19]

Toward that end, in 1987 George R. Hoffman, professor of biology at the University of North Dakota, and Robert R. Alexander, chief silviculturist at the Rocky Mountain Research Station and overseer of the Black Hills Experimental Forest, published the first classification of types of habitat (land units) for the

Black Hills National Forest. Although still primarily about trees, their research was broader than an earlier study that had divided the forest into parcels based on deer usage, but it was not as comprehensive as the study of plant communities that would be prepared by Hollis Marriott and others.[20] In general, earlier scientific papers had focused on the single species of ponderosa pine, with the aim of managing for maximum timber production; in a few cases, papers had described the general flora of the Black Hills: Rydberg in 1896, Hayward in 1928, and McIntosh in 1949.[21]

Hoffman and Alexander meant to provide a research aid for natural scientists, as well as updating Boldt's 1974 field guide for forest managers. Underlying their study, Hoffman and Alexander considered each habitat type as supporting or having the potential to support a distinctive combination of tree or shrub species that, if left undisturbed, would maintain constant populations. Each habitat type was named after its predominant association of tree and shrub. Hoffman and Alexander identified the ponderosa pine/kinnikinick (*Arctostaphylos uva-ursi [L.]K. Spreng*) combination as the most widespread habitat type and then grouped habitat types with the same predominant tree species into a distinctive series. They identified two habitats in the burr-oak (*Quercus macrocarpa* Michx.) series, seven in the ponderosa pine series, one in the aspen (*Populus tremuloides* Michx.) series, two in the white spruce (*Picea glauca* [Moench.] Voss) series, and one in the mountain mahogany (*Cercocarpus montanus* Raf.) series.[22]

In defining habitat types, Hoffman and Alexander looked for the oldest and least disturbed forest stands; examined over-story and undergrowth characteristics, topography, and soils; listed every vascular plant they could find; and estimated distributions of the more common plants. Because of timbering and natural disturbances, they acknowledged that the dominant vegetation in a given habitat type might never attain constant population. Nonetheless, they argued that understanding the differing land units in terms of their potential value could assist forest managers in predicting tree growth rates, as well as in planning for other forest uses.[23]

Alexander embraced the traditional silvicultural view that maintaining and extending varied forest uses depended on conservative timbering. Indeed, by the late 1980s, scientists throughout the national forest system were studying ways to restore and retain a multiplicity of forest values while continuing commercial timbering. Perhaps the most influential was Jerry P. Franklin, whose "new forestry" approach rested on the premise that ecology and economics could complement each other. Franklin's research contributed to resolving the spotted owl controversy in the Pacific Northwest.[24]

In the spirit of the new forestry, Supervisor Darrel Kenops (1987–91), more than any of his predecessors, pushed for an interdisciplinary rather than a strictly silvicultural approach to forest management. He spent much of his time seeking public support for such an approach and earned the reputation of being personable and outgoing, often accompanying forest user groups on field trips.[25]

In the aftermath of the 17,976-acre Galena fire in Custer State Park (July 1988) and the 14,518-acre Cicero Peak fire on mixed-ownership lands southeast of Custer (September 1990), Kenops supported the Custer County Commission in seeking voter approval of an ordinance to make homes and related structures within the national forest boundary fire resistant. The proposed ordinance required that roofs be made fire resistant (no wooden shakes); that decks and porches less than 4 feet aboveground be enclosed, with the ground below treated to prevent vegetation; that chimneys contain spark arrestors; and that vegetation surrounding buildings conform to certain heights and densities. On October 23, 1990, more than 300 county residents crowded the commission meeting room, protesting the proposed ordinance as too restrictive on use of their properties, too costly for property owners to achieve compliance, and bound to increase property taxes once improvements were made. Despite the commission's plea for help in preparing a more acceptable ordinance, the matter devolved into verbal attacks on the commissioners as individuals, forcing them to withdraw their proposal.[26] It would take another ten years and the Jasper fire for public sentiment to shift its emphasis from property rights to property protection.

Meanwhile, similar libertarian opposition, combined with the not-in-my-backyard argument, surfaced in another controversial matter, this time related to recreational use of the forest. In 1986 a local voluntary group affiliated with the recently founded national Rails-to-Trails Conservancy approached the Forest Service about taking possession of the right-of-way from Edgemont through Custer and Hill City to Deadwood and administering the former rail bed as a trail for non-motorized use. On September 11, one month before the last freight train departed from Custer (service from Custer north was discontinued in 1983), members of the voluntary group and officials of the Department of Game, Fish, and Parks organized a public meeting that attracted bicyclists, cross-country skiers, hikers, snowmobilers, adjacent landowners, representatives of the South Dakota congressional delegation, the Forest Service, the Burlington Northern Railroad, the 1880 Hill City to Keystone seasonal tourist railroad, and the timber industry. Incentive for converting abandoned rail lines to trails had come from the National Trails System Act of 1968 and from a section in the Railroad Revitalization and Regulatory Reform Act of 1976 that authorized a rails-to-trails grants program to provide monies and technical assistance.[27]

When citizens first suggested the rails-to-trails project, Supervisor James Mathers expressed surprise at the high degree of local interest. He favored converting the Hill City to Deadwood portion, mostly over Forest Service land, into a multiple-use trail and pledged to issue a special-use permit to any state agency or charitable nonprofit organization willing to take responsibility for the project. He did not, however, approve of his agency managing easements through private property. The Forest Service, he said, could not assume the financial obligations and legal liabilities. He cited the potential threats of lawsuits by adjacent landowners, the costs of bringing tunnels and trestles up to safety standards, and continuing costs of trail maintenance. These were all legitimate concerns, though perhaps the project fell outside Mathers's notion of the Forest Service's mission. As it turned out, Richard E. Lee, co-chair of the Black Hills Rails-to-Trails Association and chief warrant officer in the South Dakota National Guard, had expressed the Guard's willingness to restore trestles and tunnels as part of summer exercises and confirmed that South Dakota governor-elect George S. Mickelson enthusiastically supported the project.[28]

On April 17, 1988—the day scheduled for the governor, on behalf of the State of South Dakota, to accept title to the entire right-of-way from the Burlington Northern Railroad—several adjacent landowners, banded together as the Southern Hills Anti-Trail Coalition, obtained a restraining order. Their suit against the State of South Dakota reached the state supreme court, which ruled unanimously against them. The anti-trail group appealed to the US Supreme Court, which declined to hear the case.[29]

Members of the Southern Hills Anti-Trail Coalition, which included Forest Service employees who owned land along the right-of-way, did not want the general public passing through their properties. They based their opposition on their interpretation of certain principles of private property, as well as on legal technicalities regarding the state's proposal. Lloyd Stahl of the Black Hills Forest Resource Association warned that transfer to the state could cut access to timber stands. Rancher Richard Laue argued that the proposed trail would cross his property six times and prevent him from driving his vehicles into one of his pastures. Laue expressed the opinion that the state, desperate for economic development, had forsaken its long-held tradition of valuing the rights of people who made their living from the land in favor of hikers, bikers, and other recreationists.[30]

In the tradition of Peter Norbeck, Governor Mickelson announced that converting the rail bed into a recreation trail would provide an economic boost to communities situated along the right-of-way. He cited a study of 105 rails-to-trails projects nationwide, commissioned by the Department of Game, Fish, and Parks and prepared by University of South Dakota economist Michael K. Madden. Professor Madden had estimated that the trail would initially attract 50,000 visitors, who would spend $650,000 annually in those communities.[31] To one landowner, the governor wrote: "My feeling is that public interest and value to the state in converting the right of way to a hiking and bicycling trail is very important. The possibility of inconveniencing a few individuals may be a price we have to pay, but I would like to work with you to avoid any unnecessary conflict."[32]

Supervisor Mathers's successor, Darrel Kenops, was among the most enthusiastic rails-to-trails boosters, perhaps believing that Forest Service involvement with this project would help counter the attraction of Mount Rushmore. With Richard Lee and Sturgis businessman Guy Edwards, he traveled the speaking circuit on behalf of the project. Recognizing that the South Dakota public overwhelmingly supported the project, the state legislature authorized the sale of revenue bonds, if needed, to complete the project and passed legislation making the Department of Game, Fish, and Parks responsible for constructing fences along the right-of-way, leaving responsibility for fence maintenance to adjoining landowners but requiring that the department provide material needed for repairs.[33]

Despite a pending lawsuit over the southern portion of the right-of-way, rail-to-trail conversion began on portions north of Custer. The first 6-mile stretch, through public land near Lead, opened in fall 1991. Meanwhile, Governor Mickelson had established a Rails-to-Trails Advisory Committee consisting of four landowners, four recreationists, one recreationist/ landowner, and a non-voting chair from the Department of Game, Fish, and Parks. When making the appointments, Mickelson noted that the Forest Service was funding one-half of the entire project, the state one-fourth, and voluntary contributions one-fourth.[34] Later, in recognition of Supervisor Kenops's prominent role in support of the project, he was invited back to South Dakota to join Governor Mickelson's family (the governor had perished in a plane crash), key early supporters, and more than 200 bicyclists for the three-day inaugural ride on September 25–27, 1998. Thousands witnessed the ride from various points along the route, formally named the George S. Mickelson Trail.[35]

As part of the new generation of supervisors who saw the forest for more than just timber, Supervisor Kenops had initiated what he anticipated would be a three-year process (fall 1989 through summer 1992) to redo the 1983 Land and Resource Management Plan. His staff had compiled a list of suggested changes: improve species and age mix of trees and shrubs, increase water yields, adjust the number of stands for commercial timbering, revise allowable sale quantities, and set aside for special management 5,000 acres in the Beaver Park area.[36]

His successor, Roberta A. Moltzen (1991–94), took over the bulk of the planning process, including the recurring issue of timbering in the Norbeck Wildlife Preserve. Before Supervisor Moltzen's arrival, the Black Hills Group of the Sierra Club had appealed Supervisor Kenops's decision to allow timbering in the preserve, first to the regional forester and then to the chief forester. American Wildlands, a self-described forest reform group headquartered at Bozeman, Montana, and focused on wildlife habitat and corridors, had joined the appeal. Based on results of the required environmental analysis, Kenops had determined that, in view of declining wildlife populations, the best way to improve habitat within the preserve was through a combination of commercial logging, thinning, and prescribed burns. Except for some restrictions on off-road vehicles and snowmobiles, he allowed all existing uses—grazing, recreation, summer homes, and mining—to continue.[37]

Chief Forester F. Dale Robertson upheld Supervisor Kenops's decision but requested a supplemental environmental analysis to address the issues of wildlife habitat diversity and non-game species. In response, Forest Service staff prepared alternatives for protecting late successional stands, dead standing trees, and goshawk nesting sites. Though not listed as endangered under the Endangered Species Act, the goshawk (*Accipiter gentilis*) had been listed by the Forest Service as a "sensitive" species. Addressing the chief forester's concerns, Supervisor Moltzen affirmed her predecessor's plan to improve wildlife habitat, which included closing or obliterating some roads once timbering on stands already sold was completed. The South Dakota chapter of the Society of American Foresters supported her decision; the Black Hills Group of the Sierra Club found her decision unacceptable. Sam Clauson observed that the practice of requiring loggers to stop their work when they sighted goshawk nests came too late to protect the birds. Moltzen responded that her agency did not have the resources to conduct nesting site surveys prior to timbering. She might have added that, nationwide, more goshawk nests were lost to wildfires and insect epidemics than to timbering.[38]

Once again, expanding wilderness was behind the Sierra Club's opposition to timbering in the Norbeck Wildlife Preserve. While the Forest Service continued to oppose the designation of more wilderness areas in the Black Hills, it had issued more prescriptive rules for the Black Elk Wilderness. Given ever-increasing numbers of visitors, the Forest Service required groups of twenty-five or more to obtain special permits and prohibited all competitive events, presumably because they attracted large numbers of people. The Forest Service also prohibited the construction of new structures, halted the issuing of new permits for commercial guides and outfitters, and required that pilots flying over the preserve maintain a minimum altitude of 9,500 feet.[39]

Noting that the Black Elk Wilderness area represented less than 1 percent of the Black Hills National Forest, the Black Hills Group of the Sierra Club advocated for an additional 47,000 acres for wilderness designation: adding 10,000 acres to the existing wilderness and creating four new wilderness units, including in the Beaver Park area. Local public officials and business interests strongly opposed the Sierra Club proposal, issuing predictions that it would result in long-term devastation to the economy, endanger public safety, and destroy local culture and "life as we know it."[40]

FIGURE 10.3. Goshawk, designated a sensitive species by USDA Forest Service. Courtesy, Michelle N. Lamberson, Flickr.com.

Shortly after becoming managing director of the Black Hills Forest Resource Association, Thomas A. Troxel helped organize opposition to more wilderness acreage. A native of Virginia, Troxel had earned a degree in silviculture at the University of Montana, spent ten years in the Forest Service, then left to work for the Rocky Mountain Federal Timber Purchasers Association—the Colorado-Wyoming affiliate of the Intermountain Forest Association, through which he was attracted to the South Dakota affiliate, the Black Hills Forest Resource Association, in 1989.

In an effort to provide a unified stand in favor of forest uses, Troxel led the effort to establish the Black Hills Multiple Use Coalition, formally organized in Spearfish on June 28, 1991. He served as executive secretary of the new group, which included ranching, mining, timber, and off-road vehicle interests as well as county commissioners and other local public officials. The group opposed wilderness designations, higher grazing fees, and appeals against timber sales. Its supporters used the term *preservationists* to describe individuals who opposed development within the national forest.[41]

Brian D. Brademeyer, a brilliant software engineer, stood out among the "preservationists." His family had homesteaded in Palmer Gulch, which became part of the Norbeck Wildlife Preserve; his father had assisted Gutzon Borglum at Mount Rushmore. After earning degrees in civil engineering at the Massachusetts Institute of Technology, the younger Brademeyer returned to the family homestead, from where he operated a software consulting business. Sam Clauson recalled that, sometime in the early 1990s, Brademeyer first visited the Sierra Club office in Rapid City and offered to help stop timbering in the preserve. Clauson credited Brademeyer for introducing "scientific reasoning" to the Sierra Club's administrative and legal appeals, by which Clauson meant detailed analyses of Forest Service planning documents, discoveries of inconsistencies within those documents, discrepancies between those documents and federal rules, followed by concise and persuasive preparation of appeals documents. Others viewed Brademeyer as a selfish aesthete, seeking out the most extreme examples of spoiled views from which he generalized about the forest as nothing more than a tree farm.[42]

Brademeyer first spoke on behalf of the Sierra Club at a public meeting called by the Forest Service in November 1992 to present plans for two timber sales within the Norbeck Wildlife Preserve. Brademeyer argued that improving conditions for wildlife, the stated purpose of the sales, could best be handled if timber were left standing.[43] Three self-described forest reform groups supported the Sierra Club in appealing timber sales: two of nine sales in 1990, six of ten in 1992, ten of ten in 1995, and twelve of twelve in 1996.[44] All three groups—American Wildlands, Native Ecosystems Council (Missoula, MT), Friends of the Bow (Laramie, WY)—claimed to provide science-based technical assistance as well as legal counsel to individuals and groups challenging Forest Service timber sales. Brademeyer appeared to align most closely with Friends of the Bow, founded in 1989 to stop clear-cutting in the Medicine Bow National Forest and later expanding its geographic area of interest under the name Biodiversity Associates, then Biodiversity Conservation Alliance.

Unquestionably, the legal appeals disrupted the stable supply of timber deemed essential for efficient industry operations. Forest Service staff reassigned to assist in answering appeals had less time to mark stands for proposed sales. As a result, the appeals contributed to industry layoffs, according to Maurice Williams, manager of Hill City's major sawmill. By deflecting Forest Service staff from their normal fieldwork, the appeals had the effect of exacerbating a public perception that Forest Service employees had deliberately become little more than bureaucrats. For her part, Supervisor Moltzen wanted to give notice of timber sales at least one year in advance of planned sales dates to provide time for resolving outstanding issues, thus eliminating the need for appeals. Based on the number of appeals, one is left with the impression that negotiating compromise was not part of the anti-timber agenda.[45]

On a broader front, the required revision of the forest plan had been proceeding at a slower pace than envisioned by Moltzen's predecessor. In defense of the longer time the revision was taking, Moltzen took to the speaking circuit, explaining the deliberateness of the process, its scientific underpinnings, and the significance of the plan for the nation. Before the Custer Chamber of Commerce, mayors of Custer and Hill City, and Custer County Commissioners, she restated the Forest Service's commitment to multiple uses and, in anticipation of continuing controversy, reminded her audience of Gifford Pinchot's instructions to the agency: when conflicting interests must be reconciled, the question will always be answered from the standpoint of the greatest good for the greatest number in the long run. With rumors circulating about a likely decrease in annual allowable sale quantity, Hill City mayor Drue Vitter confronted Moltzen on the subject. She acknowledged receiving hundreds of letters requesting that the Forest Service maintain current levels for the sake of preserving local jobs but also noted that scientific analyses had suggested the need for reductions to maintain the balance of tree cutting and growth. Mayor Vitter, reportedly perturbed, raised the matter of "environmentalists" using the appeals process to halt or hold up timber sales. Moltzen responded that he was "preaching to the choir," that she had nothing to do with the filing of appeals but was being subjected to them. In a moment of political candor or perhaps sheer exasperation, Moltzen volunteered that, with the recent change in administration from President George H.W. Bush to President Bill Clinton, the number of timber industry jobs dependent on Forest Service lands would likely decline, no matter what the condition of the timber supply.[46]

Roberta Moltzen was one of only 8 women out of 200 supervisors in the national forest system. A trained forester, she had worked in the timber industry before joining the Forest Service, where she was quickly promoted. There is no question that, as a woman, she encountered some ill will from the Black Hills National Forest staff and, more pronouncedly, from individuals in the timber industry, as described to me by her former colleagues both within and outside the Forest Service.

In announcing the release of the draft forest plan on June 14, 1994, Supervisor Moltzen provided details on the advances in scientific forestry that had served as its foundation. Aside from the draft's seemingly bewildering language and inordinate length (three volumes), Moltzen explained that, in a nutshell, the plan placed all aspects of forest management into an integrated whole for the purpose of ensuring continued multiple uses of the forest while improving its ecological well-being. Most notably, she stated that the plan reflected the collective judgment of district rangers and forest specialists who had convinced her that forest stands needed to be more varied to sustain "conservative use." In practice, that translated into reducing the annual allowable sales quantity from 120 million to 80 million board feet.[47]

Reaction to the draft plan simmered until Labor Day weekend 1994, when the Black Hills Multiple Use Coalition attracted 600 supporters to Custer for a "Rushmore Rendezvous." The event began as a protest rally against the Forest Service and unraveled into a series of speeches, in the words of one organizer, against "the 'weird science' that has been used to promote excessive regulation and the unnecessary destruction of families, businesses, and communities." It concluded with an address by William P. Pendley, president of the Mountain States Legal Foundation, a politically conservative nonprofit public interest law firm. In a rambling defense of private property, free enterprise, and limited government, Pendley asserted that the Clinton administration had started a "War on the West" as part of an effort to destroy ranching, mining, and logging. The administration, he continued, meant to "lock up" federal lands so there could be no public uses except backpacking. In one of his broadsides, Pendley had described his support of multiple use as genuine conservation, which he preferred to call "wise use because the term 'conservation' has been co-opted by environmentalists to mean 'preservation only'—that is, no use."[48]

As criticism of the draft plan increased in intensity, with both pro- and anti-timbering groups marshaling their own scientists, the South Dakota and Wyoming congressional delegations requested that the public comment period be extended forty-five days. In the absence of Supervisor Moltzen, soon to be promoted to supervisor of Mount Hood National Forest, Acting Supervisor Rebecca Aus granted the extension after noting that more than 12,000 public comments had already been received.[49] It would take another three years to finish the draft with two amendments after that, for a total of sixteen years to complete what was meant to be a ten- to fifteen-year plan. One might reasonably conclude that forest plans had become working hypotheses, with policies and practices under continual revision: frustratingly difficult for all concerned, but an accurate reflection of forest dynamics and changing views about forest values.

NOTES

1. Jim D. Neiman, prepared statement concerning the future of the nation's forests, to Subcommittee on Department Operations, Oversight, Nutrition, and Forestry, Committee on Agriculture, US House of Representatives, Washington, DC, June 3, 2009.

2. Ibid.

3. Thomas A. Troxel, personal communication, January 2011.

4. *Custer County Chronicle,* July 23, 1985.

5. Ibid., October 30, 1985, January 22, 1986.

6. "The Logging Industry in the Black Hills" (1988?), typescript, 10–12, Black Hills National Forest supervisor's office, Custer, SD (hereafter BHNF).

7. James D. Rarick quoted in ibid., 16.

8. Ibid.

9. Lloyd E. Stahl to James L. Mathers, April 27, 1984, and James L. Mathers to Lloyd E. Stahl [May 1984], copies, BHNF.

10. James S. Neiman, personal communication, October 2009.

11. Jim D. Neiman, personal communication, October 2009.

12. Thomas Troxel, personal communication, October 1, 2010.

13. Jim D. Neiman, discussions with author, April 2009 and April 2011.

14. "Biomass Cogeneration Feasibility Analysis for Neiman Enterprises" (Lakewood, CO: McNeil Technologies, Inc., 2002), vi.

15. "Biomass Feasibility Study, Black Hills Region, South Dakota," prepared for South Dakota Department of Agriculture, Resource Conservation and Forestry Division, by Bilmass Energy Resource Center, Montpelier, VT 2006, at http://sdda.sd.gov/legacydocs/Forestry/publications/PDF/Biomass-Report-Final.pdf; accessed July 2014.

16. News release, Black Hills National Forest, April 4, 2007, at http://www.fs.usda.gov/detail/blackhills/news-events/?cid=FSM9_013219; accessed December 2012.

17. News release, November 9, 2009, at www.marketwide.com; accessed December 2012.

18. Jim D. Neiman, discussion with author, April 2009.

19. Robert R. Alexander, "Silvicultural Systems, Cutting Methods, and Cultural Practices for Black Hills Ponderosa Pine," USDA Forest Service, General Technical Report RM-139 (February 1987): 10.

20. John F. Thilenius, "Classification of Deer Habitat in the Ponderosa Pine Forest of the Black Hills, South Dakota," USDA Forest Service Research Paper RM-91 (May 1972); George R. Hoffman and Robert R. Alexander, "Forest Vegetation of the Black Hills National Forest of South Dakota and Wyoming: A Habitat Type Classification," USDA Forest Service Research Paper RM-276 (June 1987); Hollis Marriott et al., *Black Hills Community Inventory: Final Report* (Minneapolis: Nature Conservancy Midwest Conservation Science Center, 1999).

21. Per Axel Rydberg, "Flora of the Black Hills of South Dakota," *Contributions from the United States National Herbarium* 3, no. 8 (June 1896); Herman E. Hayward, "Studies of the Plants in the Black Hills of South Dakota," *Botanical Gazette* 85, no. 4 (June 1928); Arthur G. McIntosh, "A Botanical Survey of the Black Hills of South Dakota," *Black Hills Engineer* 19, no. 3 (May 1931).

22. George R. Hoffman and Robert R. Alexander, "Forest Vegetation of the Black Hills National Forest of South Dakota and Wyoming: A Habitat Type Classification," USDA Forest Service Research Paper RM-276 (June 1987): 6, 8–21.

23. Ibid., 3, 6, 26.

24. Alexander, "Silvicultural Systems"; Jerry P. Franklin, "Toward a New Forestry," *American Forests* 95, no. 11-12 (November-December 1989).

25. Samuel D. Clauson, discussion with author, November 2010.

26. *Custer County Chronicle*, October 24, November 21, 1990, January 16, 30, 1991.

27. Ibid., September 24, 1986.

28. Ibid., October 12, 1986.

29. Ibid., April 20, 1988.

30. Ibid., July 11, 1990; also March 7, 21, 1990.

31. Ibid., December 5, 1990.

32. Quoted in ibid., November 6, 1991.

33. Ibid., May 10, 1989, February 13, 1991, May 13, 1992; *South Dakota State Statutes*, title 41, chapter 17, section 26, at http://legis.sd.gov/Statutes/Codified_Laws/DisplayStatute.aspx?Type=Statute&Statute=41-17-26; accessed December 2010.

34. *Custer County Chronicle*, September 30, 1992, January 20, 1993.

35. Ibid., September 24, October 1, 1998; "Bikers Hit the Trail," *Deadwood Magazine* (November-December 1998): 1, at http://www.deadwoodmagazine.com/archivedsite/Archives/Bikers.htm; accessed January 1, 2011.

36. *Custer County Chronicle*, October 25, 1989.

37. Ibid., August 2, 1989, February 14, 1990.

38. Ibid., September 2, 1992, July 21, 1993.

39. Ibid., January 30, 1991.

40. Ibid., August 21, 1991.

41. Ibid., August 21, 1991, February 24, May 19, 1993.

42. Clauson, discussion with author, November 2010.

43. *Custer County Chronicle*, November 11, 1992, August 11, 1993.

44. "Project Appeals Overview," typescript, June 26, 2007, BHNF.

45. *Custer County Chronicle*, May 12, August 4, 1993.

46. Ibid., March 24, 1993.

47. Ibid., June 23, 1994.

48. Organizer quoted in ibid., September 8, 1994; William Perry Pendley, *It Takes a Hero: The Grassroots Battle against Environmental Oppression* (Bellevue, WA: Free Enterprise Press, 1994), 269.

49. *Custer County Chronicle*, October 6, 1994.

11

From Confrontation to Compromise

On a Thursday evening in October 1994, the South Dakota chapter of the Society of American Foresters sponsored a public forum on ecosystem management in Lead. Since publication of the draft forest plan in June of that year, the foresters had heard much speculation, both from within and outside their profession, as to what changes ecosystem management might bring to the forest. Because the Black Hills National Forest was regarded as the first in the national forest system formally to adopt the principles of ecosystem management, the foresters believed discussion and greater understanding of the matter would be timely and instructive for all concerned.

To be sure, ecosystem management had raised suspicion among some of the more commercially oriented forest users, especially since the term had been enthusiastically adopted by groups opposed to timbering and forest development generally. The most adamant commercial users viewed ecosystem management as part of a conspiracy to undermine the traditional purpose of forestry, namely, to ensure a continual supply of timber for the nation; they were partially correct, though not on their political grounds.[1]

Former Black Hills National Forest supervisor James Overbay, who had been promoted to deputy chief forester, had announced the adoption of ecosystem management as Forest Service policy at a seminar on the topic in Salt Lake City in 1992.[2] The Forest Service generally defined ecosystem management as managing the forest for its overall health, taking into account all the organisms living in the forest,

DOI: 10.5876/9781607322993.c011

together with those aspects of the environment—both natural and artificial—with which the organisms interacted. As such, ecosystem management represented a change in the meaning of forest conservation: from ensuring sustainable yields of forest products to sustaining the ecological values that made those products possible. For the Black Hills National Forest, the impact on forest practices would mean in time a recognition that more timber than ever needed to be cut.

Though the policy of ecosystem management had been announced under President George H.W. Bush, its champion became Jack Ward Thomas, appointed chief forester by President Bill Clinton. A research wildlife biologist and the first person with a PhD to occupy the position of chief forester, Thomas was an unabashed admirer of Aldo Leopold, best-known for *A Sand County Almanac*. In explaining Leopold's notion of land ethics to a congressional committee in 1994, Thomas intertwined the sentimental and scientific aspects of forest conservation. Leopold's land ethic, he testified, "accepts short term constraints on human treatment of land so as to ensure long term preservation of the integrity, stability, and beauty of the biotic community." Human activity consistent with that ethic "is properly within the realm of resource management options. Activities which would not be consistent with the long term preservation of the biotic community should be resisted for all but the most compelling reasons."[3] By including the ethical dimension, Thomas reflected earlier sentiments expressed by James Madison and George Perkins Marsh.

With the Clinton administration wanting to reduce timbering, it was perhaps no surprise that for the most productive national forest in the nation, the Forest Service sent John Twiss (1995–2004), director of its Wilderness and Wild and Scenic Rivers Program, to succeed Roberta Moltzen as supervisor. A twenty-five-year veteran of the agency, Twiss concluded early in his tenure in the Black Hills that because of the ponderosa pine's prolific reproductive capacity, more rather than less timber needed to be cut. That put him squarely between the chief forester, who wanted less cutting, and Senator Thomas Daschle, who wanted more. Twiss oversaw completion of the 1997 forest plan and served as Forest Service spokesperson during negotiations for the 2001 and 2005 amendments.

In comparing the 1983 and 1997 plans, Supervisor Twiss noted that the 1997 plan provided a stronger framework for improving forest health, through restoring meadows, riparian areas, and aspen-birch stands; preserving standing dead trees and maintaining more late successional (old-growth) stands; and substantially increasing prescribed burning. By focusing on forest health, he argued that the 1997 plan sought to improve species diversity and, in the process, to improve dispersed recreation by setting aside areas for non-motorized use and placing seasonal restrictions on off-road vehicle use.

On the subject of timbering, the 1997 plan did indeed reduce allowable sale quantities for saw-timber, from 118.4 million to 83.8 million board feet, according to Supervisor Twiss, based on more accurate estimates of sustainable levels of timbering. To reach the 1983 figure, the Forest Service had used 409 sites; for the 1997 figure, 30,000 sites were used. In addition, Twiss pointed out that since 1984, the actual amount of saw-timber sold had been less than the allowable sale quantities: since 1984, the Forest Service had sold an average of 95.1 million board feet per year, though for the period 1992–96 only 75.7 million board feet per year were sold.[4] Timber operators argued that the Forest Service itself was responsible for low sales volumes by keeping appraisals of standing timber unrealistically high in view of weak timber markets and accommodating anti-timber groups. The industry's Thomas Troxel suggested that the Forest Service either modify its rules to penalize groups that continued to make "frivolous appeals" or find funding for additional agency staff to "bulletproof" the 1997 plan against such appeals.[5]

On the other side, the Black Hills Group of the Sierra Club and Biodiversity Associates (formerly Friends of the Bow) declared the 1997 plan unacceptable. Speaking for the Sierra Club, Brian Brademeyer expressed the view that the 1997 plan was no different than the original 1994 draft against which twenty-two local, regional, and national organizations had petitioned Chief Thomas, unsuccessfully as it turned out, to order preparation of an entirely new version. Brademeyer seemed to take advantage of continuing grievances toward the federal government by recruiting representatives of the Oglala Sioux to support the argument that the 1997 plan failed to maintain viable populations of native species and to protect wilderness and unique ecosystems. More to the point, Brademeyer once again opposed timbering within the Norbeck Wildlife Preserve.[6]

In a guest newspaper column, Lee Stanfield of Biodiversity Associates repeated the argument that nothing had changed between the 1994 draft and the 1997 plan; both stressed "the profit of extractive industry over other forest values." Revealing her commitment to matters aesthetic, Stanfield noted that "the majestic tall ponderosa are systematically being replaced by fast-growing young trees."[7] In response, Mary Flanderka of the Black Hills Forest Resource Association cited Forest Service estimates that 71 percent of the stands in the Black Hills were older than eighty years. "Like many people," Flanderka wrote, "Stanfield evidently believes that thin trees are young trees, but tree diameter in the Black Hills is often a function of tree density, not tree age." Flanderka continued, "When too many trees grow too close together, they cannot become 'majestic tall ponderosa'—they become skinny old trees which some people think are actually young."[8]

Claiming to have been ignored by Chief Forester Thomas, the Black Hills Group of the Sierra Club, Biodiversity Associates, and other groups with similar

FIGURE 11.1. Forest stand initially cut in 1911, ca. 2000. Courtesy, USDA Forest Service, Black Hills National Forest, http://www.ForestPhoto.com.

positions petitioned his successor, Michael P. Dombeck, to order preparation of a new forest plan. The groups believed that Dombeck, a well-published conservationist, would be sympathetic and approve their request. Instead, he properly deferred to Elizabeth Estill, Region 2 forester, in her regulatory capacity as deciding officer.[9] Following her decision confirming the 1997 plan, Biodiversity Associates coordinated a formal appeal to Dombeck on September 30, 1997. The Black Hills Multiple Use Coalition, with the county commissions of Lawrence, Crook, and Weston Counties, filed their own appeals, arguing that the Forest Service had violated federal law and its own rules by not placing on sale the published limits of allowable sale quantities. Altogether, seven parties—five corporate and two individual—appealed Estill's decision.[10] Chief Dombeck sat on the formal appeal for two years.

Meanwhile, a different kind of conservation group had taken an interest in the Black Hills. In 1995 the Nature Conservancy opened an office in Rapid City and, through its Midwest Conservation Science Center, embarked on a research project (based on summer fieldwork, 1996–98) that resulted in the most comprehensive inventory of natural plant communities to that date. Plant communities meant groupings of native plants growing together, not substantially altered by human activity or by introduced organisms such as noxious plants and zebra mussels. The "Black Hills Community Inventory" built upon the Nature Conservancy's efforts, begun in the 1970s, to inventory state by state the existence and location of species, as well as natural animal and plant communities.

The credibility of the Nature Conservancy study rested on the fact of joint funding by philanthropic foundations, the timber industry, and state and federal agencies and on the reputation of the scientists involved. Hollis Marriott, a botanist associated with the Rocky Mountain Herbarium at the University of Wyoming, led the research team; a committee of scientists from all three sectors of the economy oversaw the study.[11] In keeping with the Nature Conservancy's mission to discover and protect significant sites of biological diversity, the study sought to identify the highest-quality occurrences of each community type from among 300 study plots. Using the US National Vegetation Classification, a standardized system created by the Nature Conservancy, the Black Hills study described sixty-eight different types of plant communities and placed each type in one of fifteen broader groups to illustrate ecological relationships. For example, the ponderosa pine/Oregon grape (*Pinus ponderosa/Mahonia repens*) forest plant community belonged to the dry coniferous forests and woodlands ecological group; the Black Hills montane grasslands plant community (prairie dropseed [*Sporobolus heterolepsis*], green needlegrass [*Achnatherum richardsonii*], and oatgrass [*Danthonia intermedia*]) belonged to the upland grasses ecological group.[12]

As with all credible studies, Marriott and colleagues built on prior research, including the classification of habitat types by George Hoffman and Robert Alexander that had focused on timber stands. Also, Marriott acknowledged the difficulties of ascertaining the "naturalness" of plant communities because of limited empirical evidence about the pre-settlement forest; in addition, she considered late successional conditions only one criterion for determining the "naturalness" of a given plant community.[13] Under the 1997 plan, Supervisor Twiss did designate eight botanical management areas (in total, about 8,000 acres) specifically to protect certain plant species listed as "sensitive" by the Forest Service.[14]

In early 1998 the Nature Conservancy's Black Hills program director, Bob Paulson, explained to members of the Custer Rotary Club that through the recently completed inventory, scientists had found nine rare plants in the northern Black Hills and four in the Hot Springs area; they next planned to inventory plants and birds in the Cheyenne River valley. As a practical matter, identifying threatened species and natural communities on public lands assisted public land managers in protecting biological diversity. After finding threatened species and natural communities on private properties, the Nature Conservancy sought to protect such diversity through its programs of land acquisitions, land exchanges, and conservation easements. Of special interest to developers, Paulson noted that the thoroughness of inventorying contributed to keeping certain species off the endangered species list; he gave examples of inventories that worked to the advantage of extractive industries in the nearby Powder River Basin. The Natural Heritage Program within the South Dakota Department of Game, Fish, and Parks and the Wyoming Natural Diversity Database at the University of Wyoming, both established by the Nature Conservancy, continue to serve as the standard biological inventories for industry, government agencies, and nonprofit groups.[15]

In distinguishing the Nature Conservancy, Paulson told the Custer Rotarians, "People think we are a preservationist group rather than a conservation group and when our name is used in the same sentence as the Sierra Club, we shudder."[16] He explained that the Nature Conservancy declined to engage in public policy debates or to use the legal tactics of the Sierra Club and Biodiversity Associates. Indeed, by ferreting out procedural missteps and using the courts to advance their agendas, the anti-development groups eventually antagonized forest managers and most forest users and marginalized themselves, but not before bringing forestry in the Black Hills to a virtual standstill. The precipitating incident was the Veteran-Boulder timber sale south of Sturgis.

On March 1, 1999, Supervisor Twiss issued his decision to go ahead with the sale, which included 780 acres within the 5,109-acre Beaver Park road-less area. His decision effectively eliminated the possibility of considering Beaver Park for wilderness designation because the Wilderness Act had set the minimum size at 5,000 acres. To stop the timber sale, Biodiversity Associates, the Sierra Club, and Brian Brademeyer alleged that procedural errors had been made by the Forest Service and appealed the sale. Region 2 forester Lyle Laverty rejected their appeal, allowing the sale to proceed.[17]

Then, on June 11, 1999, three days before bids were scheduled to be opened, the appellants won a stay from Chief Forester Dombeck, pending the outcome of their September 30, 1997, appeal of the forest plan. In granting the stay, Dombeck expressed the view that the Veteran-Boulder sale could thwart future actions on adding wilderness and research natural areas raised by the appeal. His decision, announced on October 12, 1999, affirmed the validity of the 1997 forest plan, except that the plan "does not fully meet all aspects of the intent and requirements of the National Forest Management Act and its implementing regulation . . . with regard to the diversity of plant and animal communities." Having made his decision on the appeal, Dombeck was required to lift his stay on the Veteran-Boulder timber sale, which allowed Supervisor Twiss to reissue his request for bids.[18]

Once again, just one day before the scheduled opening of bids, Biodiversity Associates, the Sierra Club, and Brian Brademeyer filed suit in the US District Court for the District of Colorado to stop the Veteran-Boulder timber sale. The plaintiffs alleged that the Forest Service had violated federal law and its own rules, as Chief Dombeck had implied in his criticism of the 1997 forest plan, and that Dombeck had failed to require corrective action or at least an interim solution to bring the 1997 forest plan into compliance, especially with regard to protecting native plants and wildlife diversity.[19]

By filing suit, the plaintiffs stopped for nearly two years the preparation of new timber sales, as well as thinning and timbering meant to reduce the risks of wildfires and insect epidemics during a period of extreme drought. Citing public safety as well as the health of the local economy, several parties intervened in the case on the side of the Forest Service: the Black Hills Forest Resource Association, Black Hills Multiple Use Coalition, the State of South Dakota, and Lawrence, Meade, and Pennington Counties; only the first two parties, however, agreed to the settlement mediated by the court and signed on August 1, 2000.[20]

Under that agreement, the Forest Service withdrew its decision to proceed with the Veteran-Boulder timber sale and agreed to refrain from any activity that disturbed the soil or damaged trees within the entire Beaver Park road-less area until completion of a forest-wide planning effort and an amended forest plan. The Forest Service pledged to prepare a fire prevention plan for Beaver Park and adjacent lands, in consultation with interested parties. Meanwhile, limited thinning and cutting would be permitted surrounding the Beaver Park road-less area, as would emergency fire-fighting activities within the road-less area, consistent with preserving its eligibility as a research natural area.

FIGURE 11.2. Firefighters extinguishing hotspots, Tahoma fire, 2004. Courtesy, Gary Chancey, USDA Forest Service, Black Hills National Forest, http://www.ForestPhotol. com.

Forest-wide, the Forest Service agreed to analyze other sites for possible designation as research natural areas and to undertake no management activities in those areas until approval of a final amended version of the 1997 forest plan. Concerning plant and wildlife diversity, the Forest Service agreed to conduct additional distribution studies on indicator species selected to assess the impact of management activities on given areas. Because the suit specifically mentioned possible threats to goshawk habitat, the agreement established no-trespassing or protective zones ranging in size from 30 acres around nests to a half-mile radius around post-fledging family areas. The August 2000 agreement obligated the Forest Service to prepare by the end of the year an interim amendment to the 1997 forest plan that addressed Chief Forester Dombeck's concern for species diversity; by the end of 2002 it was to prepare a final amendment addressing all the issues the plaintiffs had raised. In return, the plaintiffs agreed to drop their suit and to allow timber sales already sold, and those unsold during the appeal period, to proceed.[21]

Seeking to give a positive impression of what appeared to be a Forest Service defeat, Supervisor Twiss announced that the agency viewed amendment preparation as an opportunity to include scientific data acquired since the 1997 forest plan had been completed.[22] In fact, an enormous amount of new data would be gathered before publication of the final amendment in October 2005, much of it collected after the Jasper fire, which burned through an unprecedented 83,508 acres.

It turned out that an arsonist started the Jasper fire, just off US Highway 16, 13 miles west of Custer, shortly after 2:00 p.m. on August 24, 2000. Because of high temperatures, record low moisture, and strong winds, the fire quickly spread into treetops; windblown embers ignited spot fires as far as one-half mile ahead of the main fire. On the first day, the fire spread at the rate of 7 acres per minute, doubling in size every hour and covering 3,655 acres by day's end. Within hours on day three, the fire grew by 48,555 acres as a result of strong winds and near-firestorm conditions. Then, as weather conditions improved, the fire slowed, but it still spread over another 23,000 acres before containment on September 8 and control on September 25.[23]

Mystic District ranger Robert J. Thompson, who led the Rapid Assessment Team, summarized the fire's impact on the land: "The fire completely blackened some areas, leaving scorched, dead trees and ash-covered ground in its wake. Other areas experienced only a light ground burn, with just the base of the tree trunks and lower branches slightly burned or browned. Large areas . . . remain green, either lightly burned or completely unburned."[24]

Overall, economic damage was less than might have been expected following such a conflagration, in part because of the area's relative remoteness. To be sure, the fire burned an estimated 250 million board feet of timber, destroyed some infrastructure belonging to twenty-four grazing permittees, melted power and telephone lines, and burned poles. Around 120 miles of fire lines required rehabilitation. Remarkably, all the buildings at Jewel Cave National Monument, surrounded by the fire, were saved; only one summer cabin and three outbuildings were destroyed.[25]

Nonetheless, because of the enormity of the fire and its impact on changing habits of mind, key steps in its suppression are worth noting. Within ten minutes of the initial citizen's emergency call, fire crews were en route from Newcastle; within seventeen minutes Joe Harbach, a longtime Forest Service fire technician and former Custer volunteer fire chief, left Custer by helicopter to survey the fire. As calls went out for air tankers and more equipment, Harbach organized 250 firefighters and support personnel from various jurisdictions under a single structure, known as a Type III Management Team, that went into action late afternoon on that first day.[26]

"No doubt about it," opined *Custer Weekly Chronicle* editor Charley Najacht, "fighting the Jasper fire was like fighting a war, and for a while on Saturday [day three], the fire was winning big time." That was the day the fire grew at the rate of more than 100 acres per minute. "But then the wind settled down and friendly forces started building up. A military operation had begun."[27] On day four, a Type I Incident Management Team, the most sophisticated of all teams, arrived from the Pacific Northwest to assume control over efforts that at their peak included 1,260 personnel, 138 fire trucks, 18 bulldozers, 9 water tenders, and 6 helicopters. At the date of fire control, the Forest Service had incurred $8.6 million in fire-fighting costs; the final figure was $11.5 million.[28]

Citing a passion to protect private property (the fire burned across 2,825 acres of private property), Governor William J. Janklow threatened to order state fire crews to set backfires ahead of the fire and to order National Guard troops to use bulldozers to build fires lines, also ahead of the fire. Asked about the safety of such operations, Governor Janklow was quoted as saying that the state could buy more bulldozers and the forward crews could easily outrun the fire.[29] When Type I Incident Commander Bill Waterbury arrived on the scene, he advised the governor that he (Waterbury) was in charge of all fire suppression efforts. Waterbury later told reporters "that if it came down to a point of putting firefighters at risk or of independent actions, whether that be private citizens or the National Guard, I wouldn't hesitate to pull all of our firefighters off the line." He added, "If necessary, we'd use our federal authority to arrest people who were interfering with our firefighting."[30]

Governor Janklow was on firmer ground when he accompanied state and local authorities to oversee the evacuation of residents living within possible reach of the fire. After conferring with the governor, the Custer City Council, at 3:30 a.m. on

September 3, approved an evacuation plan dividing the town into quadrants, with a cadre of twenty-five officers assigned per quadrant from the State Highway Patrol, National Guard, and county sheriff's office to notify residents in person and direct them to Red Cross shelters in Hill City, Hot Springs, and Rapid City. Upon notification from the Forest Service that the fire had reached a point within 4 miles of Custer, the mayor would order execution of the plan; as it happened, the fire got no closer than within 6 miles of the town.[31]

While the fire still raged, some members of the public accused the Forest Service of reacting too slowly to the severity of the fire; others blamed "greenies" for tying Forest Service officers' hands with "frivolous" lawsuits: "Why not round up all Sierra Club members, hand 'em a pick and shovel and send 'em to fight the Jasper fire. They are all idiots." The "greenies" should also be forced to pay civil damages "to all of us who now suffer the loss of our wonderful hills." Arsonists may have started the fire, a citizen wrote, but political activists had prepared the setting as part of a deliberate attack on private property and the American economic system.[32]

Representative John Thune (R-SD), touring the fire on day four, blamed Clinton administration policies for fanning the flames. He singled out the road-less area initiative as preventing suppression of wildfires and generally hindering effective management: "They have replaced common sense forest management with environmental extremism."[33] On day six, Supervisor Twiss noted in a newspaper column that the Jasper fire had "little relation to any policy—the key elements fueling this intense fire are low fuel moisture, high temperatures, heavy ground fuels from the April snow storm, and erratic winds." While flying over the area, Twiss had seen the fire move with equal intensity over thinned and un-thinned areas, through meadows as well as trees. Unquestionably, policies that prevented quick action against insect epidemics, forest fires, and windstorms required immediate review; policies that led to healthier ecosystems needed to be put in place.[34]

Despite political pressure to quickly allow salvage operations while dead trees were still commercially viable, it required seven months of study before Supervisor Twiss approved the special harvest of 24 million board feet, in addition to the 44 million board feet under contract within the fire perimeter before the fire. In seeking to balance salvaging and habitat protection, Twiss noted that unburned islands of timber would be preserved for possible goshawk nesting sites (the fire had destroyed nine nests), big-game and wild turkey cover, and as seed source for forest regeneration.[35] In addition, beginning in spring 2002, a contract crew would plant approximately 150,000 ponderosa pine seedlings from the Bessey Nursery annually in places where the fire had been so hot that it sterilized the soil and destroyed seeds. As protection against deer and elk, each seedling would be surrounded by mesh tubing that decomposed within three to five years.[36]

FIGURE 11.3. Tree planting in the Jasper fire area, 2011. Courtesy, Beth Doten, USDA Forest Service, Black Hills National Forest, http://www.ForestPhoto.com.

In the wake of the Jasper fire and the earlier settlement agreement with Biodiversity Associates, combined with the policy directive on ecosystem management, Black Hills National Forest silviculturist Blaine Cook determined that the 1974 Boldt guide for foresters, supplemented in 1987 by Hoffman and Alexander, needed to be brought up-to-date. For that purpose, he recruited two silviculturists from the Rocky Mountain Research Station: Wayne D. Shepperd, who succeeded Alexander as overseer of the Black Hills Experimental Forest, and his assistant, Michael A. Battaglia.

For their research, Shepperd and Battaglia used the habitat inventory developed by Hoffman and Alexander, although the Forest Service had officially adopted the community inventory system by Marriott and others. It would be fair to state that silviculturists preferred Hoffman's "forest-driven" over Marriott's "botany-driven" approach to classification. Shepperd and Battaglia did, however, take a broader view of forestry than their silviculturist predecessors, most notably in their treatment of mountain pine beetles and wildfires, the predominant natural disturbances. With an eye to the practical, they noted that "understanding these disturbances and how they shape forest structure and influence ecological processes could allow foresters to better manage their forests by integrating disturbance history into informed management decisions."[37]

Shepperd and Battaglia explained that, at endemic levels, mountain pine beetles contribute to improved growth rates of trees through thinning and to accelerated regeneration by opening gaps in the forest cover. Beetle infestations tended to transform dense even-aged stands into irregularly spaced uneven-aged stands more resistant to epidemics. In confirming that the most effective silvicultural tool for reducing risk of epidemics remained thinning, they noted the increasing backlog of stands requiring pre-commercial thinning and deemed such thinning as "an absolute necessity" for the regeneration of even-aged and uneven-aged stands, the sooner the better for both ecological and commercial reasons.[38]

On the matter of forest fires, Shepperd and Battaglia noted that although the ecological role of fire had only recently become understood, foresters had long recognized the ponderosa pine as a species especially well adapted to fire. The thick bark of older trees protects against relatively low-intensity ground fires, while such fires destroy dense stands of seedlings and buildup of thatch. Citing recent fire studies of the Black Hills, Shepperd and Battaglia estimated that the frequency of ground fires ranged from ten to twenty-four years but that the frequency of large-scale, stand-replacing crown fires was less certain. Outside researchers, who were not always scientists, tended to view the frequency of catastrophic fires as greater than did researchers within the Forest Service.[39]

While acknowledging that the traditional shelterwood method was the most dependable for even-aged stands, Shepperd and Battaglia argued that uneven-aged stands would bring about a more aesthetic forest appearance, improve wildlife habitat, increase biological diversity, and reduce chances of insect epidemics and catastrophic fires. To achieve sustainable distributions of various diameter classes of trees, foresters needed to inventory a given stand and then mark the excess individual trees for cutting. Up to 2010, uneven stand management had occurred only within the Black Hills Experimental Forest.[40]

In view of the imperative to improve wildlife habitat, Shepperd and Battaglia devoted part of their study to a review of recent research on major wildlife species, their habitat requirements, and their management. In the case of the goshawk species, mentioned by plaintiffs in legal briefs, the silviculturists recommended that forest managers needed to review and adapt the substantial data that had been collected by researchers in the American Southwest.[41]

Although the Shepperd and Battaglia study had been commissioned as a status report on the Black Hills silviculture, separate and apart from ongoing forest planning, its recommendations proved consistent with the amendments to the 1997 forest plan. Completion of the interim amendment, scheduled for December 2000, was delayed until May 2001, suggesting debate within the agency on how best to proceed. In his decision notice, Supervisor Twiss confirmed that any forest activity that might affect species diversity and viability would be postponed until adoption of the final amendment. Because the 2000 settlement stipulated no ground-disturbing activities within or adjacent to road-less areas until completion of the final amendment, the Forest Service could not begin to reduce risks of fires and insect epidemics in the Beaver Park road-less area and the Norbeck Wildlife Preserve.[42]

Adding to the Forest Service's inability to act, on August 8, 2001, the US Court of Appeals for the Tenth District ruled in favor of Biodiversity Associates to temporarily halt the proposed Grizzly and Needles sales within the Norbeck Wildlife Preserve. The court determined that the Forest Service had yet to prove that its management plan for that area was consistent with the Game Sanctuary Act or that it met the requirements of the National Forest Management Act.[43] Although frustration over inaction was expressed privately inside the Forest Service, especially among district rangers and staff members who dealt with timber operators, frustration among elected officials and those residing near or in the national forest erupted publicly. Using its political influence, industry pressed the congressional delegation to compel the Forest Service to allow new timber sales.

On August 14, 2001, Senator Daschle, who got along well with Governor Janklow, convened a "Forest Policy Summit" in Rapid City, attended by an overflow crowd of 600. Daschle brought with him Dale N. Bosworth, newly appointed by President George W. Bush as chief forester. Bosworth was a second-generation Forest Service employee, and his appointment pleased forest administrators.[44]

At the "Summit," Chief Bosworth heard members of the public and elected officials make known their criticisms of the Forest Service on the subject of preventing and fighting forest fires. Governor Janklow, still irritated by his treatment during the Jasper fire, complained that the Forest Service had yet to fully reimburse South Dakota for its fire-fighting costs and warned that, for the next big forest fire, he would mobilize volunteer fire departments and bill the federal government for reimbursement of all expenses. Residents of two subdivisions (about 100 homes) adjoining the Beaver Park road-less area formally asked the Forest Service to construct firebreaks around the area and to implement special management of Forest Service lands adjoining the subdivisions. Representatives of groups opposed to timbering argued that rather than push the Forest Service to fireproof the forest, private property owners should fireproof around their own homes. A district ranger, apparently spontaneously, stood up to say that if procedures could be simplified and their implementation accelerated, he and his staff could devote more time to managing the forest.[45]

The conditions in and around Beaver Park highlighted the urgency of taking preventative action against catastrophic wildfires within the "wildland-urban interface," defined by the Forest Service as the place where people and their development meet or intermix with national forest lands. Toward that end, Senator Timothy P. Johnson (D-SD) directed his legislative liaison to host the first in a series of discussions that led to the extraordinary compromise that broke the impasse over management of Beaver Park and the Norbeck Wildlife Preserve and to almost universal agreement that managing for forest health was the best way to enhance forest values and sustain timbering.

A December 2001 Forest Service report on the unexpectedly rapid spread of the mountain pine beetle in the Beaver Park area precipitated political action to find timely solutions.[46] Regional Forester Rick C. Cables had taken a group, including Senator Daschle's staff member Peter Hanson, to inspect the area. With wildfires burning elsewhere in the forest, Cables recalled that when he and his group reached the center of Beaver Park, conditions were such that they feared that if a fire started nearby, they might not be able to get out in time. Cables had also learned from legal counsel that action on Beaver Park could be taken only if all parties agreed to the 2000 settlement agreement. Hanson expressed support for renegotiating that agreement.[47] Senator Daschle's legislative aide, Eric Washburn, quietly began working on a process for expediting remedial action. Long at the forefront of discussions on timber issues, Daschle remained active behind the scenes; he felt his family's imminent purchase of property near Beaver Park could be perceived by some as a conflict of interest.[48]

By early 2002, Biodiversity Associates and the other plaintiffs in the Beaver Park case suspected that Supervisor Twiss, known to enjoy a friendly relationship with congressional aides, had been advocating for congressional action to overturn the August 2000 settlement. On February 14, at the urging of Senators Daschle and Johnson, Twiss invited the plaintiffs to discuss ways—not excluding the possibility of modifying the settlement agreement—to reduce fire hazards in the Beaver Park area and the Norbeck Wildlife Preserve. "The point is," he wrote, "that public frustration is turning to desperation over the perceived threat to homes and lives from ignitions on Federal lands, and the Government's current inability to mitigate it."[49]

Biodiversity Associates and the other plaintiffs reacted negatively, accusing the Forest Service of bad faith while stating that they themselves had played by the rules. Nonetheless, they agreed to meet, together with representatives of various other forest users, for a general discussion in Custer on February 19. Regional Forester Cables, who, along with Chief Bosworth, had crafted the overall Forest Service position, reported that the discussion was constructive; as follow-up, he proposed a second meeting for which he hoped to limit the agenda to how government agencies could conduct fire prevention activities in the affected areas. Cables volunteered that the Forest Service would produce a draft action plan. The plaintiffs, wishing to prevent any human disturbances in the road-less areas, countered that the congressional delegation needed to find $10 million to establish a fund to assist homeowners and communities in protecting homes and buildings within the wildland-urban interface.[50]

Meanwhile, South Dakota lawmakers had introduced legislation authorizing municipalities to take preventative actions on national forest lands whenever the governor declared a state of emergency; in addition, Governor Janklow had renewed his threat to sue the federal government for failure to reduce fuel buildup in Beaver Park. Representative Thune had introduced a rider to the farm appropriations bill that, in his opinion, would allow the Forest Service to do its job. The proposed Black Hills Forest Preservation and Public Safety Act, cosponsored by Representative Barbara Cubin (R-WY), directed the Forest Service to use "expedited alternative processes to address forest health conditions." In the plaintiffs' opinion, Thune's rider would allow uncontrolled commercial logging in nearly any fire-prone area of the Black Hills. Senators Daschle and Johnson blocked the rider. At the same time, the senators obtained support for continuing discussions at the local level from Mark Rey, under-secretary of agriculture, who was responsible for overseeing the Forest Service. Rey's support, the threat of the Thune rider, and the need to remain on good terms with Senator Daschle combined to encourage the plaintiffs to go forward with discussions.[51]

"After considerable political wrangling and disagreement among the parties, and some preliminary meetings," Sam Clauson recalled, "we finally got together in face-to-face discussions at the Black Hills National Forest office in Custer on April 18–19, 2002."[52] Tom Troxel expressed the view that Eric Washburn had made the connections to bring all parties to the table and recalled that Washburn participated in one of the first sessions. Washburn succeeded in getting the parties to address in the same discussion two previously unrelated matters: modifying the 2000 settlement agreement regarding Beaver Park and resolving the issues posed by the lawsuit against the two timber sales in the Norbeck Wildlife Preserve.[53]

To allow for candid and unfettered discussion, Wells Burgess, representing the US Department of Justice, required that all parties sign a confidentiality agreement at the beginning of negotiations. The parties were the plaintiffs (Biodiversity Associates, Sierra Club, Wilderness Society, Brian Brademeyer, and, separately, the Black Hills Group of the Sierra Club), the counties (Lawrence, Meade, and Pennington), the state agencies (Attorney General, Department of Agriculture, Department of Game, Fish, and Parks), the federal agencies (Department of Justice, Forest Service), and the defendant-intervenors (Black Hills Forest Resource Association and Black Hills Multiple Use Coalition). Bound by the confidentiality agreement, twenty-four individuals signed up to participate in the two-day closed session.[54]

As far as can be ascertained, negotiations began in a tense atmosphere that mellowed as time went by. The plaintiffs staked out their position through a confidential draft in which they proposed no timbering and the eradication of all roads (except the scenic byway) in the Norbeck Wildlife Preserve and argued that removal of older, more fire-resistant trees would not only increase fire risk but would also damage vital habitat for sensitive species such as the goshawk. Alleging the Forest Service's unwillingness to protect wildlands, the plaintiffs requested designation of an additional 10,000 acres to the Black Elk Wilderness and 6,500 acres set aside as the Needles Natural Area. In the Beaver Park area, they asked for designation of 9,000 acres as wilderness or a combination of wilderness and natural area. They did support timbering on two stands in the road-less area, but only within strict limits and after further study of possible goshawk habitats.[55]

For the Beaver Park road-less area, the Forest Service arrived with an interim proposal to improve access for single-axle fire equipment, to create three 5-acre heliports and new fire breaks, and to cut, thin, or remove infested, dead, or downed trees within 400 feet of private properties if their landowners agreed to do likewise. For the Norbeck Wildlife Preserve, the Forest Service proposed to go ahead with the two contested timber sales, to create firebreaks along existing roads, to continue planning for wildlife habitat improvements, and to postpone for three years any cutting or thinning on 2,000 acres.[56]

While all sides gave a little, the critical concession came at the end of the second day when the Forest Service replaced its deferred timbering proposal with a recommendation to put approximately 3,374 acres of the Norbeck Wildlife Preserve into the National Wilderness Preservation System. With that concession, every party except Biodiversity Associates and Brian Brademeyer agreed to continue negotiations by telephone. On May 1, Supervisor Twiss, Bart Koehler from the Wilderness Society, and Tom Troxel from the Black Hills Forest Resource Association presented a draft modifying the 2000 settlement agreement that was acceptable to the continuing parties but still required refinements. An early forest conservation activist in Wyoming with a graduate degree in natural resources management, Koehler had long served as a troubleshooter for the Wilderness Society and was considered personable and trustworthy by all concerned. When Biodiversity Associates and Brian Brademeyer formally left negotiations on May 10, representatives of the US Department of Justice withdrew from the talks, arguing that, in the absence of two non-settling plaintiffs, the modified agreement could not be implemented administratively or through the courts. In other words, fire prevention and insect control in Beaver Park and Norbeck could be addressed only through congressional action. It is unclear whether any participant had seen the first draft of legislation prepared in early March by staff members of the Forest Service's legal department, on the chance that negotiations failed.[57]

The continuing parties, having completed a seventh and final draft of the modi-fied agreement on May 23, petitioned the South Dakota congressional delegation to introduce legislation based on that agreement. Eric Washburn put the final draft into legislative form and sent it to Supervisor Twiss for final review. With Twiss's approval, Washburn sent the final version to Kohler and David Thom, a natural resource staff officer and Twiss's principal aide in negotiations, for distribution to participants. Washburn advised no press statements until after the prepared bill had cleared all legislative hurdles. "We have come far together," he wrote, "and I think it is wise that we all coordinate press together and avoid encouraging any public discussions that could complicate our ability to get this bill across the finish line."[58]

The modified settlement agreement, also known as the Daschle rider, was attached as Section 706 to H.R. 4775, a supplemental appropriations act "for fur-ther recovery from and response to terrorist attacks on the United States." The bill was approved by the US House of Representatives on July 17, 2002, reconciled with the Senate on July 23, and signed by President George W. Bush on August 2. Based on the agreement negotiated at Custer, the Daschle rider specified management of timber sales and other prescriptions in great detail. Of highest priority for treat-ment were Forest Service lands within one-quarter mile of private properties where owners had taken or were taking actions to reduce fuel accumulations. Language in the rider encouraged state and county officials to identify "fire emergency zones" in which public safety could require postponing the issuance of new building permits until stricter fire codes were adopted.[59] The Forest Service got what it had proposed for fire prevention in the Beaver Park road-less area, but within prescribed limits; the plaintiffs gained 3,600 acres of additional wilderness but not the 10,000-plus acres they had sought.

In the Norbeck Wildlife Preserve, the two timber sales were allowed after cer-tain modifications as recommended in a "Wildlife Field Review," made part of the 2002 final negotiated settlement agreement. Prepared in October 1999 by two wild-life biologists, one from the Forest Service and the other from the South Dakota Department of Game, Fish, and Parks, the report had sought to answer two ques-tions: Were the proposed timber sales laid out to accomplish what was best for wildlife, or were they timber sales disguised as habitat improvement projects? Were the sales scientifically supportable? Their answer to the first question was ambiva-lent; the actual design of the sales would not have been their choice. They answered the second question in the affirmative but only if further recommended steps were taken to protect wildlife.[60]

With the biologists' report as their basis, the Forest Service and the South Dakota Department of Game, Fish, and Parks agreed to put wildlife biologists in charge of managing the Norbeck Wildlife Preserve. Signed on July 17, 2002, and periodically brought up-to-date, renewed, and having survived numerous appeals, the memorandum of agreement set forth procedures for monitoring the effects of forestry on wildlife and their habitats, for collaborating on habitat management, and for recommending changes as needed in forestry practices specific to the preserve. Beyond wildlife and wildlife habitat, the Daschle rider required the Forest Service to establish a committee of agency scientists to recommend by December 1, 2004, the location for a late successional research plot within the Norbeck Wildlife Preserve. Preservation of old-growth trees would be adversely affected by renewed beetle infestations.[61]

In what was perhaps an unprecedented development, the Sierra Club and the Wilderness Society had agreed with the continuing parties that because of the "extraordinary circumstances" of fire danger, the Daschle rider overrode all otherwise applicable environmental laws and related administrative procedures and explicitly superseded the August 2000 settlement agreement. Both groups agreed not to challenge the final negotiated settlement in court; they did, however, object to the addition of a sentence in the legislation: "Any action authorized by this [procedural] section shall not be subject to judicial review by any court of the United States."[62]

One month after President Bush signed the legislation that included the Daschle rider, Biodiversity Associates and Brad Brademeyer, supported by the Sierra Club and the Wilderness Society, filed suit against the Forest Service. The plaintiffs argued that the unusual specificity of the Daschle rider, together with its displacement of the 2000 settlement agreement, amounted to a legislative branch violation of the US Constitution's separation of powers. On February 4, 2004, the US Court of Appeals Tenth District decided against the plaintiffs.[63]

Though some continued to oppose forestry in the Norbeck Wildlife Preserve, they essentially marginalized themselves to the point of irrelevance. After Bryan Brademeyer, through his Friends of Norbeck organization, lost his 2010 appeal to stop thinning and other activities meant to improve wildlife habitat in the preserve, he admitted that he had filed the complaint not because he thought he would win but in retaliation against Forest Service personnel who had cited him for illegally marking for timbering more than seventy trees on Forest Service land that obscured the view of Harney Peak from his home.[64]

Meanwhile, the Daschle rider had caused both envy and resentment among members of Congress from other Western states. They argued that South Dakota wildfire threats were not unique to South Dakota and that "extraordinary circumstances" in their respective states merited the same exemptions from environmental laws and judicial reviews. Senator Larry E. Craig (R-ID) proclaimed that "what's good for the Black Hills should be good for every forest in the United States."[65] In response to congressional colleagues and to the catastrophic forest fires occurring throughout the West, at President Bush's request, Senator Daschle with Eric Washburn drafted the Healthy Forests Restoration Act of 2003, which Congress passed.

Unquestionably, the Healthy Forests Restoration Act built on the key elements of the Daschle rider: to reduce the risk of catastrophic wildfires and related insect epidemics. At the same time, the act provided for subsidies to improve commercial timber stands and thus to provide biomass for commercial purposes, such as generating heat and electrical energy. Although the rationale for the act, as well as the shift of Forest Service appropriations to fire suppression, was essentially a reaction to catastrophic wildfires, the act did allow for active forestry meant "to protect, restore, and enhance forest ecosystem components" and, within that context, to take up preventative measures "through a collaborative process of planning, prioritizing, and implementing."[66] It is tempting to conclude that, through a fortuitous set of circumstances, Senator Daschle helped to reassert the role of the Black Hills National Forest as the flagship for the entire national forest system.

NOTES

1. *Custer County Chronicle*, October 6, 1994.

2. Merrill R. Kaufmann et al., "An Ecological Basis for Ecosystem Management," USDA Forest Service General Technical Report GTR-RM-246 (May 1994): 1; Jack Ward Thomas, team leader, *Forest Ecosystem Management: An Ecological, Economic, and Social Assessment: Report of the Forest Ecosystem Management Assessment Team* (Washington, DC: USDA Forest Service, 1993), pt. 9: 10.

3. Quoted in Kaufmann et al., "Ecological Basis," 2.

4. John C. Twiss, *1996 Revised Land and Resource Management Plan; 1997 Revision Record of Decision* (Custer: Black Hills National Forest, 1997), 22; *Rapid City Journal*, December 11, 1996; *Custer County Chronicle*, December 19, 1996.

5. *Custer County Chronicle*, October 10, 1996.

6. "Hills Timber Plan Cuts Both Ways," *Rapid City Journal*, December 11, 1996, A1.

7. "Species Not Declining in Hills," *Rapid City Journal*, March 21, 1997, A4.

8. *Rapid City Journal*, April 12, 1997.

9. Black Hills Group, Sierra Club, news release, January 31, 1997, copy, Samuel D. Clauson personal files; Biodiversity Associates, "Legal and Scientific Failings of the Black Hills Revised Forest Plan," January 22, 1997, copy, Samuel D. Clauson personal files; Samuel D. Clauson, personal communication, March 21, 1997.

10. *Custer County Chronicle*, October 16, 1997.

11. Hollis Marriott et al., *The Black Hills Community Inventory: Final Report* (Minneapolis: Nature Conservancy Midwest Conservation Science Center, 1999), 1, 121.

12. Ibid., 5, 13–14, 71, 73.

13. Ibid., 11, 45.

14. Twiss, *Record of Decision*, 32–33.

15. *Custer County Chronicle*, March 25, 1998.

16. Ibid.

17. *Biodiversity Associates v. Laverty*, "Complaint for Declaratory Judgment and Injunctive Relief," US District Court for the District of Colorado, Civil Action 99–2173, filed November 10, 1999, 6–8, 17, Black Hills National Forest supervisor's office, Custer, SD (hereafter BHNF).

18. Ibid., 15–16.

19. Ibid., 20–24.

20. *Biodiversity Associates v. Laverty*, "Settlement Agreement," US District Court for the District of Colorado, August 1, 2000, 1–28, BHNF.

21. Ibid.

22. "Lawsuit Settled on the Black Hills National Forest," BHNF news release, n.d., BHNF.

23. *Custer Weekly Chronicle*, August 31, September 7, 2000.

24. Robert J. Thompson, team leader, "Jasper Fire Rapid Assessment," September 2000, p. 7, BHNF.

25. Ibid., 12, 17, 47, 49.

26. *Custer Weekly Chronicle*, August 31, 2000.

27. Ibid., September 7, 2000.

28. Ibid., August 31, September 7, October 5, 2000; Blaine Cook, personal communication, February 2013.

29. Governor Janklow quoted at http://wildfiretoday.com/2010/02/21/south-dakota-governor-vows-to-fight-fire-in-federal-wilderness-area/; accessed February 2011.

30. "Feds: Governor a Danger on Fires," *Rapid City Journal*, October 30, 2002, A1.

31. *Custer Weekly Chronicle*, September 14, 2000.

32. Letters to the editor, *Custer Weekly Chronicle*, August 31, 2000.

33. Quoted in ibid., August 31, 2000.

34. Ibid.

35. BHNF news release, April 4, 2001, BHNF.

36. Ibid., April 27, 2011, at http://www.fs.usda.gov/detail/blackhills/news-events/?cid=STELPRDB5295582; accessed December 2012.

37. Wayne D. Shepperd and Michael A. Battaglia, *Ecology, Silviculture, and Management of Black Hills Ponderosa Pine*, USDA Forest Service Rocky Mountain Research Station General Technical Report RMRS-GTR-97 (September 2002): 17.

38. Ibid., 17, 22, 78.

39. Ibid., 36–38.

40. Ibid., 68, 73–74.

41. Ibid., 58–60.

42. John C. Twiss, cover letter, *1997 Land and Resource Management Plan, Amendment 1 Decision Notice* (Custer: Black Hills National Forest, May 2001).

43. *Sierra Club—Black Hills Group, American Wildlands, and Biodiversity Associates v. U.S. Forest Service*, Court of Appeals Tenth District, 259 F.3d 1281 (2001), at http://law.justia .com/cases/federal/appellate-courts/F3/259/1281/575663/; accessed February 2011.

44. Thomas Blair, discussion with author, April 2009.

45. "Decision-Making Must Change, Foresters Say," *Rapid City Journal*, August 15, 2001, A1; "Forest Policy Summit Draws 600," *Rapid City Journal*, August 16, 2001, A1.

46. Kurt K. Allen, Daniel F. Long, and Frank J. Cross, "Evaluation of Mountain Pine Beetle Activity on the Black Hills National Forest," USDA Forest Service Biological Evaluation R2-02-02 (December 2001).

47. Rick C. Cables, discussion with author, May 2013.

48. Thomas A. Daschle to John C. Twiss, Washington, DC, March 8, 2002, Daschle rider folder, BHNF.

49. John C. Twiss to Biodiversity Associates, Sierra Club, Brian Brademeyer, and American Wildlands, Custer, SD, February 14, 2002, Daschle rider folder, BHNF.

50. Theodore Zukoski on behalf of Biodiversity Associates, Laramie, WY, February 16, 2002; Rick C. Cables to Jack R. Tuholske, Denver, CO, March 15, 2002; Sam Clauson to Senator Tom Johnson, Rapid City, SD, March 21, 2002, all in Daschle rider folder, BHNF.

51. "Public Safety Concerns and Forest Management Hurdles in the Black Hills National Forest," Hearing before the Subcommittee on Department Operations, Oversight, Nutrition, and Forestry, Committee on Agriculture, US House of Representatives, Washington, DC, June 6, 2002, 4, 7–8, Daschle rider folder, BHNF; Sam Clauson, "My Perspective on Recent Black Hills National Forest Negotiations," typescript, September 1, 2002, personal communication.

52. Clauson, "My Perspective."

53. Thomas Troxel, discussion with author, April 2011.

54. Confidentiality agreement prepared by Wells Burgess, US Department of Justice, Custer, SD, April 18, 2002, Daschle rider folder, BHNF.

55. "Plaintiffs' Confidential Draft Proposal for Beaver Park and Norbeck," April 10, 2002, Daschle rider folder, BHNF.

56. "Forest Service Beaver Park and Norbeck Proposals," April 18, 2002, Daschle rider folder, BHNF.

57. "Public Safety Concerns," 27–28; "Black Hills Legislative Drafting Service," e-mail message, March 4, 2002, Daschle rider folder, BHNF.

58. Eric Washburn to Bart Koehler and David Thom, e-mail message, Washington, DC, June 13, 2002, and Lori Potter (legal counsel to Sierra Club and the Wilderness Society) to

Kenneth Capps (Department of Agriculture, Office of General Counsel), e-mail message, Denver, CO, May 5, 2002, both in Daschle rider folder, BHNF.

59. An Act Making Supplemental Appropriations for Further Recovery from and Response to Terrorist Attacks on the United States . . ., Public Law 107–206, section 706 [Daschle rider], *US Statutes at Large* 116 (2002): 864–69.

60. Ibid., 867–68; Kerry A. Burns and Art Carter, "Wildlife Field Review, Grizzly and Needles Project Areas, Norbeck Wildlife Preserve," Custer, SD, November 10, 1999, BHNF; "Memorandum of Understanding between South Dakota Department of Game, Fish, and Parks and United States Department of Agriculture, Forest Service, Black Hills National Forest," October 20, 2009, BHNF; personal communication from Shelly Deisch, South Dakota Department of Game, Fish, and Parks, January 2013.

61. Ibid., 867–68; Kerry A. Burns and Art Carter, "Wildlife Field Review, Grizzly and Needles Project Areas, Norbeck Wildlife Preserve," Custer, SD, November 10, 1999, BHNF; "Memorandum of Understanding between South Dakota Department of Game, Fish, and Parks and United States Department of Agriculture, Forest Service, Black Hills National Forest," October 20, 2009, BHNF; personal communication from Shelly Deisch, South Dakota Department of Game, Fish, and Parks, January 2013.

62. Clauson, "My Perspective"; Daschle rider, 868.

63. *Biodiversity Associates v. Rick D. Cables*, appeal from the US District Court for the District of Colorado to the US Court of Appeals Tenth District, filed February 4, 2004, at http://ca10.washburnlaw.edu/cases/2004/02/03-1002.htm; accessed April 2011.

64. Frank Carroll, "Forest Report," May 2012, based on interview with arresting officer, personal communication.

65. Quoted in *Livestock Weekly*, August 1, 2002, at http://www.livestockweekly.com /papers/02/08/01/whldaschle.asp; accessed March 2011.

66. Healthy Forests Restoration Act, Public Law 108–48, *US Statutes at Large* 117 (2003): 1887–1915; Thomas Troxel, discussion with author, November 2009.

12

Forest Values, Forest Service

At the dawn of the new century, the front line of forestry in the Black Hills cut through the Mystic Ranger District that borders Rapid City and surrounds Hill City, Keystone, and Mount Rushmore National Memorial. Within its boundaries are 311,000 acres of national forest land and 45,000 acres of private land. District Ranger Robert J. Thompson liked to tell visitors that no point on public land within his district was more than 3 miles from private land, which means that Forest Service land borders on thousands of backyards.

Despite repeated warnings about the effects of unbridled development within the wildland-urban interface, real estate developers continued at full speed; newcomers anxious to own their piece of the Black Hills often failed to inform themselves in advance of the risks involved. The 14,495-acre Battle Creek fire in 2002 provided a reminder. At one point, winds drove embers over all four lanes of US Highway 16, casting doubts about the adequacy of recommendations concerning "defensible space" around homes and outbuildings. As with all wildfire suppression, the Forest Service underwrote most of the costs, which benefited affected property owners, their insurers, and state and local public safety agencies. In effect, the Forest Service found itself subsidizing the very development that makes its tasks extraordinarily difficult and expensive. No wonder that the affected counties felt little pressure to impose the regulations needed to lower the true costs of development or that the Black Hills National Forest, constrained to spend 40–50 percent of its budget on fire suppression, felt unable to pursue the forest-wide activities required to reduce the overall risk of catastrophic fires.

DOI: 10.5876/9781607322993.c012

FIGURE 12.1. Commercial development on private property within the Black Hills National Forest boundary, 2010. Author photo.

During the near-paralysis that affected the national forest during the Beaver Park–Norbeck Wildlife Preserve controversy, District Ranger Thompson decided to launch an experiment in landscape- rather than stand-level forestry. Its goal: to restore the forest ecosystem to the point that the forest could recover from both nat-ural and human-caused disturbances. Sustainable commercial timbering would be a secondary objective, though Thompson and others understood that achieving forest health would require more harvesting, thinning, and prescribed burns before the for-est could take care of itself. After gaining virtually unanimous public support through a lengthy and thorough process, Acting Supervisor Brad Exton approved the Prairie Project in the lower Rapid Creek area just west of Rapid City. Given its longtime preeminence within the national forest system, it is not surprising that the Prairie Project's principal goal and innovative approach would be reflected in national forest planning rules proposed in 2011 by Secretary of Agriculture Thomas J. Vilsack.[1]

At the 2001 "Forest Summit," Senator Thomas Daschle had suggested the establishment of a forest-wide advisory board as a way to resolve issues locally, without resort to the courts. After months of apparent hesitancy, Supervisor John Twiss announced his intention to recommend such a board, composed of fifteen members, to provide advice on a broad range of issues including reviewing plan revisions, monitoring and evaluating implementation of plans, and suggesting specific projects with forest-wide applications. Under a skilful supervisor, this advisory board would serve as a means to gauge public opinion and promulgate the supervisor's agenda.[2]

As it turned out, the Black Hills National Forest Advisory Board took the lead among the various groups that sought to expand the scope of the original directive for preparing the final amendment to the 1997 revised forest plan—to address more completely for the long term the issues of insect epidemics and catastrophic fires. Between 1997 and 2004, beetles had destroyed another 114,000 acres and wildfires had burned more than 150,000 acres. The 11,589-acre Grizzly Gulch fire came perilously close to destroying the town of Deadwood in 2002.[3]

Approved at long last in October 2005, the final amendment provided some accommodation to both non-timber and timber interests. To improve wildlife habitat, the Forest Service agreed to retain all dead standing trees in unburned areas, preserve snags during post-wildfire salvage operations, and protect more late-successional trees. To improve timbering, the agency agreed to increase thinning of dense stands, increase the number of post and pole stands, and retain late-successional trees as a way to gain structural diversity and lower the risks of wildfires and insect epidemics. The Forest Service deemed as outside the scope of the final amendment any changes in travel management, timber sale levels, annual allowable sale quantities, and recommendations for more wilderness areas.[4]

The most significant change in the final amendment came with the addition of an entirely new goal: to "establish and maintain a mosaic of vegetation conditions to reduce occurrences of catastrophic fire, insect, and disease events, and facilitate insect and disease management and fire-fighting capability."[5] That was precisely what District Ranger Thompson had intended for the Prairie Project, approved two years earlier, with implementation started in early 2004.

The Prairie Project came about as a reaction to catastrophic wildfires and a realization that conventional timbering had not lessened the risks, at least not in the wildland-urban interface. As Thompson explained, the timber industry reacted by advocating more pre-commercial thinning and commercial timbering; the "environmental community" argued that timbering had not reduced the risk of fires and may even have increased the risks, noting that some large fires had occurred in areas that were heavily timbered. Thompson saw merit in both arguments. He also knew that because of the relatively dense population and high property values in the project area, letting large fires burn was not an option.[6]

Thompson was in an unenviable position. By then, Pinchot's organizational model, which gave district rangers considerable authority, had given way to greater

FIGURE 12.2. Brush piles after thinning and removing ladder fuels for a firebreak, 2003. Courtesy, © Karen Wattenmaker Photography, hwwp://www.ForestPhoto.com.

centralization, most notably through unified or forest-wide budgeting; in the opinion of one longtime ranger, centralization had caused district rangers to lose much of their nimbleness, resulting in less formal authority but more responsibility. To make up for that loss, conscientious district rangers quietly went about doing what needed to be done on smaller matters and came to rely on the public through the planning process for support for larger projects.

As the basis for public discussion, Thompson directed his interdisciplinary planning team to the issue of "new forestry": not how to maximize growth and the yield of commercial timber stands but how to reduce the risk of catastrophic wildfires for the benefit of forest sustainability. William Illingworth's photographs and other empirical evidence had shown that the forest before settlement had contained fewer pines, more hardwoods, more meadows, and seemingly fewer catastrophic fires. Thompson reduced the operational question to this: how would we manage the forest if our three-part goal was to break up the continuity of fuels, reduce overall wildfire hazards, and move to a more resilient forest?[7]

Although "resilient" had replaced "productive" as the distinctive Forest Service watchword, District Ranger Thompson made it clear that the primary forestry tools remained essentially the same as the ones used under traditional forestry:

FIGURE 12.3. Thinned stand near Beulah, 2010. Author photo.

chainsaws and prescribed burns. Within the Prairie Project area, whole-tree logging would be used to reduce tree density to basal sixty or lower (not to basal eighty or seventy, once considered optimal) and to reduce fuel loads by removing slash from the forest. Likewise, mechanical means would be used to expand grasslands and meadows and make room for more hardwood. Given the fire-dependent and fire-resistant nature of the ponderosa pine, Thompson argued that by trying to mimic natural fire occurrences through prescribed burns, the Forest Service could contribute to a healthier forest and, secondarily, provide for more commercial timbering than in the past. Even in the most recent years, prescribed burns never exceeded 3,000 acres annually for the entire forest, a much lower number than copying nature would suggest.[8]

Some old-time foresters might dispute that assertion about more timbering, but others in the timber industry agreed that more timber would be cut, though in the name of forest health rather than for the sake of keeping local sawmills in operation. In fact, forest-wide standing inventory had nearly tripled since 1897, to an estimated 5.2 billion board feet in 2011, despite the fact that 6 billion board feet were harvested during the intervening years. Most foresters agreed that, for optimal forest health, the standing inventory needed to be substantially reduced. Nonetheless, the Forest Service continued its policy of allowing annual sales of 83 million board feet, based on an estimated annual growth of 119 million board feet combined with surveys showing that more than one-third of stands once thought suitable for timbering had been destroyed by wildfires and insects or made commercially unusable because of dense growth.[9] Between the approval of the Daschle rider in 2002 and the final amendment to the forest plan in 2003, the Black Hills National Forest had no permanent leadership. Planning and Public Affairs Officer Frank Carroll recalled that the timber industry used that lack to press its case for more timbering. The industry pressured the congressional delegation to demand that Chief Dale Bosworth and Regional Forester Rick Cables instruct the new supervisor to authorize an allowable sale of 110–120 million board feet annually. Instead, Bosworth and Cables informed the industry that the new supervisor, Craig A. Bobzien, had been instructed to take "a hard look" at the entire timber sale program. Supervisor Bobzien had begun his Forest Service career in the Bitterroot National Forest during a time of intense controversy over clear-cutting. He then moved to the Pacific Northwest, working during the salmon and spotted owl controversies. He went to the Black Hills after a stint as deputy supervisor of the Idaho Panhandle National Forest, where he earned the reputation of being a skilled listener and a deft diplomat, useful attributes for dealing with continuing disagreements over the level of timber sales.

When he arrived in Custer, Supervisor Bobzien, assisted by his district rangers, took that "hard look," concluding that the Forest Service could indeed meet the timber industry's demand but only for four years, after which allowable quantities would drop dramatically. Bobzien took a detailed map, prepared by District Ranger Thompson, to show the principal operators the long-term effect of their demand on timbering. At a more formal meeting that followed, the industry berated the Forest Service while Bobzien simply listened, much to the industry's consternation. The issue of commercial timber sales would be preempted by the beetle epidemic, with the urgent need to determine how to slow infestations and reduce the risk of large wildfires.[10]

Meanwhile, a secondary purpose of the Prairie Project was to address the long-standing issue of motorized and non-motorized recreational travel in the Black Hills National Forest. The Black Hills National Forest Advisory Board had wanted to deal with the issue forest-wide, but regional officials told the board to postpone discussion until the final amendment to the forest plan had been completed. A well-publicized discovery by two botanists in 2004, however, brought the issue into full view. While hiking in South Stagebarn Canyon (also known as Botany Canyon), a spring-fed box canyon near Piedmont, the botanists happened upon portions of streambed severely damaged by all-terrain vehicles. After they apparently failed to receive an immediate response from the Forest Service, the botanists interested a newspaper reporter in writing a story. Following publication, the two district rangers with jurisdiction over that area (the stream in question served as a boundary line) closed the area to all motorized traffic. The botanists presented their findings to the advisory board, which recommended the establishment of an actively managed road and trail network. The task of preparing a travel management plan fell to Craig Bobzien.[11]

Since the State of South Dakota did not require registration of off-road vehicles, reliable statistics on their numbers did not exist. The Forest Service estimated that off-road vehicle users had created more than 6,000 miles of cross-county tracks in the Black Hills National Forest, nearly twice the number of official Forest Service road miles. When legal and illegal miles were combined, the result was a road density of 4–5 miles per square mile, more than five times the average density for the national forests in Region 2.[12] Publicity surrounding the Botany Canyon discovery brought abuses to the fore. In 2005 a group of concerned citizens, initially mostly scientists and teachers, created the Norbeck Society in an effort to stop illegal and excessive use of off-road vehicles in the national forest. In 2010 the group attracted 600 volunteers to help the Forest Service inventory areas vulnerable to damage, place signs and build barriers to protect those areas, and assist with restoration of damaged areas. Norbeck Society members applauded newer methods of timbering that minimized collateral damage; society president Colin J. Paterson expressed the view that "it is not a matter of whether we log but how we log." By all accounts, Forest Service staff genuinely appreciated the work of the Norbeck Society volunteers.[13]

For his part, Supervisor Bobzien succeeded in marshaling sufficient public support for a travel plan that put forest protection first. More than his predecessors, Bobzien managed to meld his understanding of the public's wishes with the recommendations of scientists both inside and outside his agency. He had read each of the hundreds of pieces of correspondence commenting on the travel plan, listened to hundreds of individuals at meetings both formal and informal, and reviewed all of the environmental analyses before personally drafting his record of decision. With an absolute minimum of bureaucratic language, Bobzien drew special attention to suggestions with which he disagreed, as if to emphasize that he had carefully considered them.[14]

Instead of continuing the policy of keeping the entire forest open to unrestricted motorized off-road travel, except where posted as closed, Supervisor Bobzien adopted the preferred national policy of closing the entire forest to such travel, except where specifically designated as open. The travel management plan, published in March 2010, called for reducing areas open to motorized traffic from

FIGURE 12.4. User-created track restored to the forest by a youth crew, 2011. Courtesy, Beth Doten, Black Hills National Forest, http://www.ForestPhoto.com.

FIGURE 12.5. Norbeck Society volunteers building bridge for hiking and cycling trail, 2008. Courtesy, USDA Forest Service, Black Hills National Forest, http://www. ForestPhoto.com.

864,000 acres to 294,800 acres. Within that specified acreage, hunters could use motorized vehicles, but only to retrieve elk; recreationists could use motorized vehicles for dispersed camping, but only on 135,000 acres and within 300 feet of Forest Service roads. The plan reduced Forest Service roads from 3,740 miles to 3,157 miles and increased motorized trails from 36 miles to 707 miles, of which 148 miles were for all off-road vehicles, 469 miles for all-terrain vehicles only, and 90 miles for motorcycles only. The Forest Service set limits on decibel levels and assessed fees on users of motorized trails.[15]

For "leading by listening" throughout the travel planning process, Supervisor Bobzien earned recognition from the National Association of Forest Service Retirees, the first such award made to a forest supervisor.[16] With memories still alive from the Jasper fire and its aftermath, his leading by listening approach helped restore credibility with the public and improve relations with cooperating public agencies. That became even more apparent with his response to the mountain pine beetle epidemic. Between 1997 and 2012, the beetle infested an estimated 416,000 acres, almost half of the ponderosa pine stands in the national forest.

FIGURE 12.6. Black Hills near Newcastle, 2010. Author photo.

Beginning in fall 2005, Supervisor Bobzien and his staff embarked on a long campaign to inform key opinion leaders about the beetle epidemic and to obtain agreement that more needed to be done to reduce the epidemic to an endemic level. In October 2011 Bobzien issued an open invitation to interested parties to meet in Rapid City and join a Conservation Leadership Committee for the purpose of preparing a collaborative strategy to address the beetle epidemic. His refrain: the Forest Service had been doing all it could; working with others, it could do more. The genius of the ensuing "Black Hills Regional Mountain Pine Beetle Strategy" was its voluntary nature, obliging signatories to a common ideal of forest health; it was not a document binding them to any decision made by the leadership committee but simply an extraordinary expression of faith "in the spirit of cooperation and collaboration in mutual respect." The committee established a smaller working group that included participants from the Forest Service, Bureau of Land Management, National Park Service, South Dakota Departments of Agriculture and Game, Fish, and Parks, the Black Hills counties, and the Black Hills Forest Resource Association. In September 2012 the working group hired retired Forest Service officer Dave Thom as "bug coordinator." Thom had served as Supervisor Twiss's representative to the negotiations that led to the Daschle rider.[17]

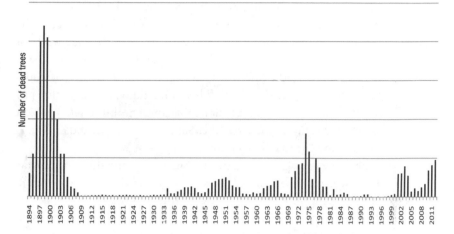

FIGURE 12.7. Estimated number of trees killed by mountain pine beetle, 1894–2012. Courtesy, Kurt Allen, USDA Forest Service, Black Hills National Forest.

Much work has been done and much money has been spent since the current beetle epidemic began: the state forestry divisions of South Dakota and Wyoming assisted private landowners with technical and financial aid; county weed and pest control boards used their federal "in lieu" funds to do likewise; Lawrence County (Deadwood and Spearfish) signed an agreement with the Forest Service that allows county crews to cut diseased trees inside forest boundaries. The Forest Service conducts timber sales in areas that need thinning, but the lumber market has been such that timber operators cannot afford to thin without federal subsidies.

To be sure, a few additional millions of dollars to underwrite thinning would be helpful, and the South Dakota congressional delegation has had some success in attracting that money. Supervisor Bobzien noted, however, that restoring the forest to health would require much more than money. Under authority of the Healthy Forests Restoration Act and again with support of the congressional delegation, Bobzien obtained agreement from the US Environmental Protection Agency and President Barack Obama's White House Council on Environmental Quality to expedite planning—including environmental assessments—for a faster, more flexible response to treat approximately 248,000 acres of forestland deemed most vulnerable to infestation.[18]

Gifford Pinchot may have been the first to recognize the unique challenges posed by the intermingling of private and public lands in the Black Hills. But it is the current beetle epidemic that demonstrates beyond doubt that managing the national forest is inextricably intertwined with the social and economic well-being of the region and that only a holistic approach—engaging all landowners and, by extension, all forest users—to the beetle issue has any chance of lasting success. The "Black Hills Regional Mountain Pine Beetle Strategy" provides the framework for such an approach: (1) reduce the mountain pine beetle epidemic to endemic levels, (2) create and maintain a healthy forest that can rebound from future epidemics and catastrophic wildfires, (3) ensure the viability of the timber industry that provides the principal management tool for maintaining forest health, and (4) protect the safety of people and communities. Whether Supervisor Bobzien and his successors can sustain such an approach remains to be seen.[19]

Underlying the beetle strategy is the notion that harvesting and thinning provide the best way to reduce and mitigate epidemics. A longitudinal study completed in 2007 by Forest Service entomologists and silviculturists confirmed for most people what had long been observed by inhabitants of the Black Hills: thinning works. In a farsighted essay written at the time the Forest Service unveiled its plan for ecosystem management, the research silviculturist Russell T. Graham expressed the view that "if society desires forests to be managed for sustainability, silvicultural prescriptions can be developed using many of the same tools that successfully produced timber crops."[20] One might go further to suggest that the only way to save the forest and commercial timbering is to create and manage for a biologically diverse forest. When asked what Gifford Pinchot would have said about this new approach, District Ranger Bob Thompson responded that the chief forester would be proud of the changes because of the continuing emphasis on the greatest good for the most people in the long run.[21]

NOTES

1. Frank Carroll, Black Hills National Forest (BHNF) planning and public affairs officer, personal communication, March 2011.

2. "Twiss Announces Advisory Committee," BHNF news release, June 3, 2002, at http://www.fs.usda.gov/detail/blackhills/news-events/?cid=FSM9_013081; accessed December 2009; Thomas Blair, discussion with author, April 2009.

3. USDA Forest Service, Black Hills National Forest, *Record of Decision, Final Environmental Impact Statement, Phase II Amendment, Revised Land and Resource Management Plan* (Custer, SD: US Department of Agriculture [USDA] Forest Service, 2005), 1.

4. Ibid., 2–3, 13–14.

5. USDA Forest Service, Black Hills National Forest, *Revised Phase II Amendment, Black Hills National Forest Land and Resource Management Plan* (Custer, SD: USDA Forest Service, March 2006), I: 35–36.

6. Robert J. Thompson, personal communication, January 2013.

7. Ibid.

8. Robert J. Thompson, discussions with author, November 2009, April 2011.

9. Blaine Cook, discussions with author, February 2011, February 2013.

10. Frank Carroll, discussion with author, February 2013.

11. "ATVs Threaten Plants, Serenity," *Rapid City Journal*, July 3, 2004, A1; USDA Forest Service, Black Hills National Forest, *Record of Decision, Black Hills National Forest Travel Management Plan* and same agency, *Final Environmental Impact Statement, Black Hills National Forest Travel Management Plan* (Custer, SD: USDA Forest Service, March 1910).

12. "Norbeck Society Comments on USFS Proposed Action: Black Hills National Forest Travel Management Notice of Intent to Prepare an EIS," Rapid City, November 8, 2007, 10, Black Hills National Forest supervisor's office, Custer, SD.

13. Quoted in Colin Paterson, "Don't Treat Forest Like a Tree Farm," *Rapid City Journal*, October 20, 2010, E4; Thompson, discussion with author, November 2011.

14. Frank Carroll, discussion with author, September 2010.

15. USDA Forest Service, Black Hills National Forest, *Record of Decision, Black Hills National Forest Travel Management Plan*, 4–7.

16. "Bobzien Earns Honor from National Forest Group," *Rapid City Journal*, August 5, 2011, B8, at http://rapidcityjournal.com/sports/bobzien-earns-honor-by-being-leader-who-listens/article; accessed January 12, 2013.

17. "Black Hills Regional Mountain Pine Beetle Strategy [Summary]," Black Hills National Forest, May 2l, 2012, 8, at http://www.rcpcem.com/assets/docs/beetle/MPB%20BlackHillsRegionalMPBStrategy5-21-12.pdf; accessed December 2012; Carroll, discussion with author, February 2013.

18. "Forest Service to Expedite Pine Beetle Fight," *Rapid City Journal*, December 18, 2012, A1.

19. "Black Hills Regional Mountain Pine Beetle Strategy," 5–8.

20. J. M. Schmid et al., "The Influence of Partial Cutting on Mountain Pine Beetle-Caused Tree Mortality in Black Hills Ponderosa Pine Stands," Rocky Mountain Research Station Paper RMRS-RP-68 (November 2007); Russell T. Graham, "Silviculture, Fire and Ecosystem Management," *Journal of Sustainable Forestry* 2, no. 3-4 (1994): 347.

21. Thompson, discussion with author, November 2009.

Bibliography

A NOTE ON PRINCIPAL SOURCES

The Black Hills National Forest Historical Collection, Leland D. Case Library for Western Historical Studies, Black Hills State University, Spearfish, South Dakota, consists of file cabinets filled with papers, reports, maps, and photographs moved from the forest supervisor's office in Custer; preservation work is in progress. Supplementing this collection are historical materials located at the Black Hills National Forest supervisor's office, Custer, and, for more recent activities, on the Black Hills National Forest website (http://www.fs.usda.gov/blackhills). In addition to those principal repositories, I used the United States Forest Service Collection 74, series 1, box 1, folders 1–36, at the Denver Public Library. I also depended on microfilm copies of the *Custer County Chronicle*, continued as the *Custer Weekly Chronicle*, for the years 1897 through 2001, which I found to be the most complete run of local weekly newspapers.

"Albert F. Potter." *American Forestry* 16, no. 2 (February 1910): 107–8.

Allen, Shirley W. "E. T. Allen." *Journal of Forestry* 43, no. 3 (March 1945): 222–23.

Alleger, C. N., ed. *Civilian Conservation Corps, South Dakota District History*. Rapid City: Johnston and Bordewyk, ca. 1935.

Alexander, Robert R. "Silvicultural Systems, Cutting Methods, and Cultural Practices for Black Hills Ponderosa Pine." US Department of Agriculture (USDA) Forest Service General Technical Report RM-139 (February 1987), 32 pp.

DOI: 10.5876/9781607322993.c013

Averill, Clarence C. "The Civilian Conservation Corps as a Fire Suppression Organization." *Black Hills Engineer* 24, no. 1 (December 1937): 38–47.

Ayers, George V. "Lawrence County Roads and How They Were Done." *Pahasapa Quarterly* 5, no. 1 (December 1915): 9–15.

Badè, William Frederic, ed. *The Life and Letters of John Muir*, vol. 2. Boston: Houghton Mifflin, 1924.

Berisford, C. Wayne. "Andrew Delmar Hopkins—a West Virginia Pioneer in Entomology." *West Virginia University Agricultural and Forestry Experiment Station Circular* 155 (January 1992): 20–26.

Boldt, Charles E., and James L. Van Deusen. "Silviculture of Ponderosa Pine in the Black Hills: The Status of Our Knowledge." USDA Forest Service Research Paper RM-124 (June 1974), 45 pp.

Bonilla, Carleton L. "A South Dakota Rendezvous: The Sturgis Motorcycle Rally and Races." *South Dakota History* 28 (Fall 1998): 123–43.

Briggs, Harold E. *Frontiers of the Northwest: A History of the Upper Missouri Valley.* New York: D. Appleton-Century, 1940.

Brown, Greg, Jay O'Laughlin, and Charles C. Harris. "Allowable Sale Quantity (ASQ) of Timber as a Focal Point in National Forest Management." *Natural Resources Journal* 33 (Summer 1993): 569–94.

Brown, Peter M., and Carolyn Hull Sieg. "Fire History in Interior Ponderosa Pine Communities in the Black Hills, South Dakota, USA." *International Journal of Wildland Fire* 6, no. 3 (1996): 97–105.

Bunkers, Matthew J. "L. Ronald Johnson, James R. Miller, and Carolyn Hull Sieg. "Old Black Hills Ponderosa Pines Tell a Story." *South Dakota Academy of Science Proceedings* 78 (1999): 149–62.

Burroughs, John Rolfe. *Guardians of the Grasslands: The First Hundred Years of the Wyoming Stock Growers Association.* Cheyenne: Pioneer, 1971.

Buttrick, P. L. "The Probable Origins of the Forests of the Black Hills of South Dakota." *Forest Quarterly* 12 (1914): 223–27.

Camp, Charles L., ed. *James Clyman, Frontiersman: The Adventures of a Trapper and Covered-Wagon Emigrant as Told in His Own Reminiscences and Diaries.* Portland, OR: Champoeg, 1960.

Campbell, Robert Wellman. "Wishlist: Wilderness Endgame in the Black Hills National Forest." *Great Plains Quarterly* 30, no. 4 (Fall 2010): 287–305.

Carroll, John M., and Lawrence A. Frost, eds. *Private Theodore Ewert's Diary of the Black Hills Expedition of 1874.* Piscataway, NJ: CRI Books, 1976.

Chapman, Herman H. "Edward Merriam Griffith, 1872–1939." *Journal of Forestry* 38, no. 1 (January 1940): 62–63.

Clements, Kendrick A. "Herbert Hoover and Conservation, 1921–33." *American Historical Review* 89, no. l (February 1984): 67–88.

Clepper, Henry. *Professional Forestry in the United States*. Baltimore: Johns Hopkins Press, 1971.

Clow, Richmond L. "Timber Users, Timber Savers: The Homestake Mining Company and the First Regulated Timber Harvest." *South Dakota History* 22, no. 3 (Fall 1992): 213–37.

Cravens, Jay H. "Who Is the Guilty Party?" Paper presented at the Canadian Institute of Forestry/Society of American Foresters Convention, Edmonton, Alberta, October 5, 2004. Typescript.

Deland, Charles E. "The Vérendrye Explorations and Discoveries." *South Dakota Historical Collections* 7 (1914): 99–332.

Derscheid, Lyle A. *The Civilian Conservation Corps in South Dakota, 1933–1942*. Brookings: South Dakota State University Foundation Press, 1986.

Donaldson, Aris B. "The Black Hills Expedition." *South Dakota Historical Collections* 7 (1914): 554–80.

Duthie, George A. "The Origin of Deadwood's Name." *Black Hills Engineer* 18, no. 1 (January 1930): 4–11.

Duthie, George A. "Timber, an Economic Resource of the Black Hills." *Black Hills Engineer* 16, no. 2 (March 1928): 101–9.

Elkins, James R. "Strangers to Us All: Lawyers and Poetry." West Virginia University, at http://myweb.wvnet.edu/~jelkins/lp-2001/robinson.html. Accessed August 2010.

Fanebust, Wayne L. *Echoes of November: The Life and Times of Senator R. F. Pettigrew of South Dakota*. Freeman, SD: Pine Hill, 1997.

Fielder, Mildred. *Railroads of the Black Hills*. Seattle: Superior, 1964.

Fite, Gilbert C. *Peter Norbeck: Prairie Statesman*. Pierre: South Dakota State Historical Society Press, 2005 [1948].

Franklin, Jerry P. "Toward a New Forestry." *American Forests* 95, no. 11-12 (November-December 1989): 37–40.

Freeman, John F. *High Plains Horticulture, a History*. Boulder: University Press of Colorado, 2008.

Froiland, Sven G. *Natural History of the Black Hills and Badlands*. Sioux Falls: Center for Western Studies, Augustana College, 1990.

Furniss, Malcolm M. "American Forest Entomology Comes on Stage: Bark Beetle Depradations in the Black Hills Forest Preserve, 1897–1907." *American Entomologist* 43 (Spring 1997): 40–47.

Furniss, Malcolm M. "A History of Forest Entomolgy in the Intermountain and Rocky Mountain Areas, 1901–1982." USDA Forest Service General Technical Report RMRS-GTR-195 (2007), 40 pp.

Gore, Bancroft. "Conserving Lumber Products by Fuel Economy." *Black Hills Engineer* 16, no. 2 (1928): 147–58.

Grafe, Ernest, and Paul Horsted. *Exploring with Custer: The 1874 Black Hills Expedition,* 3rd ed. Custer, SD: Golden Valley, 2005.

Graham, Russell T. "Silviculture, Fire and Ecosystem Management." *Journal of Sustainable Forestry* 2, no. 3-4 (1994): 339–51.

Graham, Russell T., and Theresa B. Jain. "Application of Free Selection in Mixed Forests of the Inland Northwestern United States." *Forest Ecology and Management* 209 (2005): 131–45.

Graves, Henry S. "The Black Hills Forest Reserve." In US Geological Survey, *Nineteenth Annual Report, 1897–1898*, Part V: *Forest Reserves,* 67–164. Washington, DC: Government Printing Office, 1899.

Griffith, Edward M. "The Black Hills Forest Reserve." *The Forester* (November 1901): 287–90.

Hanson, Jeffrey R., and Sally Chirinos. "Ethnographic Overview and Assessment of Devils Tower National Monument, Wyoming." *Intermountain Region, National Park Service, Cultural Resources Selections D-36* (1997): 1–62.

Hassrick, Royal B. *The Sioux: Life and Customs of a Warrior Society.* Norman: University of Oklahoma Press, 1964.

Hays, Samuel P. *The American People and the National Forests: The First Century of the U.S. Forest Service.* Pittsburgh: University of Pittsburgh Press, 2009.

Hays, Samuel P. *Wars in the Woods: The Rise of Ecological Forestry in America.* Pittsburgh: University of Pittsburgh Press, 2007.

Hayward, Herman E. "Studies of the Plants in the Black Hills of South Dakota." *Botanical Gazette* 85, no. 4 (June 1928): 353–413.

Hirt, Paul W. *A Conspiracy of Optimism: Management of the National Forests since World War Two.* Lincoln: University of Nebraska Press, 1994.

Hoekstra, Thomas W., A. A. Dyer, and Dennis C. LeMaster, eds. *FORPLAN: An Evaluation of a Forest Planning Tool.* Rocky Mountain Forest and Range Experiment Station General Technical Report RM-140 (April 1987), 164 pp.

Hoffman, Arthur F.C., and Theodore Krueger. *Forestry in the Black Hills.* USDA Yearbook. Washington, DC: US Department of Agriculture, 1949.

Hoffman, George R., and Robert R. Alexander. "Forest Vegetation of the Black Hills National Forest of South Dakoa and Wyoming: A Habitat Type Classification." USDA Forest Service Research Paper RM-276 (June 1976), 48 pp.

Homestake Centennial, 1876–1976. Lead, SD: Homestake Mining Company, 1976.

Hood, A. B. "Logging Operations in the Black Hills." *Black Hills Engineer* 16, no. 2 (March 1928): 120–35.

Hopkins, Andrew Delmar. "The Black Hills Beetle, with Further Notes on Its Distribution, Life History, and Methods of Control." *USDA Bureau of Entomology Bulletin* 56 (1905): 1–24.

Hopkins, Andrew Delmar. "Insect Enemies of the Pine in the Black Hills Forest Reserve: An Account of Results of Special Investigations, with Recommendations for Preventing Losses." *USDA Bureau of Entomology Bulletin* 32 (1902): 1–24.

Hornibrook, E. M. "A Modified Tree Classification for Use in Growth Studies and Timber Marking in Black Hills Ponderosa Pine." *Journal of Forestry* 37, no. 6 (June 1939): 483–88.

Hough, Franklin B. "On the Duty of Governments in the Preservation of Forests." Proceedings of the American Association for the Advancement of Science, August 1873, Portland, ME, at http://memory.loc.gov/ammem/amrvhtml/cnchron2.html. Accessed February 2008.

Ise, John. *The United States Forest Policy.* New York: Arno, 1972 [1920].

Jenney, Walter P. "The Mineral Wealth, Climate and Rainfall, and Natural Resources of the Black Hills of Dakota." *US Geological and Geographical Survey of the Black Hills.* Washington, DC: General Printing Office, 1876.

Johnson, Arthur I. "Scenic Highways." *Pahasapa Quarterly* 8, no. 3 (April 1915): 50–55.

Julin, Suzanne Barta. *A Marvelous Hundred Square Miles: Black Hills Tourism, 1880–1941.* Pierre: South Dakota State Historical Society Press, 2009.

Julin, Suzanne Barta. "South Dakota Spa: A History of the Hot Springs Health Resort, 1882–1915." *South Dakota Historical Collections* 41 (1983): 201–8.

Kaufmann, Merrill R., and 10 others. "An Ecological Basis for Ecosystem Management." USDA Forest Service General Technical Report GTR-RM-246 (May 1994), 22 pp.

Kaufmann, Merrill R., William H. Moir, and Richard L. Bassett. *Old Growth Forests in the Southwest and Rocky Mountain Regions: Proceedings of a Workshop.* USDA Forest Service General Technical Report GTR-RM-213 (1992), 201 pp.

Kellar, Kenneth C. *Seth Bullock: Frontier Marshall.* Aberdeen, SD: North Plains, 1972.

Kelleter, Paul D. "The National Forest of the Black Hills." *Pahasapa Quarterly* 2, no. 4 (June 1913): 9–12.

Kime, Wayne R., ed. *The Black Hills Journals of Colonel Richard Irving Dodge.* Norman: University of Oklahoma Press, 1996.

Kingsbury, George W. *History of Dakota Territory*, vol. 1. Chicago: S. J. Clarke, 1915.

Knize, Perri. "The Mismanagement of the National Forests." *Atlantic Monthly* 268, no. 4 (October 1991): 98–100, 103–4, 107–8, 111–12.

Krick, Brian G. "Mountain Farmers: Supervisors of the Black Hills National Forest, 1898–1995." MA thesis, University of South Dakota, Vermillion, 2001.

Krueger, Theodore. "The CCC in the Black Hills and Harney National Forests." *Black Hills Engineer* 24, no. 1 (December 1937): 14–25.

Krueger, Theodore. "Practices and Problems in the Disposal of Brush Resulting from Thinnings in Ponderosa Pine in the Black Hills National Forest." *Journal of Forestry* 32, no. 7 (October 1934): 757–59.

Lamar, Howard R. *Dakota Territory, 1861–1889: A Study of Frontier Politics.* New Haven: Yale University Press, 1956.

Langston, Nancy. *Forest Dreams, Forest Nightmares: The Paradox of Old Growth in the Inland West.* Seattle: University of Washington Press, 1995.

LeMaster, Dennis C., and John H. Beuter, eds. *Community Stability in Forest-Based Economies: Proceedings of a Conference in Portland, Oregon, November 16–18, 1987.* Portland, OR: Timber, 1989.

Linde, Martha. *Sawmills of the Black Hills.* Rapid City: Fenske, 1984.

Lundgren, Stewart. "The National Fire Management Analysis System (NFMAS) Past 2000: A New Horizon." USDA Forest Service General Technical Report PSW-GTR-173. Albany, CA: USDA Forest Service, Pacific Southwest Research Station, 1999, 7 pp.

Marriott, Hollis, Don Faber-Langendoen, Amanda McAdams, Diane Stutzman, and Beth Burkhart. *Black Hills Community Inventory: Final Report.* Minneapolis: Nature Conservancy Midwest Conservation Science Center, 1999.

Marsh, George Perkins. "Address Delivered before the Agricultural Society of Rutland County, Sept. 30, 1847," at http://memory.loc.gov/ammem/today/sep30.html. Accessed March 2010.

Marsh, George Perkins. *Man and Nature or, Physical Geography as Modified by Human Action.* Ed. David Lowenthal. Cambridge: Harvard University Press, 1965 [1864].

Mattox, Robert. "Pennington County Wildfire Protection Plan." Prepared for Pennington County fire administrator Dennis Gorton. Deadwood, SD: Black Hills Land Analysis, 2007. 29 pp.

McAdams, Amanda G. "Changes in Ponderosa Pine Forest Structure in the Black Hills, South Dakota, 1874–1995." MS thesis, Northern Arizona University, Flagstaff, 1995.

McCandless, Philip. "The Black Hills Lumber Industry." *Black Hills Engineer* 19, no. 1 (January 1931): 11–16.

McCarthy, G. Michael. "The Forest Reserve Controversy: Colorado under Cleveland and McKinley." *Journal of Forest History* 20, no. 2 (April 1976): 80–90.

McClintock, John S. *Pioneer Days in the Black Hills.* Ed. Edward L. Senn. Norman: University of Oklahoma Press, 2000 [1939].

McDermott, John D. "The Military Problem and the Black Hills, 1874–1875." *South Dakota History* 32, no. 3–4 (Fall-Winter 2001): 188–210.

McIntosh, Arthur G. "A Botanical Survey of the Black Hills of South Dakota." *Black Hills Engineer* 19, no. 3 (May 1931): 159–278.

McLaird, James D., and Lesta V. Turchen. "Exploring the Black Hills, 1855–1875: Reports of the Government Expeditions, the Dakota Explorations of Lieutenant Gouverneur Kemble Warren, 1855–1856–1857." *South Dakota History* 3, no. 4 (Fall 1973): 360–89.

McLaird, James D., and Lesta V. Turchen. "Exploring the Black Hills, 1855–1875: Reports of the Government Expeditions, the Explorations of Captain William Franklin Raynolds, 1859–1860." *South Dakota History* 4, no. 1 (Winter 1973): 18–62.

McLaird, James D., and Lesta V. Turchen. "Exploring the Black Hills, 1855–1875: Reports of the Government Expeditions, the Scientist in Western Exploration, Ferdinand Vandiveer Hayden." *South Dakota History* 4, no. 2 (Spring 1974): 161–97.

McLaird, James D., and Lesta V. Turchen. "Exploring the Black Hills, 1855–1875: Reports of the Government Expeditions, the Scientists Search for Gold, 1875: Walter P. Jenney and Henry Newton." *South Dakota History* 4, no. 3 (Summer 1974): 280–319.

Meeker, E. W. "Highways in the Black Hills." *Black Hills Engineer* 18, no. 2 (March 1930): 142–47.

Miller, Char. *Gifford Pinchot and the Making of Modern Environmentalism*. Washington, DC: Island, 2001.

Miller, Char, ed. *American Forests: Nature, Culture, and Politics*. Lawrence: University of Kansas Press, 1997.

Moulton, Gary E., ed. *The Journals of the Lewis and Clark Expedition*, vol. 3. Lincoln: University of Nebraska Press, 1987.

Myers, Clifford A., and James L. Van Deusen. "Growth of Immature Stands of Ponderosa Pine in the Black Hills." Rocky Mountain Forest and Range Experiment Station Paper 61 (July 1961), 14 pp.

Myers, Clifford A., and James L. Van Deusen. "Site Index of Ponderosa Pine in the Black Hills from Soil and Topography." *Journal of Forestry* 58, no. 7 (July 1960): 548–55.

Newport, Carl A. *Forest Service Policies in Timber Management and Silviculture as They Affect the Lumber Industry: A Case Study of the Black Hills*. Pierre: South Dakota Department of Game, Fish, and Parks, 1956.

O'Toole, Randal. *Reforming the Forest Service*. Washington, DC: Island, 1988.

Oliver, William W., and Russell A. Ryker. "*Pinus ponderosa* Dougl. ex Laws." In *Silvics of North America*, ed. Russell M. Burns and Barbara H. Honkala, 1: 413–24. Washington, DC: USDA Forest Service, 1990.

Otis, Allison T., William D. Honey, Thomas C. Hogg, and Kimberly K. Lakin. *The Forest Service and the Civilian Conservation Corps, 1933–1942*. Washington, DC: USDA Forest Service, 1986.

Parker, Watson. *Gold in the Black Hills.* Norman: University of Oklahoma Press, 1966.

Parkman, Francis. *France and England in North America,* vol. 2. New York: Literary Classics of the United States, 1983 [1892].

Parrish, J. Barry, Daryl J. Herman, and Deanna J. Reyher. "A Century of Change in Black Hills Forest and Riparian Ecosystems." *South Dakota Agricultural Experiment Station Bulletin* 722 (February 1996): 1–20.

Pearson, Gustav A., and Raymond E. Marsh. "Timber Growing and Logging Practice in the Southwest and the Black Hills Region." *USDA Technical Bulletin* 480 (October 1935): 1–80.

Peck, Frank S. "Roads: Past, Present, and Future." *Pahasapa Quarterly* 8, no. 3 (April 1919): 15–20.

Pendley, William Perry. *It Takes a Hero: The Grassroots Battle against Environmental Oppression.* Bellevue, WA: Free Enterprise Press, 1994.

Pinchot, Gifford. *Breaking New Ground.* Washington, DC: Island, 1998 [1947].

Pinchot, Gifford. "How Conservation Began in the United States." *Agricultural History* 11, no. 4 (October 1937): 255–65.

Pinchot, Gifford. *The Use of the National Forest Reserves, Regulations and Instructions.* Washington, DC: US Department of Agriculture, 1905, at http://www.foresthistory.org/ASPNET/Publications/1905_Use_Book/1905_use_book.pdf. Accessed February 2008.

Pinkett, Harold T. *Gifford Pinchot, Private and Public Forester.* Urbana: University of Illinois Press, 1970.

Progulske, Donald R., and Richard H. Sowell. "Yellow Ore, Yellow Hair, Yellow Pine: A Photographic Study of a Century of Forest Ecology." *South Dakota Agricultural Experiment Station Bulletin* 616 (July 1974): 1–169.

Progulske, Donald R., with Frank J. Shideler. "Following Custer." *South Dakota Agricultural Experiment Station Bulletin* 674 (1983): 1–99.

Pyne, Stephen J. *Fire in America: A Cultural History of Wildland and Rural Fire.* Seattle: University of Washington Press, 1997 [1982].

Rasker, Ray. *Solutions to the Rising Costs of Fighting Fires in the Wildland-Urban Interface.* Bozeman, MT: Headwaters Economics, 2009, at http://headwaterseconomics.org/wphw/wp-content/uploads/HeadwatersFireCosts.pdf. Accessed February 2010.

Robinson, Doane A. *Doane Robinson's Encyclopedia of South Dakota.* Pierre, SD: by the author, 1925.

Robinson, Doane A. "Inception and Development of the Rushmore Idea." *Black Hills Engineer* 18, no. 4 (November 1930): 334–43.

Roeser, Jacob J., Jr. "The Role of Timber Stand Improvements in the Black Hills." *Black Hills Engineer* 24, no. 1 (December 1937): 48–54.

Rom, Lance, Tim Church, and Michele Church, eds. *Black Hills National Forest Cultural Resources Overview*. 2 vols. Custer: USDA Forest Service, Black Hills National Forest, 1996.

Roosevelt, Theodore. *An Autobiography*. New York: Library of America, 2004 [1913].

Roskie, George W. "State Game Preserve." *Pahasapa Quarterly* 4, no. 3 (April 1915): 9–14.

Rydberg, Per Axel. "Flora of the Black Hills of South Dakota." *Contributions from the U.S. National Herbarium* 3, no. 8 (June 1896): 463–540.

Sargent, Charles Sprague. *The Silva of North America*, vol. 11. New York: Peter Smith, 1947 [1897].

Schell, Herbert S. *History of South Dakota*, 3rd ed. Lincoln: University of Nebraska Press, 1975.

Schmid, J. M., S. A. Mata, R. R. Kessler, and J. B. Popp. "The Influence of Partial Cutting on Mountain Pine Beetle–Caused Tree Mortality in Black Hills Ponderosa Pine Stands." Rocky Mountain Research Station Paper RMRS-RP-68 (November 2007), 19 pp.

Shepperd, Wayne D., and Michael A. Battaglia. *Ecology, Silviculture, and Management of Black Hills Ponderosa Pine*. USDA Forest Service Rocky Mountain Research Station General Technical Report 97 (September 2002), 112 pp.

Shinneman, Douglas J., and William L. Baker. "Non-equilibrium Dynamics between Catastrophic Disturbances and Old-Growth Forests in Ponderosa Pine Landscapes of the Black Hills." *Conservation Biology* 11, no. 6 (December 1997): 1276–88.

Snow, Elva A., and Jacob Roeser Jr. "The National Forests of the Black Hills." *Black Hills Engineer* 26, no. 3 (December 1940): 245–59.

Soylent Communications. "John Gutzon de la Mothe Borglum," ca. 2005, at http://www.nndb.com/people/610/000166112/. Accessed March 2011.

Stanley, John A. "South Dakota's State Park." *Pahasapa Quarterly* 10, no. 4 (June 1921): 179–86.

Steen, Harold K. "The Beginning of the National Forest System." USDA Forest Service, History Unit FS-488 (May 1991), 37 pp.

Steen, Harold K. *The U.S. Forest Service: A History*. Seattle: University of Washington Press, 2004 [1976].

Steen, Harold K., ed. *The Conservation Diaries of Gifford Pinchot*. Durham, NC: Forest History Society, 2001.

Sterling, E. A. *Attitude of Lumbermen toward Forest Fires*. USDA Yearbook. Washington, DC: US Department of Agriculture, 1904.

Sundstrom, Jessie Y. *Pioneers and Custer State Park: A History of Custer State Park and Northcentral Custer County*. Custer, SD: by the author, 1994.

Sundstrom, Linea. "The Sacred Black Hills: An Ethnohistorical Review." *Great Plains Quarterly* 17, no. 3–4 (Summer-Fall 1997): 185–212.

Taliaferro, John. *Great White Fathers: The Story of the Obsessive Quest to Create Mount Rushmore*. New York: Public Affairs, 2002.

Tallent, Annie D. *The Black Hills, or, the Last Hunting Ground of the Dakotahs: A Complete History of the Black Hills of Dakota, from Their First Invasion in 1874 to the Present*. St. Louis: Nixon-Jones, 1899.

Thilenius, John F. "Classification of Deer Habitat in the Ponderosa Pine Forest of the Black Hills, South Dakota." USDA Forest Service Research Paper RM-91 (May 1972), 28 pp.

Thomas, Jack Ward, team leader. *Forest Ecosystem Management: An Ecological, Economic, and Social Assessment: Report of the Forest Ecosystem Management Assessment Team*. Washington, DC: USDA Forest Service, 1993.

Todd, Edgeley W., ed. *Astoria, or Anecdotes of an Enterprise beyond the Rocky Mountains by Washington Irving*. Norman: University of Oklahoma Press, 1960 [1836].

Twiss, John C. *1996 Revised Land and Resource Management Plan; 1997 Revision Record of Decision*. Custer, SD: Black Hills National Forest, 1997.

USDA Forest Service. "National Forest System Land Management Planning: Proposed Rule." *Federal Register* 76, no. 30 (February 14, 2011): 8480–528.

USDA Forest Service, Black Hills National Forest. "Black Hills Regional Mountain Pine Beetle Strategy," May 2012, at http://www.fs.usda.gov/Internet/FSE_DOCUMENTS /stelprdb5392402.pdf. Accessed December 2012.

USDA Forest Service, Black Hills National Forest. Decision Notice, 1997 Land and Resource Management Plan, Amendment 1 [Phase I]. Custer, SD: USDA Forest Service, May 2001.

USDA Forest Service, Black Hills National Forest. *Black Hills National Forest, 50th Anniversary*. Washington, DC: General Printing Office, 1948.

USDA Forest Service, Black Hills National Forest. *Final Environmental Impact Statement, Black Hills National Forest Land and Resource Management Plan*. Custer, SD: USDA Forest Service, 1983.

USDA Forest Service, Black Hills National Forest. *Final Environmental Impact Statement, Black Hills National Forest Revised Land and Resource Management Plan*. Custer, SD: USDA Forest Service, December 1996.

USDA Forest Service, Black Hills National Forest. *Final Environmental Impact Statement, Black Hills National Forest Travel Management Plan*. Custer, SD: USDA Forest Service, March 2010.

USDA Forest Service, Black Hills National Forest. *Final Environmental Impact Statement, Phase II Amendment, Black Hills National Forest Land and Resource Management Plan*, 2 vols. Custer, SD: USDA Forest Service, October 2005.

USDA Forest Service, Black Hills National Forest. *Final Environmental Impact Statement, Prairie Project Area (Lower Rapid Creek Area)*. Custer, SD: USDA Forest Service, October 2003.

USDA Forest Service, Black Hills National Forest. *Final Environmental Statement, Timber Management Plan for the Black Hills National Forest.* Custer, SD: USDA Forest Service, March 1977.

USDA Forest Service, Black Hills National Forest. *Land and Resource Management Plan, Black Hills National Forest.* Custer, SD: USDA Forest Service, 1983.

USDA Forest Service, Black Hills National Forest. *Record of Decision, Black Hills National Forest Revised Land and Resource Management Plan.* Custer, SD: USDA Forest Service, March 1997.

USDA Forest Service, Black Hills National Forest. *Record of Decision, Black Hills National Forest Travel Management Plan.* Custer, SD: USDA Forest Service, March 2010.

USDA Forest Service, Black Hills National Forest. *Record of Decision, Phase II Amendment, Black Hills National Forest Land and Resource Management Plan.* Custer, SD: USDA Forest Service, October 2005.

USDA Forest Service, Black Hills National Forest. *Revised Phase II Amendment, Black Hills National Forest Land and Resource Management Plan.* Custer, SD: USDA Forest Service, March 2006.

USDA Forest Service, Black Hills National Forest. *Summary Final Environmental Impact Statement, Black Hills National Forest Land and Resource Management Plan.* Custer, SD: USDA Forest Service, August 1983.

USDA Forest Service, Black Hills National Forest. "Timber Management Plan, Black Hills National Forest." *Rocky Mountain Region* 2 (1986): 1977–86.

Walker, Ronald, Gary Brundige, William Hill, and Richard Sparks. *Custer State Park Resource Management Plan, 1995–2010.* Pierre, SD: Game, Fish, and Parks Commission, 1995.

Warren, C. J. "The Manufacture of Black Hills Forest Products." *Black Hills Engineer* 16, no. 2 (March 1928): 135–46.

Western Pine Association. *Ponderosa Pine: The Pick o' the Pines: Its Properties, Uses and Grades.* Portland, OR: Western Pine Association, 1953 [1938].

Western Wood Products Association. *Western Lumber Grading Rules 88.* Portland, OR: Western Wood Products Association, 1988.

Williams, Gerald W., and Char Miller. "At the Creation, the National Forest Commission of 1896–97." *Forest History Today* (Spring-Fall 2005): 33–37.

Williams, Roger L. *Aven Nelson of Wyoming.* Boulder: Colorado Associated University Press, 1984.

Williams, Roger L. *A Region of Astonishing Beauty: The Botanical Exploration of the Rocky Mountains.* Lanham, MD: Roberts Rinehart, 2003.

Wolff, David A. *Seth Bullock, Black Hills Lawman.* Pierre: South Dakota State Historical Society Press, 2009.

Woodward, Harry R. "Forest Management versus Recreation Management." *American Forests* 63 (January 1957): 32–33, 51–53.

Wulf, Andrea. *Founding Gardeners: The Revolutionary Generation, Nature, and the Shaping of the American Nation*. New York: Alfred A. Knopf, 2011.

Index